SIMPLE THINGS WON'T SAVE THE EARTH

Simple Things

Won't Save the Earth

BY J. ROBERT HUNTER

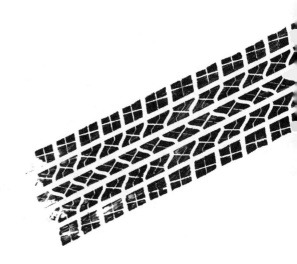

University of Texas Press • Austin

First edition, 1997

Requests for permission to reproduce material from this work should be sent to
Permissions, University of Texas Press, Box 7819, Austin, TX 78713-7819.

⊗ The paper used in this publication meets the minimum requirements of
American National Standard for Information Sciences — Permanence of Paper
for Printed Library Materials, ANSI Z39.48-1984.

Library of Congress Cataloging-in-Publication Data

Hunter, J. Robert (James Robert), 1921–
    Simple things won't save the earth / by J. Robert Hunter. — 1st ed.
        p.   cm.
    Includes bibliographical references and index.
    ISBN 0-292-73112-4 (cloth : alk. paper). — ISBN 0-292-73113-2 (pbk. : alk. paper)
        1. Hevea.   2. Rubber industry and trade.   3. Rain forest conservation.
    4. Human ecology.   I. Title.
    SD397.H54H86   1997
    363.7—dc20   96-35689

For Nancy — of course!

CONTENTS

PREFACE

SINCE THE END of World War II, the Union of Concerned Scientists (UCS) has been one of our most outspoken advocates for the prevention of any nuclear misfortune. In order to emphasize what they considered an alarming and precarious situation, in this regard, the members of that assembly proposed a 24-hour "Doomsday Clock" as a symbol to depict how close we might be to some atomic disaster. The hands on this clock were moved in accordance with each increase in global disharmony, such as the Cuban missile crisis during the Kennedy administration, and were usually set very close to midnight.

In November 1992, at a well-attended meeting in Washington, D.C., the leaders of this group made a statement that, although the threat of nuclear conflict clearly remains, we are now faced with a far more serious menace: the potential destruction of our global environment. This was embodied in their "Warning to Humanity," which stated that "human beings and the natural world are on a collision course."[1]

In recent years, there have appeared a number of similarly disturbing publications also predicting probable catastrophic futures for human society everywhere on Earth.[2] For this reason, one might have thought that programs or projects of an equally serious nature would, by now, have been organized and under way to take action which might lead to the avoidance of some possible environmental Armageddon. Because such has not been the case, the question now appears to be not whether such catastrophes will occur but simply when.

We have long resorted to the use of omens and symbols to draw attention to problems of this scale. For example, the Pacific Northwest has its spotted owl, the Tennessee Valley its snail darter, Kenya its elephants, China (together with the World Wildlife Fund) the panda. In each case, symbols are employed in an attempt to make as many people as possible aware of some unfortunate happenstance or occurrence, either here at home or on some far distant shore, with the hope that measures could soon be adopted (and funds soon received) to remedy or improve the situation. Not only is this technique now increasingly prevalent, but these symbolic messages are unfortunately often quite misleading as well — to the detriment of everyone, except those making the high-pressure pitch. This is especially true of the dubious, even blatantly false advertising schemes contrived by numerous commercial institutions that take advantage of these new trends by touting "ecologically friendly products." [3] In other instances, the symbol and its proposed remedial action often seem designed simply to protect one particular species or habitat reported to be in jeopardy. Furthermore, the impression created by these ad campaigns suggests that the purchaser of each of these special indulgences will find peace of mind and soul knowing that the whole distressful matter will be handled promptly and efficiently — by someone else. We are also left with the impression that financial participation of this kind will leave the world a much better place in which to live — even in cases where there is only a remote possibility that the declared goal could ever be attained.

Indeed, instead of viewing the future with some alarm and concern it now appears to be the belief of many that if we were but to make an effort to reduce deficits and increase employment, while simultaneously providing sufficient funds and capital to refuel our economic engines (but always with a balanced budget in mind), we could look ahead to a bright and rosy tomorrow — not at all the kind of future the scientists, referred to above, did gravely forewarn. The optimistic phrase "sustainable development" tends to creep into many prognostications; and when most of us in the United States examine life about us, it is difficult to come to grips with the distressing prospect of doom-and-gloom conditions. While we do admit that the world is troubled, as in the case of the former Yugoslavia, and nuclear upstarts continue to threaten us, we generally believe that adequate steps are being taken to rectify such situations and that the world will soon be a better place in which to live. In addition, we are such inveterate optimists that we often believe it will; for as Pope wrote, "Hope springs eternal from the human breast." The world, it would seem, is following the modern advertising trend of having a ditty or jingle as a theme song to promote everything from coffee and toilet-bowl cleaners to insurance companies, and its anthem is rapidly becoming the tune "Wishing Will Make It So."

Far in the back of the minds of many, though, lies the fear that something indeed is amiss and that the global engine is not exactly operating on all cylinders. While a few would argue that current conditions are moving rapidly toward a point so critical that *Homo sapiens* may have to add itself to the list of endangered species, the majority of us suffer a form of denial — either ignoring or scoffing at such an idea. After all, each time humans were previously confronted with crisis situations we were able, in some manner, to overcome most of them once we put our minds to the task — so why worry? Solutions are all about us — right?

I must confess I am one of those who are convinced that such currently popular slogans as "Help Save the Planet!" are absurd, at best, and generally quite misleading, even deceptive, since the earth could, I suppose, get along very well without us. What such slogans or buzzwords actually mean — whether or not those who shout them out realize it, or have the courage to admit it — is "Help save *us* from disaster and provide *us* with the sort of life we would like to live." The fact is, until the last minute of another hypothetical 24-hour clock — one representing the totality of *global* history — there were no people present, and planet Earth and all living matter thereon presumably got along rather well. Now, however, during those final few seconds, when human beings finally arrived on the scene, we have demonstrated an absolutely amazing incapacity to care a whit for a world we take pretty much for granted, and an unbelievable propensity to harm, or at best ignore, our individual environments, including the lives and future of others like ourselves.

Any number of emblems or symbols, ranging from whales to chickadees to butterflies, could be used to draw attention to this serious human shortcoming. These species are now, each in its own way, also facing extremely tenuous futures due, in some degree, to a certain amount of callousness but principally ignorance on our part. However, instead of such common, perhaps obvious and well-known figureheads, I have chosen to utilize a plant species — the Para rubber tree — which I believe to be not only a more appropriate standard to demonstrate our continued abuse of nature but also one which hints at a variety of novel approaches that might be taken to avoid or at least mitigate such ill-treatment.

I know this species well and have often shown it to a wide range of people. Their immediate reaction on observing even the tapping of a single tree has convinced me that it could easily serve as an unusual and exotic emblem, and thus perhaps one more able to attract the requisite high degree of attention. This Amazonian species, originally known as caoutchouc (rhymes with Groucho — as in Marx), may also be regarded as special and unique in that it can be shown to represent a wide gamut of topics and could thus provide a more complete and unifying starting point to portray currently serious and multifaceted global environmental problems as well as possible solutions to these.

So, let me count its ways. To begin with, while this tree can be said to depict the wonder and mystery of an entire tropical rain forest ecosystem, it is also the epitome of a naturally derived or extracted product — rubber — on which our complex, modern technologically oriented societies are virtually completely dependent. Additionally, and perhaps of even greater importance, there is the little-understood role played by isoprene, a gaseous chemical compound often identified with rubber, found in many non-latex-bearing plants. Also a byproduct of animal physiology, this substance may help maintain a critical balance not only within these organisms but, once expelled or emitted from them, in the earth's atmosphere as well. When we fathom and comprehend these functions more thoroughly, it is hoped that we will be induced to pay more attention to the argument that we must soon assume not a sovereign but rather a holistic and cooperative relationship with all living things or suffer some form of disagreeable retribution.

Since most of us, in the United States at least, are from a culture in which we were originally admonished to "have dominion over the fish of the sea and over the birds of the air and over every living thing that moves upon the earth,"[4] we face a serious and trying predicament in this regard. It is perhaps difficult, after all these years, for many to understand that the verb *to dominate* should have a broader and more profound meaning than the self-serving anthropocentric one to which we have so long been accustomed. Fortunately, there is some precedent in another definition, since the fundamental tenet of democracy, after an abortive beginning in ancient Greece and a slow and anguished comeback, is that those who dominate today's governments do not obtain this position either by means of force or through heredity but instead are, or should be, honestly elected by a majority to assume the role of public servants, not masters. Thus, the word *dominate* implies not only a ruling position but a leading, guiding, and managing one as well. Furthermore, many are just beginning to understand that to execute any dominant or key role seriously and efficiently is a challenge which allows little margin for error.[5]

It is additionally frustrating that a look at our track record over the past several centuries reveals such a lack of intelligent leadership in the carrying out of programs that benefit humanity as a whole (and not just the leader or leaders themselves). Fortunately, there have been a few successes to which we can point with some pride, during this same period, that can provide adequate guidelines, or be used as models. These may give us a good enough idea of what we must do. Despite these indications as to which paths to follow, the question remains whether we are capable of choosing competent leaders to escort us to a less threatening environmental future and then working with them toward achieving this end. A serious obstacle today is that for too many, "Looking Out for Number One" is the prevailing "ethic"; calls for action and pleas to assist in improving the general welfare are viewed as a complete bore and a waste of time — to be avoided whenever and wherever possible.

I began these essays in preparation for a series of lectures on tropical ecosystems — and probably also as an exercise in readying myself for imaginary confrontations with those not trained or prepared to take their environment seriously. From the start, I had hoped that these might be dialogues through which the facts of the matter could be debated in an unbiased, reasonable way. I have utilized, as examples for discussion, ideas gained from personal experience and observation, as well as the thoughts of others, on where we might be erring or mismanaging our world — all with variations on the theme of the Para rubber tree, its ecology and byproducts, as points of departure.

In this I had considerable advice and counsel from many but particularly E. P. Imle, a friend for more than 40 years who first taught me about rubber. I am indebted, of course, to my wife Nancy Hunter, who — though she was never really enchanted with tropical forests and jungles (which she usually referred to as "green monsters") and more often than not was quite offended by the sanctimonious behavior of those (scientists and academicians in particular) who too often attempted to hide such an unflattering attribute behind the transparent shield of "searching for the truth"[6] — always made a concerted effort to keep me honest in my quest. While I have learned to agree with her in many respects, and have attempted to stick simply to my own views, I must also acknowledge my gratitude for the help I received from many of this particular group including Bil Alverson, Edilberto Camacho, Mo Donnelly, Hugh Iltis, Francesco Loreto, Gene Manis, Jorge Mora, Eldon Newcomb, Tom Sharkey, Steve Solheim, Bob Voertman, and Allen Young. I should also like to thank David Tenenbaum for his assistance in editing portions of this book.

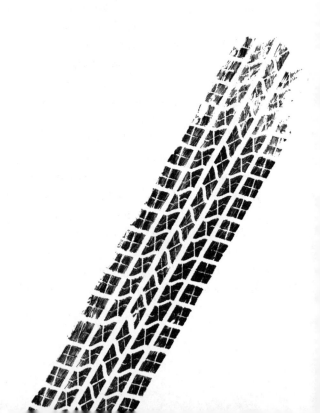

SIMPLE THINGS WON'T SAVE THE EARTH

1

A SYMBOL
OF OUR ENVIRONMENTAL DILEMMA

ANYONE WHO HAS watched the touchdown of a space shuttle must surely have observed those twin puffs of smoke coming from the tires when the wheels hit the ground. These instantaneous, transitory flashes of vaporizing rubber, while nowhere near so dramatic as a flame-engulfed launch, have always been, for me, the key indication of the safe execution of one of the most difficult and crucial aspects of a space mission: the landing. As most of us are probably aware, the same sort of display, but with less drama, occurs when the tires on commercial aircraft strike the runway on landing. The intense heat from the friction caused when the rubber of the tires engages the surface of the runway produces the smoke — for rubber does burn. What, perhaps, is not so well known is that the tires of commercial aircraft, like those of space shuttles, are almost 100 percent natural rubber, whereas only about 30 to 40 percent of the rubber in an ordinary automobile tire is natural — most of it is synthetic.

The majority of drivers are now so accustomed to take the safety of their cars for granted, with large sums of advertising money being spent each year to maintain this attitude, that not many would find the discrepancy between the composition of automobile and aircraft tires of any great consequence. Actually, vehicles — significantly called "wheels" by some of the more youthful among us — are such an integral part of our culture that few ever contemplate what is involved in the production and manufacture of the tires on which they run or question the availability of raw materials required for their construction.

In truth, though, as the result of countless engineering studies by a number of individual companies, but particularly the Malaysian Rubber Research and Development Board,[1] natural rubber has been shown to retain its elastic properties through rapid changes in temperature and pressure in a manner superior to that of synthetics. It has therefore been accepted as the material of choice in tires that may not only have to go through such changes but must be counted on to be able to withstand sudden and violent shocks without sacrificing their integrity. Shuttlecraft, aircraft, racing car, and truck tires, all of which suffer greater abuse than ordinary car tires, are thus constructed for the most part from natural rubber.

I have come to realize that few people are really knowledgeable about these facts and so was only slightly surprised to discover, during the recent and highly publicized[2] struggle of Francisco (Chico) Mendes and other Brazilian rubber tappers to prevent the destruction of the environment which provides them with their humble livelihood, that the majority among us are also not at all certain as to just where natural rubber comes from nor how it is processed. But then, the manufacture of synthetic polymers — the technical term for any compound of high molecular weight that is produced by the coupling of many smaller molecules of the same kind (like so many links of sausages) — must also be a rather mysterious process. By the same token, I wonder how many of us are aware that not only the tires on shuttle spacecraft but many other items, including millions of examination gloves and the more than three billion condoms produced annually on a worldwide basis, are made exclusively from natural rubber latex.

Heartbreaking and senseless as the Mendes murder was, it must be recognized as but a single example of a growing number of similar tragic confrontations which are now being played out all over the earth. Indeed, during the past 20 or 30 years, acknowledgment of increasing injury to and misuse of distinct aspects of the earth's ecosystem (including terrible abuse of millions of human beings) is evidenced by a spate of programs, articles, television specials, and gatherings all presented and organized with the hope of rectifying some dilemma, such as acid rain, global warming, or ozone depletion, now threatening our physical existence.

Nevertheless, "Earth Days" have come and gone and all we are really left with is the disturbing realization that after the tree plantings, high-powered political photo opportunities, sit-ins, and folk music devoted to proclaiming support for the health of our planet, there has been little ecological improvement.[3] Actually, for the largest percentage of our rapidly burgeoning numbers, especially those in developing countries, life not only continues to be as grim as it has always been, but is actually deteriorating — slowly, silently, yet inexorably. While there are those from the more affluent sectors of society who may view the future as a disturbing one, most members of such fortunate communities are sufficiently content with their current lifestyles as to shrug off any worry about what might be in store for the earth as a whole.[4] In this connection, a recent Roper Poll indicates that 70 percent of U.S. consumers do not shun or abandon products considered environmentally irresponsible.[5] Even more to the point are the results from a Gallup Poll, which show that while 76 percent of Americans identified themselves as environmentalists, only 4 percent cited the environment as a major problem. When asked about future concerns, replies showed that taxes, jobs, prices, and interest rates took up 91 percent of the answers and ecological or environmental matters none at all![6]

What, one might ask, does all this have to do with such a common and ordinary commodity as rubber? To begin with, it is becoming increasingly clear that both natural and synthetic rubbers, so necessary to most of us, and yet so much taken for granted, appear to have very uncertain and threatened futures. If this is the case, I hope to rectify this serious gap in our general knowledge. To begin with, the recent aggressive and petulantly destructive actions of Saddam Hussein in the Persian Gulf should remind us of the possibility that the production of synthetics of any kind could be placed in some jeopardy, since many substitutes for natural products, including synthetic rubber, are manufactured from petroleum. So far as natural rubber is concerned, assurance of a readily available future supply is in doubt as well. According to a World Bank prediction, published well before the Persian Gulf crisis of the early 1990's, our needs for this product, even under normal conditions, will double before the year 2000, and the output of natural rubber is not increasing sufficiently and at a pace to meet future demand.[7]

As so many recent alarmist statements regarding the supposed demise of our environment have produced no sudden and dramatic change in the manner by which we live, some may wonder whether such predictions about rubber are really based on facts or whether they are, perhaps, based instead on observations similar to those that caused the anguished cries of Chicken Little that "the sky is falling." The actions and pronouncements of our politicians — who, one might think, should certainly be knowledgeable about such subjects — tend to support these same doubts. Elected officials in general have shown a surprising lack of interest, not only in studying or evaluating environmental degradation, but also in demonstrating strong leadership on this extremely important issue.

Furthermore, when considering this generally pessimistic view as it specifically relates to rubber, we must accept the reality that we are indeed approaching a very critical period with regard to the availability of adequate raw materials.[8] The prospect of this impending crisis of supply is supported by many who have carefully studied this situation over a period of years, and should provoke more than modest concern. For what we are facing is not just a shortage of supply but a failure of imagination: that is, it is almost impossible for any of us to think what it might be like to drive a car — even a solar-powered, hydrogen-powered, or electric car on the technological cutting edge — that is not equipped with rubber tires of some sort. After all, what other material is there for this purpose?

I am proposing here that this single tree species may serve as a meaningful symbol for the larger issue of global devastation. In addition to the important but rather familiar or mundane use of the exudate from Para rubber trees as a key and intrinsic component of modern-day life, the chief constituent of this latex, a hydrocarbon called isoprene, may play a key role in the maintenance of the chemical balance of the earth's atmosphere. Another aspect to be considered is the labor required to extract this substance, as this embodies all the unfortunate attributes associated with the menial and onerous tasks of other similar extraction industries, such as mining, lumbering, and fishing.

Thus, those who are truly disturbed, as I am, by the increasingly ominous outlook for the earth's environment may well agree with me that an ideal starting point for analyzing some of these difficulties may well be this tree, scientifically known as *Hevea brasiliensis*. Its common name comes from the state of Para in Brazil; in the local Indian dialect, *para* means river — in this particular case, the mighty Amazon itself. Also, while perhaps not quite so grand as the Brazil nut tree or other giant dominants of these tropical jungles, with its tall, straight bole and full crown, Para rubber is a sufficiently noble example of the Amazon rain forest to merit being the emblem not only for the forests in this region but for forests everywhere. As these vital ecosystems are now rapidly disappearing, I believe that an understanding of the best means of establishing rubber and increasing the total acreage planted could provide much needed insight as to how to better manage forests, as well as diverse natural landscapes in other locales.

Since each of these examples should be a matter of considerable importance and consequence to everyone, let us turn to a brief review of the history of this particular tree species and of our dependence on and relationship to it.

2

THE
PARA RUBBER TREE

OUR CURRENT USE of and growing demand for natural rubber is a classic example of the discovery, exploitation, and ongoing development of a natural product. Over the course of slightly more than two and a half centuries, rubber sprang from obscurity, was improved from a curiosity into an essential industrial product, and has become one of the most important crops in the world. During this brief period, this commodity even enjoyed a status worthy to be the subject of explorer's myths. Furthermore, it has provided one of the better tales relating to economic botany in our literature.

Rubber was almost completely unknown in Europe and North America until Charles-Marie de La Condamine, the French explorer and mathematician, returned to Paris from a trip to South America in 1735 with samples in hand. Actually, he had just completed a rather difficult and trying expedition to Ecuador (then a province of Peru) at the request of the French Academy of Sciences to measure and determine the exact shape of the earth from its equator and took the dangerous, difficult route, one almost never traveled by Europeans, descending the eastern slopes of the Andes to the Amazon River. From there he was able to proceed across to the Atlantic with relative ease. During this trek through tropical jungles, he was in an excellent position to collect samples of the unique plant he spoke of as "caoutchouc."[1] It is interesting that the name he used is still the common one for rubber in French-speaking countries today. In Germany it is known as *das Kautschuk* and in Italy as *caucciú*.

It should be noted here that a rather complete and entertaining outline of the history of rubber, up to World War II, is to be found in Vicki Baum's novel *The Weeping Wood*.[2] This title is a translation of the indigenous Quechua word *caucho, cahutchu,* or *caoutchouc,* which denotes the manner by which this product is basically derived from trees in the Amazon basin; they are cut so as to bleed, or "weep." These trees belong to the spurge family, or Euphorbiaceae, of which a common characteristic is that they contain latex. If you snap a leaf from a more available spurge, the poinsettia plant, you will quickly see this milky substance ooze from the wound.

As there are so many different local and scientific names for this product and the plants from which it is obtained, one should properly begin with a discussion of its nomenclature. To begin with, in 1775, another Frenchman, Fusée Aublet, established the scientific name of the genus in which the most important source of natural rubber is to be found as *Hevea*. He derived this name from the Carib Indian word *hevé*, which subsequently led to a minor turmoil in botanical taxonomy, as this was actually the common name used for another species of latex-bearing tree to be described later. Both are still called by this appellation, or *hebe* in Peru and Ecuador.[3]

Aublet, along with such other plant explorers and botanists as the Englishman Richard Spruce, the Germans K. F. P. von Martius, Jacob Huber, and E. H. G. Ule, and the Austrian Alfonse Ducke, all of whom actually worked in South America — together with George Bentham in England and the Swiss Jean Mueller (known in the literature as Mueller-Argoviensis), who devoted themselves exclusively to herbarium material — eventually recognized up to 24 different species of this genus. More recently, R. J. Seibert from the United States, whose work centered mainly in eastern Peru during the 1940's, greatly reduced this number to 8 species and 2 varieties.[4] At approximately the same time, J. T. Baldwin, Jr., also an American, accepted 9 *Hevea* species but pointed out, as had Seibert, the tendency of this genus to hybridization. Finally, Richard E. Schultes, another American, who also worked for lengthy periods along the Amazon before, during, and after World War II, accepted 9 species and 4 varieties. Schultes, however, questioned the thinking of both Seibert and Baldwin on the importance of hybridization.[5]

Of all these species and varieties only *H. guianensis*, *H. benthamiana*, and *H. brasiliensis* yield commercially valuable rubber and have been exploited in the wild. From the standpoint of latex production, the last is by far the most important. Indeed, a number of authors indicate that the yields and quality of the first two species are inferior, and thus command a much lower price than that paid for *H. brasiliensis*, better known as the Para rubber tree.

In Brazil, where Portuguese is the national language, the tree and its exudate are referred to as *borracha* (bottle) but are more commonly called *seringa* (syringe). These names derive from the ancient practice by Amazon Indians of forming small bottles or syringes from fresh latex which, following coagulation, they filled with water and used as toys (just as youngsters play with squirt guns today) at their celebrations. When the Portuguese conquistadores arrived in Brazil in the sixteenth century and observed this custom, they naturally applied their own words for the toy to the tree and its product.

Plants of this genus, however, are not the only source of rubber. Another New World tree, *Castilla*, commonly called *hebe* by the Indians of Peru and Ecuador (here is where Aublet made his terminological mistake), as well as by the Quechua word *caucho*, has also been a source of commercial rubber. In Central America and Mexico it is also called *caucho* but more commonly *hule* after its Aztec name — *ule*. It is a member of the mulberry family, or Moraceae, and as in the example above, a leaf snapped off any ornamental *Ficus* from this same family will also bleed latex from the wound.

If all one wishes, however, is to see latex, dandelions will do quite well, and a number of other plants from the composite family, or Asteraceae — such as guayule (*Parthenium argentatum*) or the Russian dandelion (*Taraxacum koksaghyz*) — have been used commercially to produce latex when demand and price were high.

To return to the Moraceae, it could have been a ball made out of the rubber from *Ficus elastica*, an Asian member of this family, that was so much coveted by King John in A. A. Milne's poem — "And oh, Father Christmas, if you love me at all, bring me a big red India rubber ball."[6] Others claim that the use of "India" when speaking of this rubber refers to the West Indies, since Columbus, following his second voyage, wrote of seeing Indians in what is now Haiti playing with rubber balls that had to have been obtained from the *Castilla* tree. The use of "India" in this connection may also have been due to the fact that it was Indians from South American jungles who were, at that time, chiefly responsible for the collection of this product. Robert Friedel writes that during the first "rubber boom," which took place early in the nineteenth century, the largest of several factories to open was that of the Roxbury India Rubber Company just outside Boston.[7]

It is certain, though, that when Joseph Priestley, the chemist and discoverer of oxygen, used bits of dried latex to rub out mistakes he had jotted in his notebooks with a lead pencil, he called the material a "rubber" instead of using the perhaps more cumbersome, yet quite proper English word *caoutchouc* (which is still in our dictionaries).

English-speakers everywhere were soon using "rubber" for eraser. This new convenience was, however, rather high-priced. In 1770, Priestley wrote that "a cubical piece of about half an inch cost 3 shillings." This equates to about $200 a pound for dried rubber latex at that date — the highest recorded price for this product. It is curious, though, as P. W. Allen has pointed out, how this name caught on and persisted as the result of such a trivial use.[8]

Before we return to the Para rubber tree, other factors that led to a rapidly growing demand for this commodity at that time should be noted here. The key breakthrough was Charles Goodyear's serendipitous discovery of vulcanization in the early 1800's when he accidentally spilled one of his experimental concoctions on a hot stove top. Once he had pried this mixture loose and let it cool, he noticed that certain properties of rubber change when it is heated with sulfur. Instead of a gooey mass, Goodyear had produced a resilient, pliable, and tough material that continued to retain its new configuration — in this case, the shape of the stove top. By the middle of the century, large and well-attended exhibitions were held in both London and Paris to promote a variety of new vulcanized products. This not only stimulated demand but also demonstrated the potential of this substance, and other novel uses soon appeared.

For example, a raincoat made from rubberized cloth is often still called a mackintosh more than 150 years after Charles Mackintosh made waterproof garments in England by dissolving rubber in naphtha, spreading the resulting liquid on cloth and allowing the naphtha to evaporate.

The mackintosh was followed by the invention of rubber-working machinery by Thomas Hancock that, by means of mastication or grinding up of odd lots and bits of dried latex with sulfur and other additives such as lampblack (carbon) under heat and pressure, produced standard and uniform sheets of rubber. This technology soon led to the most important invention of all — the tire — by John Dunlop, first for bicycles and later for horseless carriages.

These discoveries and innovative applications quickly boosted demand to the point that a frantic search for new sources of natural rubber outside the Amazon basin was soon under way. For example, a vine, from the milk-weed family (Asclepiadaceae), discovered in the early nineteenth century in the humid forests of central Africa by a French botanist, who identified and named it *Landolphia*, was shown, in the late 1850's, to be a good source of latex. (As an aside, it should be emphasized that the scientific names are not used here to bore or annoy the reader. These will be of considerable importance later, and as the saying goes — one really can't tell the players without a scorecard.)

Before long, Leopold II, king of Belgium, began making a fortune off this crop on what amounted to his private farm — the Belgian Congo. A good part of his economic success is attributed to his barbaric treatment of native latex gatherers. Workers who did not harvest their unrealistic daily quotas lost their hands as a punishment.[9] Despite this incredibly but rather routinely harsh treatment of African laborers by European overlords, neither this source of latex nor any of the other plants tested up until then could really compete with the Para rubber tree.

Latex collectors in Brazil, known as *seringueiros*, suffered exploitation that was only slightly less brutal than that experienced in the Belgian Congo. This frenzied quest to produce ever-increasing amounts of latex to meet the rising demand for rubber in Europe and North America, depicted in Werner Herzog's movie *Fitzcarraldo*, caused the rapid growth of the two Amazon river towns of Manaus and Belém into large and important cities. The former was resplendent with its Opera House, where Galli-Curci, Caruso, and many other world-famous artists performed. Under such boom situations, the so-called local rubber barons[10] demonstrated a most savage treatment of those who worked to bring this product out of the jungle. I argue that this form of what amounted to indentured servitude of rubber tappers by a wealthy and powerful few — who appeared to be interested only in the amount of latex produced and not in the workers' welfare, in the possibility of horticultural innovation, nor in the condition of the rubber trees themselves — was a major reason the New World is now in the backwater of rubber production, while this crop has become one of the principal jewels of the Southeast Asian agricultural crown.

The true account of the transfer of the Para rubber tree from the Ama-

zon to Asia and later to other tropical areas is fascinating, but the oft-told
tale of how this occurred is undoubtedly apocryphal — probably the result
of effective propagandizing on the part of an adventurer who had dabbled
in rubber in various parts of South America and was later knighted for his
role in transferring the seeds. The Englishman, Henry A. Wickham, did
not really smuggle rubber seed from Brazil by calling them "rare botanical
plants for the Queen's private garden." In recounting this exploit, Wickham
was acting, I am convinced, as his own public relations man.[11] The record
shows that he embellished the facts regarding his problems in harvesting
the seeds and getting them out of Brazil. The major factor was not skull-
duggery or smuggling but a series of remarkably fortunate happenstances,
which in themselves make for quite a story.

In the first place, there was then no law regarding exports of plant material. P. W. Barker and E. G. Holt of the U.S. Department of Commerce
wrote that the "romantic story that Wickham obtained the rubber seeds
against the orders of the Brazilian government is not supported by fact or
by any prohibition against exportation of rubber seeds at the time of this
incident."[12] R. E. Schultes substantiates these remarks, and W. E. Klippert, a former manager of Goodyear's Central American operations, wrote,
in an attempt to clear up this matter: "The truth was available to any re-
searcher who cared to sift through an official report prepared for the
Brazilian Ministry of Agriculture, Industry and Commerce in 1913 by Dr.
O. Laboy. This government publication titled A Borracha no Brasil (Rubber in Brazil) states, on page 42 in the chapter concerning the development of cultivated rubber, 'And it was an Englishman, Wickham, then a res-
ident of Santarém, to whom must go the honor of having exported to Kew
Gardens the first fresh seed of Hevea brasiliensis, thanks to the benevo-
lence of the Brasilian Government, which arranged to have the seeds collected for him by Indians in the forests of the uplands of the lower Tapajós
River.'"[13]

The old legend, even including the cunning manner by which Wickham plied the Belém customs officers with liquor so that the S.S. Amazonas could sail away while they lay in a drunken stupor, has the makings
of a good yarn, but the true account is equally intriguing. To begin with,
Wickham was just plain lucky. For example, the timing for his gathering
the seed crop was an absolute fluke. These acorn-sized, shiny, speckled

seeds (generally sought for the oil they contain or, more often, for use as a crop in some drug-plant substitution program) are only available at one particular, brief harvest period each year.

Rubber trees are deciduous and form their little green, scented flowers after each annual leaf fall. The fruit, a three-compartmented seed pod, matures about six months after pollination. These pods will rupture on hot sunny days with a loud pop and shoot the enclosed seeds away from the parent tree to scatter about the forest floor. These either soon germinate, are eaten by a wide range of jungle life, or perish, for their viability is quite brief. This seed dispersal occurs but once a year and lasts about two to three weeks.

But to return to Wickham and his luck, here we have a man, who at that period in his life was practically destitute, upon whom was thrust a good solid order for rubber seed, just when a British ship, empty of any cargo, was on its way back to England. On the basis of this commission from Sir Joseph Hooker, director of Kew Gardens, Wickham was able to sign what amounted to a C.O.D. contract with Captain Murray of the S.S. *Amazonas* to transport the seed to Liverpool. Next, the local government provided him with the labor to collect the seed. Finally (and why this is never mentioned is beyond me), all these events coincided exactly with the very brief yet critical period of seed dispersal.

For some time, there had been growing interest in establishing rubber as a commercial crop in the Far East. As early as 1861, the Dutch had grown India rubber trees and later *Castilla* rubber from the Americas on plantations in the East Indies, but with poor yields. Their efforts were due not only to a heightened demand for rubber in Europe at that time, but also to a disaster in the many coffee plantations. During the 1800's, the Dutch East Indies was the world's major producer of this commodity, with the result that for some time, even in the United States, a "cup of Java" was synonymous with a cup of coffee. In an attempt to improve the quality and production of this crop, the Dutch sent agronomists to the upland forests of Ethiopia (the true home of coffee) to bring back superior varieties. In short order, these specialists identified heavy-bearing plants in the African forests, dug these up, planted them in wooden barrels and shipped them back to Java, while carefully watering them during the entire trip. Unfortunately and unknowingly, however, they also returned with a coffee rust disease, caused by the fungus *Hemileia vastatrix*, on the leaves of their selected trees.[14] This leaf rust (which, in its most lethal form, kills off its host by causing complete leaf fall) soon shattered Java's prominent position in the coffee world, leaving a trail of devastation through the Malay Peninsula, Ceylon (now Sri Lanka), and southern India.[15] While Ceylonese planters originally replaced their coffee crop with tea, the Dutch chose to cultivate rubber.

The British were more fortunate with the type of rubber they selected, although they also suffered initial reverses in attempts to transfer rubber seeds or plants from the Americas to Asia. It was only when Sir Joseph Hooker of Kew Gardens — on the advice of a number of people, particularly Sir Clements Markham, who had attempted unsuccessfully to transfer rubber to India (but had been instrumental in bringing the quinine-producing cinchona tree from Peru to Asia) — made arrangements with the government of India to provide Wickham with the commission referred to above that things slowly began to move forward. From the 70,000 seeds Wickham sent to Kew in 1876, however, only 2,700 plants were actually raised — an extremely low percentage of success. From this meager number, a total of 1,919 seedlings were shipped in Wardian cases (small portable greenhouses) to the Botanic Gardens of Peradeniya in Ceylon in August 1876. Two days later, 50 of these plants were shipped to Singapore, but due to poor handling all eventually died. In June of the following year, according to John Purseglove, 22 additional plants were shipped from Kew to Singapore, of which, this time, only 3 were lost.[16] In any case, the millions of acres of rubber trees found today throughout Southeast Asia all descended from these few trees raised from the seeds that Wickham had collected during one brief annual harvest period from a single locality on the banks of the Tapajós River near Santarém, Brazil.

To continue this series of fortuitous episodes, E. P. Imle, former director of the USDA Rubber Research Station at Turrialba, Costa Rica, states that Wickham (although he had collected rubber seed in other areas, including the banks of the Orinoco River) was probably unaware that only *H. brasiliensis* grew in the vicinity of Santarém.[17] Had he collected elsewhere and obtained seeds from another species, the development of rubber culture could have been delayed everywhere, perhaps for decades.

Equally important, during this seed transfer, neither leaves, bark, nor other parts of the tree (which might have carried diseases) were shipped. Thus, when the seeds arrived at Kew Gardens, they were germinated and grown in what was, for all practical purposes, an intermediate plant quarantine center of which none then existed in the world, almost guaranteeing that all pests and diseases of this tree were left behind in Brazil.

However, not everything was as providential as it might have been; for, again according to Imle, Wickham's choice of his collection site was certainly not ideal, as the yield potential of the Tapajós populations of *H. brasiliensis* is considerably lower than that of sources found farther to the west in the Acre region of Brazil near the Peruvian border. However, to be fair, Wickham was not aware of these more productive trees; they were not discovered and incorporated into breeding gene pools until the 1940's.

Despite this minor setback, fortune continued to follow rubber as it spread throughout Southeast Asia. The first bit of luck, according to Allen M. Young, entomologist with the Milwaukee Public Museum, was that Ceratoponogid midges, a rather ubiquitous group of tropical insects, were already present in the forests of Asia and able to pollinate the rubber once the trees were old enough to flower.[18] This might not appear to be so remarkable until one considers that such ecological circumstances have not always been the case in the transfer of plant specimens. For example, since no pollinating insects awaited vanilla when these climbing vines of the orchid family were taken, soon after the Spanish conquest, from Mexico and Central America to other parts of the tropical world, it is not surprising that no eagerly hoped-for vanilla beans were produced. I learned from Robert Dressler of the Smithsonian Institution that it is the male euglosine bees (indigenous to and found only in Mexico and Central America) that pollinate the small, green flowers of this vine. They carry out this task as part of their strategy to obtain from the flowers and ripe beans essences that are then converted into pheromones used to attract female bees.[19] Today, in such places as Madagascar, where the greatest amounts of vanilla are grown, flowers must be pollinated by hand, contributing to the substantial cost of this spice.

Next in this saga of rubber development came Henry Ridley, director of the Botanic Gardens in Singapore in the late 1880's. Of all the Englishmen working on the development of rubber at that time, Ridley was, in my estimation, unjustifiably passed over for knighthood. I am by no means alone in this opinion: in 1941, O. F. Cook of the USDA Bureau of Plant Industry went so far as to publish a paper urging a change in the name of the Para rubber tree to *Siphonia ridleyana* in honor of Mr. Ridley. Cook pointed out that "without Ridley's discovery (of his method for tapping) there would have been no commercial planting of *Siphonia* in the East Indies, higher prices would have ruled, and some of the *Castilla* plantations in Mexico and Central America would have been profitable." [20]

There is little doubt that through his continual persistence "Rubber Ridley," or "Madman Ridley," was chiefly responsible not only for the development of plantation rubber plantings for Southeast Asia but also for a superior tapping system, modifications of which are still used today. Prior to Ridley's efforts, latex was extracted by butchering the trees with machetes or axes — with no concern for regrowth of bark — to obtain the maximum latex in the shortest time. Since rubber trees seemed a limitless resource in many Amazonian jungles, *seringueiros*, whose lives were dismal at best, gave little thought to tapping trees (which they did not even own) carefully or systematically. When tapping the *Castilla* tree, which gave far more latex at one tap than Para rubber trees (but which could only be tapped a few times during a year), the *seringueiros* literally killed these geese which laid golden eggs, by cutting the trees to the ground to tap every bit of the trunk and even some larger branches. After viewing the havoc done to Para and *Castilla* rubber trees in the Amazon in 1926, Carl D. La Rue, a rubber specialist with the USDA, wrote that "if there ever were *seringueiros* who were careful in using the *machadinho* (tapping ax), the tribe has vanished from the soil — and the waters — of the Amazon area!" [21]

John Purseglove, who later became director of the Botanic Gardens in Singapore, points out in his two-volume *Tropical Crops: Dicotyledons* that the botanical key to the tapping problem is in the "latex vessels, which are modified sieve tubes . . . formed from the cambium as cells, which fuse and the cross-walls disintegrate. They [the vessels] run in concentric cylinders in a counter-clockwise direction at an angle of about 3.5° to the vertical." [22]

Realizing that this was probably the case, Ridley perfected a system, after an intense effort of trial and error, of making diagonal cuts to the right down the trunk of the rubber trees perpendicular to the latex vessels, assuring maximum flow. These cuts were carefully and delicately made (women are as good or better than men at this task) with a special V-shaped knife called a jebong. An identical instrument is sold in the United States today by a number of outlets, including A. M. Leonard of Piqua, Ohio, which advertises it as a "wound cleaner for easy tree surgery."

In rubber tapping, only a $\frac{1}{16}$-inch strip of bark, which contains the latex vessels, is removed to reach, but not pierce, the cambium layer which is responsible for new growth. Any damage to this layer will prevent normal bark regrowth and possibly kill the tree. Ridley found that successive cuts could be made after a day's "rest" — to allow the tree to recuperate from the previous tapping. After two to three years, when a tapper has finished working from a height of about five feet down one side of the trunk to half a foot above ground (this allows room for the cup, suspended below the cut, in which the latex is captured), new bark will have regenerated and may once again be tapped.

A further boon to the industry was due to the efforts of the Dutch (traditionally excellent horticulturists, who had, nevertheless, experienced such poor success in their initial attempts with other rubber-bearing trees, and dismal failure with coffee) to bud-graft the seedling Para rubber trees that they had been able to obtain from Ceylon. This is a common horticultural technique in which a shoot or bud from one plant (scion) is carefully inserted into the bark or stem of another plant (stock) usually of the same species. Once this scion has "taken" (continues to grow as part of the stock plant), the remainder of the stock plant is cut away, leaving the growth from the new bud to develop into the permanent plant: a clone of the donor. In this connection, I recall asking Daymon Boynton, when he was dean of agriculture at Cornell University, for his estimate of what percentage of high-quality orchard crops in the United States including apples, almonds, and citrus were bud-grafted. He replied immediately, "If it's anything less than a hundred percent it must be a pretty poor farm."

Bud-grafting is such a predominant horticultural technique because it permits planting a seed of unknown potential and then grafting on the resulting seedling a bud from a plant that was carefully selected for precocity, production, and resistance to disease and insects. For all practical purposes the tree will grow and later perform in a manner similar to the donor tree. Prior to the work of the Dutch in Java, in the latter part of the nineteenth century, this technique had never been applied to Para rubber. Soon budwood from outstanding rubber trees in the Far East was grafted to ordinary seedlings, and once these clones were transplanted from the nursery to the field, they guaranteed greatly increased yields.

Another example of rubber's good fortune in Asia was the adoption of plantation farming, as opposed to helter-skelter New World jungle-gathering ventures. The story of coffee and tea plantations of the nineteenth and early twentieth centuries, together with the planters, bearers, coolies, godowns, agents, and shippers, is well documented in the writings of such authors as Joseph Conrad and W. Somerset Maugham.[23] While there was definitely a strict class stratification from plantation owners down to the humble field hand, provision was also made for the necessities of food, clothing, and shelter for the tappers, other workers, and their families. Hospitals, schools, temples, shops, and other components of correct infrastructure were also an integral part of successful plantations. Indeed, rubber plantations in the Far East progressed so well that workers soon had to be imported. By 1934, for example, a total of 61,845 Indians and 41,138 Chinese had immigrated into the Malaya Straits to answer the demand; the Chinese were often considered the most able tappers. Furthermore, these plantings of neat, well-cultivated, straight rows of rubber were a world away from the *estradas*, or random plots of 50 to 200 rubber trees connected by a narrow, overgrown trail through the Amazon jungle. In the Far East, a good tapper could easily handle 350 trees each day, and a total of 700 (on an alternate-day tapping schedule), while his counterpart in Brazil or Peru would visit a maximum of about 100 to 150 trees and these only every third or fourth day, as he was obliged to smoke the collected latex and spend considerable time hunting, fishing, and growing his own food as well. It would be many years before plantation rubber would reach the tree's home in the New World.

Despite all this, because rubber was a completely new crop for Southeast Asia and one that required considerable capital investment, especially during the first six or seven years after planting, as well as before tapping, an additional push would be required before plantation rubber would take hold as an enterprise of any great economic promise. During 1899, the first British official year of record for this region, the overall yield was only 4 tons of processed rubber produced from some 4,000 acres — the total area under cultivation in all of British East Africa. That necessary push was to come with a soaring demand for rubber during World War I.

3

NATURAL

TO SYNTHETIC

FOLLOWING THE RAPID and overwhelming acceptance of vehicles (first horse-drawn, then motor-propelled) that moved about almost exclusively on wheels now protected by rubber, demand for this product soon began to skyrocket. These coverings were initially made of solid rubber and only later became pneumatic, or air filled. Incidentally, the French, who were quite instrumental in perfecting this innovation, still speak of a tire as a *pneu*. Naturally, with the increasing call for this product, prices rose correspondingly, and by 1910 No. 1 Ribbed Smoked Sheets were selling in New York for almost $3.00 a pound. As a point of comparison, while the price on the commodity markets has decreased somewhat recently, by the spring of 1995 rubber had risen from a low of $0.40 in the early 1990's to a range of $0.90–$0.96 a pound in New York.

With the advent of World War I, demand for rubber and rubber products, especially tires, increased even further. Until that time, mass movement of troops and material was either by railway or by horse-drawn carriages with wooden wheels, often iron clad. But the necessity for greater speed and range changed this now-antiquated system rapidly. A classic example of this change was when Paris was under attack, early in the war, and its taxis had to be called to duty to move all available soldiers to the front.

With the armistice, market quotes for rubber eventually began to slacken off, but even so, returns continued to be sufficiently high to stimulate a flurry of planting in Asia. It was, after all, a crop which did not have the disease difficulties that had plagued coffee, was not perishable nor subject to attack by pests and insects once harvested, and furthermore had complete and solid government backing. Thus as coffee, first developed on any scale in the Far East, found a haven from *Hemileia* leaf rust in the New World, rubber escaped its principal diseases when it was cultivated in Southeast

Asia and, under increasingly technicalized management, became an important and prominent crop in this region.

The Far East soon had a monopoly on natural rubber, turning out three-quarters of the total world output, rapidly outdistancing the primitive and inefficient efforts at production of the American tropics. The Opera House in Manaus closed down, and many from this region began to complain that their birthright had been stolen. Eventually the Brazilian government shut the barn door by enacting a law prohibiting the export of rubber seeds, which was in effect until only a few years ago.

The cyclical up-and-down pattern typical of many commodity prices soon took hold on rubber, however, and its value slowly began to decline, reaching a low of $0.14 a pound in 1921. This was due, to some extent, to the increasingly abundant amounts of high-quality product now being supplied by the Far East but probably more to a slackening of demand caused by the generally depressed global economy immediately following World War I. With hindsight, it is now obvious that this recession was stimulated by the first significant rise in petroleum prices on world markets — an ominous harbinger of things to come. Since most of the plantations in the Far East at that time were under British suzerainty, planters naturally turned to London for help. In response, the British Colonial Office quickly appointed a special committee, under the chairmanship of Sir James Stevenson, to look into the matter. The result was a plan designed to limit exports of rubber from the Far East, by means of taxation, until prices rose to a planned-for $0.30 a pound.

Not very much actually took place, however, until the then British secretary of state for the colonies, a gentleman named Winston Churchill, put his full weight behind what had now become known as the Stevenson Restriction Act. With his interest and backing, prices again began to rise.

The Dutch, who by this time were also producing quite a bit of rubber in the Netherlands East Indies (now Indonesia), simply chose not to go along with the Stevenson plan, leaving it to the Americans, who were by then consuming about three-quarters of the entire world output, to single-handedly oppose this restrictive policy. By 1925, when the price had climbed to almost $0.75 a pound, Thomas Edison, Henry Ford, and Harvey S. Firestone, Sr., each in his own way, had been seeking means to challenge and thwart the effects of what they considered to be a rather monopolistic British program. The government of the United States also became involved when Congress appropriated half a million dollars so that the USDA could study areas in the New World (and thus closer to the United States) suitable for growing rubber.

Thomas Edison, then late in life, set out, through his Edison Botanic Research Corporation, to systematically develop some plant which could easily be grown in the United States that might compete with the Para rubber tree in the production of latex. By the time of his death, Edison had developed a variety of goldenrod of the genus *Solidago* (another composite, like the dandelion), from which he is reported to have obtained almost 7 percent pure rubber. While this may seem like a promising start, it implies replanting a crop each year, from which but a single harvest can be made, in comparison with a onetime planting operation from which, once they are of proper age, the trees of a rubber plantation can be tapped for decades.

Both Ford and Firestone opted for sticking with Para rubber, but planting it nearer to home—Firestone in Liberia, and Ford in Brazil. It should be mentioned here that Goodyear was close behind and chose, in addition to its new plantations in Sumatra and the Philippines, to develop farms in Costa Rica and Panama, and later near Belém in Brazil and in Guatemala.[1]

By 1925, Ford had already obtained two large tracts of land very close to the spot where Wickham had obtained his famous seed, one of which, called Boa Vista, was subsequently renamed Fordlandia. The other was later to be called Belterra. Then—in a manner surprisingly similar to that by which Donald Ludwig established a monocultural pulp farm many years later, even towing a processing factory across the oceans from Japan, where it had been built, to the Jari, another tributary of the Amazon—Ford sent ships from the United States that contained the total requirements for his two new rubber plantations near Santarém.[2]

On the Ford plantations, everything went by the book of modern technology. As specially collected rubber seeds were germinated and the resulting seedlings planted out in nurseries waiting to be bud-grafted with the best (or highest-yielding) genetic material the Far East had to offer, schools, hospitals, slaughterhouses, sawmills, and an ice plant were already under construction. Workers were provided with proper housing as well as stores and a church. Hotels, parks, and a theater (shades of the Opera House at Manaus?) together with areas where the workers could produce their own subsistence and garden crops were all properly planned for. This was a far cry from the old days of the rubber barons and their entrapped *seringueiros*, and as nurseries expanded and straight lines of rubber trees were set out in properly prepared fields cut out of the jungles along the banks of the Amazon, prospects appeared most promising.[3]

However, before there was any significant production, disaster hit. A fungus indigenous to the American tropics, with the scientific name of *Dothidella ulei*, which attacks the new young leaves of many *Hevea* species (in a manner quite analogous to that by which leaf rust ruined coffee plantations in Southeast Asia 75 years previously) quickly decimated the new Amazonian rubber plantations. The plants had all been properly budded to what turned out to be very susceptible Far Eastern clonal material (the parent stock of which had originally been collected from this very area).

In the constant process of scientifically upgrading the taxonomic naming of plant and animal species the word *Dothidella*, which I always thought had such a nice ring, was abandoned in favor of *Microcyclus*, but the common name, South American Leaf Blight (SALB), remains the same. These promising and costly efforts to establish Para rubber under plantation conditions in the New World by major U.S. corporations all generally ended up as expensive failures because SALB, a disease of only minor importance on widely scattered *Hevea* trees in the forest, caused complete disaster to these same trees when grown under monocultural conditions. According to Imle, a small 50-acre planting would have been adequate to demonstrate this fact and would have provided a site for research on the control of the disease. Hindsight, he insists, indicates that Ford would have saved many millions had he used some good botanical and pathological advice rather than treating the whole enterprise as simply a large-scale engineering project. The Ford Motor Company eventually abandoned any direct involvement in the business of growing rubber to make its own tires.[4]

The availability of natural rubber in the United States suffered its most serious setback, however, on 7 December 1941, when the Japanese Navy struck at Pearl Harbor. Within days of this attack, and with a seriously damaged U.S. Navy no longer an immediate threat to their flank, Japanese troops were on their way down through French Indochina (now Vietnam) and the Malay Peninsula to the Netherlands East Indies, taking over the productive source of most of the world's natural rubber. To keep things in proper perspective, while rubber was extremely important to the Japanese as well, Admiral Isoroku Yamamoto's chief goal was control of the oil fields of the Netherlands East Indies, since the United States had, at that time, effectively cut off petroleum supplies to Japan.

To overcome the loss of such a critical commodity as rubber, a concerted effort was made to promote the collection of wild rubber in the American tropics through the Rubber Development Corporation of the U.S. Department of Commerce, and many thousands of tons of this vital material were eventually obtained and shipped to the United States. The Cooperative Rubber Research Program of the USDA, while developing a scheme to stimulate the production of guayule in certain of the southwestern states, also initiated, at about this same time, a project aimed at overcoming the ravages of South American Leaf Blight through the use of fungicides, breeding, selection, and a variety of novel horticultural techniques.[5] This was, of course, a long-term effort, following Ford's failure, to make possible the cultivation of Para rubber in the Western Hemisphere.[6] The vital contribution to the emergency needs of a nation at war came, however, not so much from work with different latex-bearing plants but rather from the forced birth of a synthetic rubber industry in the United States, whereby organic products similar to natural isoprene were artificially produced.

Ever since 1826, when Michael Faraday assigned the empirical formula of C_5H_8 to rubber, chemists had been challenged to reproduce this molecule in their laboratories. In 1956, Harry L. Fisher wrote that in 1879, G. Bouchardat, a Frenchman, discovered that by heating natural rubber to a high temperature he could obtain a volatile substance called isoprene, which he reasoned (correctly) might be the building block of rubber. Three years later, in 1882, W. A. Tilden, in England, obtained isoprene from turpentine, which he converted, following Bouchardat's methods, into "a tough substance resembling caoutchouc." He later discovered that isoprene "unites with sulfur in the same way as ordinary rubber, forming a tough elastic compound."[7]

These combining properties of isoprene are due to its molecular structure. Methane, which is far more abundant in nature and extremely stable, does not have the double bonds of isoprene. It is these double bonds that give isoprene the potential for combining with other atoms or molecules. In this connection, it is interesting to note that isoprene, which has a molecular weight of only 68, has never been found, as such, anywhere inside a rubber plant. Latex has an average molecular weight of approximately

1 million and—in addition to its long chain polymer, made up of many links of isoprene—also contains proteins, organic acids, fats, salts, and water. Naturally occurring isoprene is an extremely important constituent of living matter and is eventually emitted into the atmosphere in gaseous form not only from many plants (natural rubber being an important exception) but from a number of animals (including human beings) as well. Actually it is one of the principal atmospheric gases, equaling in volume the more familiar gas methane (CH_4), although its presence is difficult to detect, since it quickly unites or combines with a number of other gases in the atmosphere, as will be more fully discussed later.

Utilizing the basic information developed during the late 1800's and early 1900's, German chemists were able to synthesize from petroleum first isoprene and then butadiene in sufficient quantity to make tires from it. Butadiene, the simplest of all hydrocarbons of this class and superior to pure isoprene for many purposes, was first produced by S. V. Lebedev in Russia in 1910. Later, during World War I, when the Germans were cut off from natural rubber supplies, they produced a substance called methyl rubber, a synthetic polymer similar to butadiene, which they were forced to use as a natural rubber substitute, although they soon discovered this was a quite inferior and much less satisfactory product than that obtained from the Para rubber tree. This synthetic polymer was eventually upgraded to what was known as Buna rubber (Bu = butadiene; Na = sodium, the catalyst used for polymerization), with the formula C_4H_6 and later to the butadiene-styrene copolymer of the 1930's. However, with the termination of hostilities in 1918, relatively little attention was devoted to the production of synthetics, as almost everyone went back to natural rubber because it was abundantly available at low prices and possessed properties and characteristics definitely superior to synthetic rubber.

But then in early 1942, with the Japanese threatening to gain control of those areas that produced most of the world's natural rubber, the other warring nations were forced to fall back once again on synthetic rubber—soon spoken of as SR. This was a severe blow to the United States, for by the time of the U.S. entry into World War II, Americans had become so completely dependent on natural rubber that there was not a single plant or factory in North America expressly established for the manufacture of SR. FDR's hastily appointed Rubber Survey Committee, made up of Bernard M. Baruch, James B. Conant, and Karl Compton, soon recommended, as the most promising means of overcoming the strategically critical problem of a greatly diminished supply of natural rubber, the development and manufacture of a general-purpose synthetic similar to Buna-S (butadiene, sodium, and styrene). While the administration of this program was assigned to William M. Jeffers, president of the Union Pacific Railroad, the actual day-by-day direction of this large-scale, complex chemical engineering effort was assumed by Robert R. Williams, a Bell Telephone chemist, who had had considerable prior experience with natural rubber.

The key to the success of this venture was a remarkable cooperative effort that almost certainly could not have taken place during peacetime. According to Peter J. T. Morris, this was a project in which diverse chemical, oil, and rubber companies joined with research personnel of 12 different universities, the Bell Laboratories, and the National Bureau of Standards under the leadership of Williams to achieve a satisfactory goal in a relatively brief period of time.[8] The success of this operation can only give one pause to contemplate what might be accomplished today with similar group participatory action.

The U.S. government soon constructed a factory at Institute, West Virginia, which by December 1943 was turning out a good supply of Buna-S, later to be known as GR-S (government rubber-styrene). This was quickly followed by additional output from other newly constructed factories; these facilities produced the synthetics that greatly assisted in the crucial job of supplying the armed services, as well as the nation as a whole, with a large percentage of their rubber requirements.

Despite an increasing output of synthetics, these were, unfortunately, not completely satisfactory for some of the more vital aspects of the war effort. Furthermore, as was only later to be discovered, many chemicals involved in the fabrication of synthetics, such as carbon disulfide and butadiene, are toxic — the latter listed today by the National Institute of Occupational Safety and Health as carcinogenic, although there is some disagreement concerning the believed severity of its attack on the human body. To overcome such deficiencies, and as previously indicated, efforts to obtain natural rubber from every available source in this hemisphere continued wherever possible.

James Brooke writes of how Brazil (possibly under pressure from the United States) attempted to develop a cadre of workers to increase rubber output, estimated in the early 1940's at a figure of possibly 100,000 tons a year, simply by seeking out and working over the thousands of untapped trees scattered throughout the Amazonian jungles. These men, soon known as "rubber soldiers," were promptly issued a uniform (of sorts) and a very modest allotment of equipment.[9] Some, including Warren Dean of New York University, have termed the venture a colossal failure, since only about 25,000 of an anticipated 100,000 workers actually made the trip from the northeastern part of Brazil up the Amazon to where wild rubber trees abounded.[10] W. E. Klippert also pointed out that this program was certainly not a successful one, for by the end of the war the entire residual stockpile of natural rubber in the United States amounted to only 60,000 tons, far below the absolute minimum established by the War Production Board.[11]

Once peacetime conditions returned, however, and with natural rubber once more flowing through normal commercial channels, the U.S. government, in an effort to recoup part of its original investment of $677 million, auctioned off to private industry the plants and facilities constructed to produce synthetic rubber, leaving the problem of the development of any new synthetics to the military. At about the same time, possibly because government economic planners had become convinced that synthetics would provide all of our future rubber needs, other projects, such as the USDA Regional Rubber Research Program (chiefly dedicated to work on *Hevea*, but also on such other crops as guayule), were terminated. The most serious result was not so much the discontinuance of these programs as the eventual loss and destruction of clonal collections of natural rubber trees from a number of experiment stations. The enormous amount of time and effort involved in bringing together, then studying and breeding a wide range of distinct *Hevea* varieties from different localities in the Amazon basin was dismantled in a short time span. Little or no thought was given, it seems, to the question of whether we might have to repeat such efforts at some future date.

There was a brief period following the dramatic increase in the price of petroleum in the early 1970's when the U.S. government once again became involved in research on substitutes and alternative sources of energy. However, to our present sorrow, when oil prices began to decline a few years later, still during the Nixon administration, this newly rejuvenated program was hastily and illogically terminated. The result was not only that large numbers of well-trained chemical engineers were suddenly out of work but also that our knowledge and capacity in this field was lost to the perception that oil resources were infinite and that petroleum was the only raw material required to produce all our rubber needs.

From the beginning of the twentieth century, world demand for rubber has shot up exponentially, more or less doubling about every decade. Since the end of World War II, of the total amount of rubber produced in the world, synthetic has varied between 50 and 75 percent. In 1981, total world production of all types of rubber came to 12.6 million tons. By 1988, a total of over 5 million tons of natural rubber was produced and consumed, while during that same year, slightly more than 10 million tons of different types of synthetic rubber was also fabricated, bringing the total used to 15 million tons. One might ask at this point why synthetic rubber never completely took over the entire rubber market and whether it could ever do so. The simple answer is that, as with other uses of synthetics, synthetic rubber, although similar in character, lacks many of the desired properties of natural rubber. (Despite the production of a wonderful range of synthetic fibers, for example, demand for wool, cotton, and silk remains high; and likewise, synthetic vanillin produced from the wastes of pulp mills does not, to the true connoisseur, have the taste, flavor, or aroma of pure natural vanilla.) As previously pointed out, natural rubber has both greater strength and a superior capability for retaining its elasticity through abrupt changes in temperature; moreover, for this reason it is the current choice for aircraft, racing vehicle, and heavy-duty truck tires. Actually, synthetic and natural rubbers can be blended together in any amount; and in the early days of the synthetic program a humorously critical statement used to be made to the effect that synthetic rubber was a remarkable product, as it could be blended with natural rubber in any proportion, but the more natural rubber in the mix, the better the product.

According to P. E. Hurley, president of the Malaysian Rubber Bureau's regional headquarters in Washington, D.C., today's average radial passenger tire weighs about 24 pounds, of which half is made up of rubber and the remainder of carbon black, zinc, sulfur, nylon (or rayon), and steel.[12] The rubber polymer itself is manufactured from a blend of 5 pounds of natural rubber and 7 pounds of synthetic. Natural rubber latex also makes superior examination gloves (so critical in this era of the AIDS epidemic), and all of the condoms presently sold each year on a worldwide basis are made of natural rubber latex. This near universal preference for natural rubber is due to the fact that no synthetic product has yet been found that can so successfully impede the passage of the HIV virus, responsible for the scourge of AIDS.

On 30 January 1995, a memorandum went out from a large distributor of tires to its clients stating the following points, which it considered to be of some concern:

- Tire shortages, though presently severe, could be more pronounced in March and April.
- Extreme rise in the cost of raw materials has caused most tire lines as well as independents to announce tire increases by March, and more are expected.
- Supply is nowhere close to market demands.
- Outlook for those on strike is not at all encouraging. Firestone is presently rehiring to bring up its production staff by replacing union workers.[13]

The content of this memo confirms the current perception that demand will follow the previous pattern and double during the coming decade. In the context of the present argument, the debate can no longer be as to whether technologically fabricated synthetics or natural rubber is more important. The key question now must relate to the availability and abundance of the raw materials used in the fabrication of these two similar, yet different products.

Let us begin, therefore, by first examining the situation as it pertains to natural rubber.

4

DREAM

THE IMPOSSIBLE DREAM?

MIGHT IT ACTUALLY be possible to extract the world's total future rubber needs from a single species of tropical tree and thus achieve some of the oft-touted myth of sustainability for the benefit of all? If such an accomplishment were ever brought to fruition, it would have to be described as the culmination of an environmentalist's or even a practical forester's dream. For converting a reverie of this magnitude into reality would imply the solution of a great many of our most difficult and gnawing ecological problems. An added benefit might be the enhanced possibility of solving a wide range of related social, economic, and political matters that increasingly plague us. In short, the outcome of such an effort could well embody the sort of practical touchstone that many have long been seeking — and even go a long way toward obviating the fear, as expressed by the Union of Concerned Scientists, that we "may so alter the living world that it will be unable to sustain life in the manner that we know it."[1] Yet, since such a hopeful outcome — and the effort needed to attain it — has all the appearance of being too tall an order for us to fill at this point in our history, it should be carefully and thoughtfully analyzed, lest the dream turn into a nightmare.

Let us begin, then, by noting that, according to Colin Tudge, botanists now suggest a theoretical maximum potential yield of 9,000 pounds of natural rubber latex per acre (9,000 kg/ha) per year.[2] This figure is based on some very sophisticated research and developmental work in molecular biology and genetics — coupled with improvements in plant breeding, disease control, and horticulture — carried out over the past 30 to 40 years by private companies, such as Goodyear, Michelin, and Dunlop, as well as such government institutions as the USDA, but particularly the Malaysian Rubber Research and Development Board (formerly, when under British guidance, the Rubber Research Institute — RRI).

Even SALB has finally been brought under control through the selection and breeding of ever more resistant clones as well as by means of topworking (or crown-working) highly productive but nonresistant trees. Topworking is a technique in which a bud from a disease-resistant but not necessarily high-latex-producing selection of *Hevea* is grafted at a height of about 6 to 7 feet on a base-budded, high-yielding (but not necessarily disease-resistant) rubber tree. This nursery tree will have been assisted, since its emergence as a seedling, in attaining this size through constant care, including protection against such diseases as *Phytophthora* and SALB, by various means including the use of fungicides. Once this second bud has taken, the newly formed three-component, or sandwich, tree—in which the trunk (the ham in the sandwich), where tapping takes place, is actually from a clonal selection with the ability to produce large quantities of latex and the top, or crown, is from a SALB-resistant variety—may then be removed from the nursery and planted in the field.

Today, on many commercial plantations in the Far East, the adoption of such new horticultural improvements is helping increase yields dramatically. Also, owing to the following additional techniques, yield figures are now close to 3,000 pounds per acre per year: miner's lamps are employed to permit early morning tapping (latex flows best from predawn hours until about 10 to 11 A.M.); plant growth stimulants are applied to the tapping panel to increase latex flow; electrically driven precision instruments, which are quicker and more efficient than the old jebong knife, are used for puncture tapping; finally, the best tappers are permitted to devote themselves solely to this task, leaving such jobs as the retrieval of latex from the cups on each tree to others. And there are presently under test other innovative projects dedicated toward making the production and collection of latex more efficient.

Even without the use of many of these innovations, the present average in Malaysia is already in the 2,000-pound-per-acre range. This exceeds by a very wide margin the very best average production of *seringueiros*, like the late Chico Mendes, in the Amazon basin. Actually, the Amazonian tappers—who operate under jungle conditions where rubber trees are scattered, some distance apart, and intermixed with a variety of other trees and shrubs—consider themselves lucky when they tap 200–300 pounds to the acre each year.

Another idea, which had actually been tried as much as 50 years ago,[3] relates to the development of some means or scheme to utilize the area between the rows of rubber trees, rather than having to constantly waste time and money cultivating or mowing these strips of land. One method has been to plant corn, bananas, or manihot (cassava) between the rows of rubber trees when these are still young and not yet tall enough to block the sunlight from reaching the "companion" crops. When the rubber trees are more fully grown, these annual crops are abandoned, and something like cocoa (which is more permanent and definitely shade tolerant) is then planted.

In some cases, the interplanting has tended toward providing pasture for animals of some kind. Sheep, goats, chickens, and turkeys have all been tried—with the latter especially effective at the time of seed dispersal in gobbling down these highly nutritious and seldom-used annual offerings. Rubber seeds themselves could provide a source of income from the oil they contain, but harvesting, especially by hand during the single brief seed-distribution period each year, is most time-consuming and arduous. While diversified farming using livestock may not appear too practical a venture except for smallholders, it must be pointed out that between 60 and 70 percent of all rubber planted, even in Malaysia, is on "plantations" under 40 acres in size and is thus obviously in the hands of individual farm families who are usually anxious for any possible extra income from their land.

Though it may seem redundant to mention this fact, Para rubber is a tree and thus can also be used for its lumber.[4] The optimum productive life span of a rubber tree at the present time is approximately 25–30 years, after which latex production begins to decrease. The obvious management decision to take, once trees attain this age, is to remove them and replace them with new ones. During the period when the old trees were in production, it may be presumed that new varieties will have been developed in research and breeding centers that promise such superior performance and higher yields as to certainly justify this replacement.

By the time of latex diminution, the bole, or trunk, of the trees is of good timber size, and the semihard wood itself, light blond to tan in color, is, according to Regis Miller of the USDA Forest Products Laboratory, quite suitable for furniture and paneling.[5] Indeed, for many in East Asia from Japan to Singapore, rubber is now becoming the lumber of choice for such purposes; the only trees not being sought after are those from places like Vietnam where the logs often contain bullets and shrapnel fragments. In a world where timber is being destroyed, burned, or cut in one fashion or another, more rapidly than it is being replaced, the utilization of non-productive trees offers an added economic as well as environmental incentive to increase the acreage of this crop.

But to return to the main topic of discussion, let us, for the sake of argument (and simpler calculations), use the figure of one metric ton, or 2,240 pounds, of dry natural rubber per acre per year as the goal to be harvested by the beginning of the twenty-first century as the basis for this dream.

Estimated world requirements for rubber, including synthetic as well as natural, tend to vary to some degree. This is understandable, taking into consideration the peculiarities and uncertainties of current economic conditions. For example, barring any economic collapse or apocalyptic catastrophe of a global nature, the World Bank has set a figure for global rubber demand in excess of 30 million tons, or over 60,000 million pounds, for the beginning of the twenty-first century. P. E. Hurley, president of the Malaysian Rubber Bureau's Washington office, believes that this figure is too high, and that even an optimistic figure for that date would be considerably lower.[6] However, Dartmouth College professor of environmental studies Noel Perrin has suggested, particularly in relation to the pollution they will cause, that "as recently as 1950, when there were 53 million motor vehicles registered in the world, their emissions could float away with only modest effects. But now the planet has well over half a billion cars and trucks to deal with. Before the year 2000 it will have a full billion."[7]

Taking into account the rubber requirements for only the tires of these vehicles (at an average of 5 tires per vehicle with a composition of 15 pounds of polymer each), this would amount to 33.5 million tons. It is true that the tires will last for more than a year in many cases, but since the consumption of rubber for other needs has been increasing and will undoubtedly continue to do so, it is safe to assume from this evidence that global rubber requirements by the year 2000 could very easily reach a figure of more than 30 million tons. This would imply that, if we were to rely solely on natural rubber for all our needs, we should plan for at least 30 million acres of high-grade plantation rubber trees to supply the estimated demand — providing yields could be in the 2,000-pounds-per-acre range.

At 640 acres to the square mile, this amounts to 46,875 square miles, or about the combined size of Costa Rica and Panama. To bring these figures closer to home, an area almost exactly equal to the total land area of New York State would have to be set aside exclusively for the production of a single commodity — large, yes, but not really overwhelming, considering that the entire moist and humid tropics of the world would be taken into account. Actually, the area in question is less than 1.5 percent of the total land area of Brazil and could easily fit into a corner of the Amazon basin. However, the situation in the tropical regions of the world is rapidly changing; they are no longer empty, unused jungles but are rapidly becoming filled with people.

It should be pointed out here, simply for comparison purposes, that in a recent series of advertisements, the International Paper Company claims it can meet its needs for raw material for paper "through a practice called 'sustainable forestry' which includes planting 50 million SuperTree™ every year."[8] In a similar manner, with a color picture showing schoolchildren viewing a seedling nursery, Georgia-Pacific also states that it is growing the same number each year. Guessing that in both cases these would be planted at approximately the standard Forest Service spacing of 900 trees to the acre, it is simple to calculate that for just these two, admittedly large companies only about 175 square miles of land would be required for such annual plantings.

A metric ton of rubber to the acre at present prices of about $0.85 a pound in New York works out to $1,904.00 gross income per acre. The average plantation tapper can handle 700 trees — 350 each day in an alternate-day tapping schedule. On a recommended 2×10 (meaning 2 meters between each tree with rows 10 meters apart) or 4×5 planting, this comes to slightly more than 5 acres of mature tappable trees; the other 50 to 75 of about 200 planted to the acre will have died or will have been suppressed or removed for one reason or another by the time the trees are of an age and size to tap. Thus each tapper can bring in a yearly gross of about $9,500 for the rubber he or she would presumably be able to produce, when this is placed in New York or London. This figure is actually about twice the present per capita annual income in Costa Rica, six times that of Nicaragua, and higher yet than that of Madagascar, the large island off the southeast coast of Africa, which is predicted to lose all of its forest cover in about 50 years, primarily due to the effects of overpopulation. Even more difficult to comprehend, this income is almost 40 times that of Bangladesh, the South Asian country the size of Wisconsin with a population almost equal to half that of the United States, and which has no forest cover to speak of.[9] These nations are mentioned, in passing, since they are all places capable of producing natural rubber.

Although this gross income figure is considerably higher than the world poverty line set by the United Nations, in addition to the worker's wages, this income must, of course, include transportation and handling, commissions, plantation profits, debt repayment, and so on. Although at first glance the numbers looked quite good, they are, admittedly, not so bright and promising once these costs have been factored in and deducted from the total. In general, the rule of thumb is that the original farm producer receives somewhere between 8 and 12 percent of the final price paid in some importing country. Thus, at best, only about $760 to $1,142 would accrue to each worker per year. While this is considered a rather good wage for most rubber tappers throughout the world, it is certainly nothing to brag about.

As partially spelled out above, yields of natural rubber can probably easily and efficiently be improved, without adding any financial burden to the consumer in the process. The best suggested means for carrying out such changes in order that plantation rubber might be a more attractive agricultural proposal, especially with regard to employees' salaries, would be to use more agricultural chemicals in the form of fertilizers, fungicides, and stimulants, select and breed trees that will produce more latex per cut, and somehow induce workers to increase their tapping tasks. Each of these proposals has obvious drawbacks in terms of cost and human effort. While the yields on small holdings are generally not as great as those on large-scale plantations, many smallholders, especially if they own their farms, have been shown to tap more than do paid workers. It is presumed that because they are working for themselves, they make a greater effort for success. In many endeavors, it has been shown that private ownership (or some scheme that induces workers to believe they are truly in charge of their own destinies) provides an important incentive for extra labor inputs.

Perhaps, then, by developing a satisfactory combination of all the factors mentioned above, but particularly by providing some form of worker incentives, a goal of 5,000 pounds per acre per year may be possible in the not too distant future, and the gross income of each tapper could then be increased to $5,000.00 per year—in today's terms a rather good salary in regions where winter (with all of its economic problems) never comes. However, since this may seem, to many, like a dream too good to be true, for the sake of the present argument, we should probably stick to the original goal of a metric ton per acre per year and consequently lower worker incomes.

To extract the projected total amount of rubber that will soon be needed, including planting out the acreage suggested above, would require engaging the services of approximately 5 million tappers, in addition to the thousands presently engaged in this work, who will have to be trained and on hand by the beginning of the twenty-first century. Large as this number may appear, it does not even come close to putting a dent in the 825 million people the World Bank predicts will be unemployed and living in poverty by the year 2000. A question which could be asked now, for it eventually will have to be dealt with, is whether we can continue to ignore and overlook the plight of this large number of human beings, or are they also part of the overall enigma? Obviously, within the confines of the current presentation, this inquiry will have to be delayed.

The potential employment of close to 6 million people for the one specific task of tapping rubber is one of the social and economic ramifications of this project. This would obviously provide an incredible financial boost to many nations in the tropical regions of the world, such as Haiti, where rubber grows well. An operation of this magnitude, while not to be carried out in one single locality, would also have to involve hundreds of thousands more in ancillary service, supervisory, and administrative positions, to say nothing of those who would be involved in supplying all the rubber workers with their basic wants of food, shelter, and clothing. Hiring on this scale would certainly go a long way toward reducing the ominous unemployment estimates projected by the World Bank.

In addition to considering these special and distinct labor requirements for a global latex-extraction operation, a total of at least 4 billion high-grade new rubber trees, for supplemental plantings as well as replacements, would be required. Naturally, more labor and funds would be needed to produce, bud, and generally care for these nursery plants.

We should pause for a moment to contemplate, again for comparison purposes, that simply producing this enormous quantity of seedlings would actually require far fewer trees than President George Bush once suggested, in an environmental dream of his own, he was going to see planted in the United States.[10] He called not for a single planting of a billion trees, but for this same number to be added each year for the next 10 years at a cost of $175 million a year. Admirable as the gigantic Bush project might have appeared on the surface, it was never carried out as planned. Furthermore, despite what Barbara Bush later said about using this "America the Beautiful" plan as a model for environmental reform and reforestation in other areas,[11] little or nothing actually came of it. Why?

To continue to dream an impossible, quixotic dream as to what might happen when supplies of rubber, rubberlike products, and materials for the production of rubber are unlimited, let us turn to the matter of the availability of the products needed to manufacture an average radial passenger-car tire. A single Para rubber tree will produce, during a year, slightly more than enough rubber (13.33 pounds) to supply the total polymer needs for one car tire.[12] Using this average, 5 billion producing natural rubber trees (out of a total of 6 billion planted) would produce the 60 billion pounds (30 million tons) of rubber estimated to be needed by the beginning of the twenty-first century.

Now, to view this from a different perspective, according to the Rubber Manufacturers Association of America, about one barrel of oil is required to produce a tire in which the polymer is exclusively synthetic rubber. Employing the same numbers as were used above would imply setting aside a billion barrels of petroleum per year, if we were to manufacture all the tires needed out of this nonrenewable fossil fuel. Current figures indicate that the United States has somewhere between 25 and 30 billion barrels of proven reserves left for all of our multiple needs, from gasoline to fertilizer, from here on out.

It is difficult for many, so accustomed to driving into the gas station and filling up the tank, to realize that these numbers imply that when the proven U.S. reserves have all been depleted, there just won't be any more for any purpose. Using these figures for proven reserves, it is easy to calculate that we have between 25 and 30 years of oil reserves left: *if* we were to use every drop just to produce all of our vehicular tire needs exclusively from synthetic rubber, there would be none of this nonrenewable resource available for all those other items, including diesel and gasoline, on which we have come to rely so heavily.

This points up the basic, underlying reason the Bush administration was so reluctant to permit Saddam Hussein the possibility of controlling a large percentage of the source of supply. It is for this reason also that so many other countries, concerned as to Saddam's motives, participated both financially and militarily in the recent Persian Gulf War. In this connection, many have cynically pointed out that the tragic events now taking place in the former Yugoslavia would long ago have been terminated if there had only been known oil deposits there.

It seems wise, then, to at least review the implications of the proposed dream, for what better way would there be to save an enormous quantity of petroleum each year than by not consuming this nonrenewable resource — simply by planting a sufficient amount of a truly renewable one? Contemplate all the benefits which might accrue, ranging from no longer having to contend with pollution from synthetic rubber factories to improved income distribution on a worldwide basis to the marvelous economic opportunities for joint ventures (shades of World War II cooperation to produce synthetic rubber?) between such giant multinationals as British Petroleum, Michelin (which makes one out of every five tires produced in the world today), and some Brazilian land company (to say nothing of a highly improved public image for each), with the establishment of plantation rubber on burnt-over forest or worn-out pasture land in the humid tropics of the world. Think also of lending agencies receiving a much higher return on their loans for such ventures than they are presently accustomed to earn. Pause for a moment to contemplate the volumes of carbon dioxide these trees would absorb from the earth's atmosphere.[13] Just visualize what a glorious (not to mention kinder and gentler) future would be in store for all of us.

We have recently become so inundated by voluminous outpourings of books, pamphlets, and other offerings of how-to projects to save our environment—where hope reigns supreme and verbs such as *should* and *could*, together with such adverbs as *possibly* and *perhaps*, proliferate — that this dream may not sound completely impossible. We may have been led so far down the pathway of being told all the little tasks each individual can perform to save the global ecology or promote an individual green lifestyle that a gigantic project for planting millions of trees of a single species might appear completely feasible.

However, since there may be more than a few doubting Thomases hiding in the background who would scoff at the general argument and may even have little or no use for any type of ecological venture of this nature, perhaps we should stop for a moment to question whether anything even remotely approximating this utopian reverie could possibly take place. Under present conditions and with attitudes the way they are now, we must concede that the practicality of such abstract musing is more than highly doubtful; it is probably a completely nonsensical scenario. And so, to explain why something we are ostensibly eagerly striving for will, in all likelihood, not soon be achieved, we must now examine a host of major social, economic, as well as environmental issues that face us today in search of the answers.

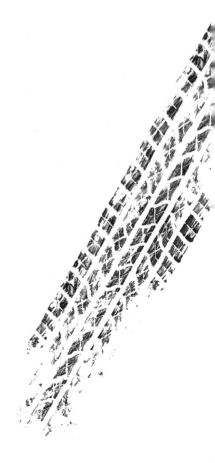

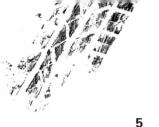

5

DISAPPEARING
JUNGLES—AND FORESTS

EXPANDING THE ACREAGE of rubber throughout the world or even reforesting cutover and damaged tropical jungles as well as degraded temperate areas are practices which should merit our approval. Unhappily, it is cause for growing concern that very little of this is presently taking place. What is happening instead is that natural rubber production is decreasing and not keeping pace with demand, and both tropical and temperate forests are being decimated at a far more rapid rate than replanting or natural replacement can ameliorate.

It is not my intention to present an in-depth analysis of the reasons for, nor the causes by which, ever-increasing areas of both jungles and forests are disappearing. Articles and exposés dealing with this subject have been and are presently being paraded before us in a quantity to satisfy any need. It should probably be pointed out here, though, that unfortunately the level of this publicity has reached the point of overkill, and the tone of what is written often contains a high degree of sanctimonious finger-pointing. This misunderstanding or misrepresentation of the evidence tends to leave the public with a plague-on-all-your-houses attitude and a disinterest in or indifference to environmental matters. What follows is an attempt to determine the reasons or causes for this growing and serious lack of interest in these issues.

Obviously, a good place to begin would be the Amazon basin, since it is not only the original home of our designated symbol—the Para rubber tree—but also one of the earth's most critical areas, so far as the disappearing forests syndrome is concerned. Alarm over the demise of the Amazon basin did not really begin, surprisingly enough, until quite recently—about the 1960's. Up to that time, owing primarily to a lack of overland routes in this region, the only means of transportation was along the Amazon itself and some of its principal tributaries. There were, of course, a few roads and railroads, such as the railroad constructed almost a hundred years ago to bypass the rapids on the Beni River in both Bolivia and Brazil. This railway began just below Riberalta, Bolivia, and terminated at Pôrto Velho in Rondônia, Brazil. Here, the Beni becomes the Madeira River, which flows unimpeded to the Amazon. Thus, except for the slight, almost negligible, impact of scattered groups of indigenous peoples who have inhabited these jungles for thousands of years, really very little damage attributable to humans was done to the environment except perhaps along the banks of the main waterways. However, during the past 40 years a number of things fell into place that changed the situation with amazing rapidity.

Undoubtedly, the most important of these was the world's population explosion, which following World War II was especially evident in Latin America. In this particular case, the reason was not that people were having more babies (they were having just as many as before) but rather that fewer, by far, were dying when young. Some scholars, such as René Dubos, argue that a decrease in infant mortality was already well under way prior to World War II.[1] Others disagree, claiming that this change came later. In any case, if we were to seek some group that might be responsible for what took place during the recent past, one of the chief candidates could well be those involved with all aspects of modern public health.[2] This recent and rapid decrease in worldwide death rates may largely be attributed to the widespread use of penicillin, sulfa, and other wonder drugs, coupled with growing cadres of trained people who went about administering these remedies, even in remote areas. At the same time, these medical workers also advocated and promoted such new prophylactic measures as boiling water for drinking and immunization. The result has been that a growing number of the babies born stayed alive and, when these matured to child-bearing age, outdid their parents in producing a new and larger generation.

In many of the poorer and drier areas of South America, from the Altiplano regions of Bolivia and Peru to the by-now worn-out northeastern rim of Brazil, an eruption of young people, the majority with no jobs nor land of their own, were forced to seek out parcels in the unclaimed regions of the Amazon basin on which to make their living.[3] And these areas, unfortunately, were generally not ideal for even subsistence farming; all of the best land had previously been taken over by the wealthier claimants. The same may be said about frontier areas in many other tropical regions of the world.

This invasion of pristine lands amounted, in many cases, to an almost planned colonization movement. Many South American governments actually encouraged this economic migration as a means, they thought, of developing their own lightly populated regions. This was by no means a unique phenomenon though, for a similar thing occurred in the United States during the latter half of the nineteenth century after the passage of the Homestead Act. The discovery of gold and other minerals in the Amazon region only added to the flood of migrants.[4] Such incursions were soon followed by a rush to build new roads to and through these regions — many financed by such institutions as the World Bank.[5] It now seems to be politically correct to accuse these kinds of development and lending agencies of being responsible for much of the current decimation of forest and jungle.[6] They certainly must take some of the blame, as it is now easy to look back and note, as others did before loans and grants were being made for highway construction, what the rule of thumb had fast become: where a road is built into any jungle area, destruction will soon follow.

In the case of Brazil, which is both petroleum and coal poor, this trend of wanton ruination of substantial areas of the environment was exacerbated by the conversion of thousands of acres of forest trees into charcoal as a coal substitute for use in steel and iron production, as well as for export.[7] This disappearance of timber was further aggravated by the construction of large dams designed especially for the production of hydroelectric power. These structures caused the inundation of many more thousands of acres of jungle.[8]

According to Nathaniel C. Nash, "Forestry experts say that up to 500,000 acres of native forests are being cleared every year in Bolivia. For its size, that is only slightly below the rate in Brazil." He continues by stating that "researchers for the Inter-American Development Bank have estimated that more than 11 percent of its forests have been either wiped out or damaged by logging and agribusiness, compared with 5 percent in Brazil."[9]

At the same time, what might be called a deadly impact on a number of Indian tribes by unwelcome invaders was also taking place. In addition to those seeking minerals and gems, these intruders included others such as proselytizing missionaries[10] and anxious anthropologists, both of which groups, ostensibly out to do good, may have irreparably altered many native cultures (for better or for worse, who knows). As a result of the efforts of these outsiders, not only were the Indians subjected to novel, often upsetting, ideas; they were also put in contact with a variety of decimating diseases, from which they had so far escaped.[11]

As previously noted, far too many of these reports, such as *Time* magazine's "Torching the Amazon,"[12] come rather close to being questionable and melodramatic reporting of almost a purple-prose nature. There was, for example, only one brief mention in the *Time* article of population pressure on jungle resources—the crux of the overall problem. H. Jeffrey Leonard, director of the International Development Program of the Conservation Foundation, has been quick to point out that this sort of environmentalist hysteria could well hasten further Amazonian destruction. The only sane answer to the present problem, he believes, lies in an all-out effort to assist those settlers already there, together with the swarm that will soon settle in this region, to stabilize and intensify their agriculture, and to help them get their products to market.[13] And any way one looks at it, from the thousands of acres destroyed for conversion to pasture or for a temporary site to be used solely to produce such a crop as cocaine, the jungle is disappearing. Meanwhile, much of the current debate on forest and jungle demise seems to focus simply on the polemic as to how fast this is taking place and how many species might become extinct as the result.[14] It is true that there are others who claim they have a scheme or system that will assure sustainable development in this region, but since few seriously consider the impact of population increase, the majority of these tend to be almost ludicrous. Moreover, as many have pointed out, the expression "sustainable development" is an economic oxymoron to be avoided or ignored by anyone who is serious about effectively dealing with these situations.[15]

As we should well know by now, the matter of jungle and forest devastation is by no means exclusively a South American tragedy. According to a news article, Maine, the most heavily forested of the United States, will be 20 percent short of its needs for spruce and fir by the beginning of the twenty-first century, and in 2020 less than 5 percent of Maine's forests will have trees suitable for industrial use.[16] In another article, Page Stegner decried the fact that "in the forests of New England, noble stands of oak and hemlock are being torn asunder for second homes and subdivisions."[17]

Moving to the center of our nation, a debate has been going on for some time in Wisconsin, another important lumbering state, over how to manage national forests there. On one side, a group of botanists from the University of Wisconsin advocate that large, contiguous parcels of land must be preserved intact and unmanipulated to protect the ecological systems which harbor plants and animals that require "deep woods" habitats.[18] The timber industry together with many others, even some in the U.S. Forest Service itself, opposes such a proposal, arguing basically that clear-cutting or selective harvesting followed by either seeding or allowing natural regeneration to take place is quite enough to maintain all the diversity that is needed.[19] This dispute reached the courts, which sufficiently demonstrates how contentious the entire matter has become.[20]

Farther west, we quickly discover that the intensity of the confrontation over forest use and misuse has been raised to another, higher level of acerbity. In the debate over the use of forests in Alaska and the Pacific Northwest, the intellectual level has fallen and emotional name-calling has taken over; for example, Representative Don Young of Alaska has called both Representatives Bob Mrazek of New York and Jim Jontz of Indiana "pimps for Eastern environmentalists." This was in response to Jontz's rather innocuous pronouncement that he considered "the forests of the Northwest to be as much a national treasure as the Grand Canyon" and Mrazek's statement that "trees (from Alaska) were being sold to the Japanese for the cost of Big Mac hamburgers."[21]

An article such as "The Ancient Forests" by Catherine Caufield[22] leaves little doubt in the reader's mind that cutting on public lands has gotten out of hand, and even such a sage and well-recognized columnist as Tom Wicker of the New York Times chastises us by claiming that "the U.S. has long done what Brazil is now being criticized for."[23] More recently, Nancy Langston has pointed out how much of the problem has been due to an arrogant disregard of these special ecosystems and a decided lack of knowledge as to how to properly manage them over the long run.[24] The other side of the coin is the message to be seen on the bumpers of many cars and trucks from this region urging us to "Eat an owl—Save a logger's job."

In certain respects, at least one part of this particular story may be headed for a rather happier ending—as of now. Someone in the state of Oregon obviously saw the handwriting on the wall and made the decision to initiate training programs for loggers and sawmill operators to learn about other skills and professions.[25] Now, while the forests there are no longer being cut so rapidly as before and lumber sales are reduced, Oregon appears to be enjoying a minor economic boom that few would have thought possible only a few years ago — and the habitat for the northern spotted owl has not been destroyed.

This modest prosperity has been due primarily to the emergence of a small but growing cadre of personnel trained to work in non-timber-related industries and service organizations. While many who are not so sanguine point out the large number of loggers who have not landed other jobs, with some luck this model may provide a guide or key to other regions. If a community will take the initiative to similarly rectify the labor situation, it may be able to rescue or transform its depressed lumber-based economy before it is too late.

Moving over to Asia, one may search without success to find a situation similar to the Oregon story described above. Actually, there does not now appear to be even a glimmer of hope for truly overcoming forest destruction in much of that region. Accessible forests in most of China had been depleted by the early 1900's, due to increasing pressures from a growing population. While the Communist government under Chairman Mao early instituted large-scale reforestation projects, many regions are now reported to be cutting more than is being replanted.[26]

When I visited the northeastern province of Heilungjiang in the fall of 1989, I was quickly made aware of the extreme pressure on the part of Japanese, Korean, and Taiwanese lumber concerns to avail themselves of what forest resources remain there, as well as across the Amur River in eastern Siberia. Despite the fact that the Chinese and Russians desperately need this resource as well, timber extraction for export was in full swing.[27] The grim reality here is that the outsiders have the funds required, and both China and Russia are strapped for cash.

The formerly bountiful forests of teak and Philippine mahogany in Burma (or Myanmar), Thailand, and the Philippines have now largely been cut and exported, with the greatest percentage going to Japan.[28] Indonesia is presently under constant pressure to export, and the new focus of attention centers on the island of Borneo, which at one time may have contained perhaps the largest and richest tropical forest on earth. This island, the third largest in the world, is divided between Kalimantan, which occupies the southern two-thirds and is part of Indonesia, and Sarawak and Sabah (separated by the rather small sultanate of Brunei), both part of

Malaysia, in the northern third. I use the past tense in categorizing the rain forest there, since it is now being decimated at an astonishing rate, particularly in Sarawak. This problem is now becoming so grave that the Malaysian government in Kuala Lampur is making serious efforts to keep it from becoming public knowledge. This cover-up approach is certainly understandable since half of the timber concessions in Sarawak are owned by Abdul Taib Mahmud, the country's chief minister, and his family and friends, including Abdul Rahman Yakub, his uncle and the past minister.[29]

However, secrets of this nature are difficult to keep: Greenpeace made this disaster the lead story in its bimonthly journal in the summer of 1990, and *The New Yorker* published in the late spring of 1991 an article, "Logging the Rain Forest,"[30] relating basically to the same problem. The principal focus in each of these articles was not so much the demise of the forest (with the majority of the logs being shipped to Japan) as the effects of this sort of timber extraction on the lives and culture of the indigenous Penan peoples on this island. This concern is similar to that now being directed to the slow but steady disruption and breakdown of other primitive tribes clamoring for land, including the Yanomami in northern Brazil and growing numbers of Indians in Guatemala.[31] If only partially correct, the information provided on the often extremely inhumane system of outright wasteful logging and blatant disregard for the basic rights of the Penan people is reminiscent of the many other horror stories of resource extraction during the past few centuries in which rampant greed has been a key ingredient.

Bruno Manser, a shy young man from Switzerland who — pictured with long hair, quite naked except for leg bands, a loincloth, and his steel-rimmed glasses — has become well known in environmentalist circles, insists that the loggers are using (stealing) the resources of the Penan to promote their own way of life. He and others claim that of those who might merit the seventeenth-century ideal of the "Noble Savage" — someone who lives in complete harmony with nature and is thoroughly knowledgeable about almost every phase of the jungle habitat — the Penan exceed and outstrip all others. Now the very environment or habitat of these people and, to a degree, their heritage are rapidly being looted by outsiders.

But a general lack of concern, based on an obvious deficiency of knowledge regarding basic ecology, is not the preserve of any particular group. Returning to the debate in Wisconsin, it is reported that the fallback argument of Ralph Saperstein, vice president for forest planning of the Northwest Forest Industries Association of Portland, Oregon, was that the Wisconsin botanists' "concern is not diversity or rare plants. They're looking for a surrogate to advance their cause. Their concern is stopping logging in the national forests."[32] The publicly stated position of the botanists, however, is not that the Forest Service should cut back on logging activities but that it should permit this cutting to take place, in such regions as the Chequamegon National Forest, on 80 percent of the total area, leaving 20 percent only to remain untouched.

All of this raises a serious question as to Saperstein's motives as well as his knowledge and understanding of the basic problem. And here, perhaps, lies a key to the entire dispute; for the interest of the botanists referred to above truly relates to the long-term environmental effects of excessive timber extraction. They believe logging must include the maintenance of at least a minimum area of irreplaceable "deep woods" habitats so critical for the future of forests.

This approach was clearly and publicly stated before the Committee on Agriculture of the U.S. Senate in November 1993 by Professor D. M. Waller of the University of Wisconsin.[33] The rebuttal of this testimony by the Forest Service (in the same report) was a pathetically standard one that served merely to make apparent that this governmental institution, presumably one devoted to the public welfare, is obviously much more interested in the short-term gains of the timber companies while yet continuing to maintain a belief (hope?) that the future will somehow take care of itself.

In this matter of extracting limited resources from their natural habitat, it would be instructive to consider, for a moment, the difficulties facing the fishing industry in the North Atlantic.[34] The present situation there — a result of overfishing with little apparent regard for providing some means of natural regeneration of stocks ("deep waters" for "deep woods"?) — has become so critical that the decision to completely prohibit fishing for a time in certain areas is becoming one of the only viable alternatives. In this case, we need only substitute "fishermen" for "loggers," and "cod" for "Douglas fir." Ignorance of the fact that "limits to growth are nature's own"[35] remains the same.

The crux of an efficient operation of almost any extraction industry over the long term thus appears to lie in being able to comprehend the principles of ecology involved. To some this may be as difficult as attempting to unravel the mysteries of the "bottom line" — a factor which so often determines forest policy. While the "bottom line" is actually simpler in nature and generally only important over the short run, a knowledge of all that is implied in the meaning of "deep woods" may be extremely vital to all of us over the long haul. Fortunately, Sallie Tisdale has described the vital importance to all life (including human) of maintaining large areas of undisturbed wilderness not simply as monuments or recreational areas but rather as wellsprings for future generations of all organisms (again including us) appropriate to the particular ecosystem in question. She has done this not only in a straightforward and simple manner but also in a lovely, almost poetic one. Her article "In the Northwest," in a recent issue of *The New Yorker*,[36] should be required reading for all—foresters and ordinary citizens alike.

Dr. Jerry Franklin, ecologist at the University of Washington, who has long been involved with programs of forestry management, has espoused a similar ecological approach. He recently stated that in order to understand clearly what is now taking place in the Pacific Northwest, so far as the timber industry is concerned, one must first examine the overall aquatic environment there. The abundance or disappearance of salmon as well as many other stream and river dwellers serves as a sort of "miner's canary" relative to the well-being of the forests of the region.[37] Today, the status of these riverine environments clearly demonstrates the detrimental effects of forest decimation and presently portends, according to Professor Franklin, an ominous picture for the future of forests in that region.

To complete the argument here, we should return to Brazil, where Sr. José Lutzenberger, then special secretary for the environment, is reported to have stated publicly: "We are signing IOUs that our children cannot pay. We are acting as if we were the last generation on the planet." Statements of this nature should, at least, give us pause to reflect for a moment on this entire matter of the use and misuse of our natural surroundings, too often the result of unwise resource extraction for immediate economic gain. To begin with, this maltreatment of our environment is nothing new. Humans have been doing this sort of thing for centuries, inevitably with quite unsatisfactory results. That we were able to continue at all along this same line, greedily gobbling up available resources, has not been due to a strong conservationist philosophy but rather to the fact that once we had decimated one area, a new one was discovered in which we could repeat the process.

One of the more interesting examples of a group who were unable, because of their isolation, to avail themselves of a new resource and what occurred as a result is that of one advanced Polynesian society. At the height of their civilization, these prehistoric people constructed, moved, and erected 20-foot-high stone figures, presumably idols, on what is now known as Easter Island. It is assumed that a great deal of their building activity depended on the existence of abundant forests, the trees from which were used for construction materials and especially rollers by which the heavy, intact stone figures were transported from quarry to site. By the eighteenth century when Europeans discovered this isolated island, the forests were gone and the few people left were reduced to a miserable subsistence living, with suggestions of cannibalism and no sign of any attempts to erect more huge idols—there were simply no trees left to do the job.[38]

That we are now faced with a growing number of environmental difficulties is basically because we are rapidly destroying more and more areas of the earth that were formerly under some form of tree cover—whether through inefficient extraction techniques, forest cutting, or burning to clear land for crops. We are now reaching a point where we have all but run out of new and undisturbed areas to develop. A simple, enjoyable way to understand this dismal historical process is through reading such a book as *A Forest Journey* by John Perlin.[39] While Perlin asserts that his book is basically a discussion of the role of timber, wood, and wood products in the development of civilization, in my view it is concurrently a description of how civilizations rose and fell as the result of an avaricious, often downright gluttonous, exploitation of woods and forests throughout the globe as different civilizations abused their environment. This is obviously exemplified, as earlier reported, by the manner with which *seringueiros* sacrificed rubber trees for a quick, onetime exploitation of whatever latex could be obtained.

In Perlin's presentation, there is a strong, underlying Malthusian bent: as populations increase, forests and jungles (indeed, all of our natural resources) diminish correspondingly. It is also clear, when reading this volume, that there is an additional warning to those who will heed it. As in the case of Paul Johnson's thesis presented in his book *The Rise and Fall of the Great Powers*—that when nations, apparently at the height of their power, expend ever more of their resources to maintain their military might in an effort to protect their power, they begin to crumble[40]—so we too run an increasing risk of jeopardizing our present standard of living by avoiding difficult decisions relating to conservation and attempting to snatch away every bit of the resources we can from nature in any way possible.[41]

What are we now being told as to the most promising ways to proceed? What examples are there that can serve as guides or markers to follow in order that we could begin to slow the steady degradation of the global environment?

6

JUNGLE MYTHS
AND TALL TIMBER TALES

IT IS UNFORTUNATE that those who wish to gain a true picture of what is presently taking place in the jungles and forests of the world must usually obtain this information secondhand. There are always a few, of course, who can afford to make a Jungle Safari to Africa, camp out in a national forest, or even take a cruise on a ship up the Amazon. While on such trips and journeys, the participants must surely be aware that they are not thus automatically privy to a thorough understanding of these novel environments any more than those who spend a weekend in New York immediately become experts on the life and times of that metropolis. At the very least, their mere presence in such distinct natural surroundings, often with a throng of others, always provides a sufficiently distracting note to disrupt normal patterns of life. The photos of bored lions lying in the dust of the Serengeti, surrounded by hordes of tourist-filled vehicles — the occupants of which, expensive cameras hung round their necks, are all anxious for some dramatic action shots — substantiate this point.

At the same time, it is obvious that significantly large segments of the public have become quite interested in matters relating to the environment whether or not they are able to see raw nature at firsthand. Just consider the enormous amount of television time, voluminous articles (written in both yellow and purple prose), conferences without end on all kinds of ecological matters, and untold government committees given over to the self-proclaimed arduous task of "hammering out policy" that are now engaged in dealing with some aspect of our environment. And more and more people, everywhere, obviously would like to know what they might do to help and which way to proceed.

A tragic drawback in this, I believe, is that far too much information now being foisted upon us is questionable, spurious, and even false. These untruths and misinformation can only add to the general aura of confusion that clouds the entire dilemma of disappearing jungles and forests. What should be of concern is the outburst of information and articles claiming to be God's truth that are too often nothing more than fables themselves. If we are sincerely troubled about jungle or forested environments and believe something positive and effective must be done to improve or at the very least save what remains of these habitats, we cannot begin to make proper judgments on what action to take if we do not have true facts and honest information about them.

These fables or "jungle myths and tall timber tales," as I call them, are often spun by people who not only claim to be properly certified scientists, but who should know better. A serious difficulty arises when these fictitious or unfounded reports are told often enough (especially by some well-recognized narrator): they actually begin to be accepted and thus perpetuated as truth. I will agree that the motive for such propaganda is often a desire to improve or ameliorate some difficult or trying situation. But since the information utilized is simply not true or exact, eventually these inaccurate myths can not only return to haunt the instigator but also add detriment to the very causes that were the original target of the remedy. Oscar Wilde put it well when he said:

> Yet each man kills the thing he loves,
> By each let this be heard,
> Some do it with a bitter look,
> Some with a flattering word.[1]

Let us begin at home. In our own temperate forests we find a prime example of the tall timber tales to which I refer. The Greek physician Galen is reported to have known about and used, as long ago as the first century A.D., an extract from juniper trees (conifers) to treat certain forms of cancer. Today, hardly a magazine or newspaper can be found that has missed the opportunity to write about the novel and dramatic effects on a variety of malignancies that could be obtained by using an extract from another conifer—the Pacific yew (*Taxus brevifolia*). An article in the January–February 1991 issue of *Nature Conservancy* reports Gordon Cragg, acting head of the National Cancer Institute's Natural Products Branch, as stating, "It takes 20,000 pounds of bark—that's 2,000 to 4,000 trees—to produce one kilogram of taxol (a promising anti-cancer drug). And the trees must be sacrificed to produce the bark."[2]

Publicity of this nature has unwittingly promoted the theft of thousands of Pacific yew trees or the simple yet fatal scalping of the bark of many others. This decimation is obviously caused by the extreme efforts of many who are thoroughly convinced that the only source for the cancer-"curing" taxol is the bark of these specific trees. It is now clear that destruction of this extent need not have happened, and it is quite surprising that Dr. Cragg made his pronouncement without at least mentioning other avenues of approach to the matter. Could he and his staff have been unaware of other research projects taking place in this field? An article in the *Journal of Natural Products*, reporting the results of one such project, concluded that other tissues, including the needles, of a number of different and distinct yew trees contained amounts of taxol in quantities comparable to the bark of the Pacific yew.[3] Jane E. Brody, in the November 20, 1990 issue of the *New York Times*, wrote of a scheme for laboratory extraction of this drug by means of tissue culture.[4] This well-known process is now being utilized for the production of a number of other drugs and medicines from plants.

The Pacific yew may yet soon be saved, however, by another similar approach. During the spring of 1991, the U.S. Patent and Trademark Office awarded a patent to Dr. Robert A. Holton and the University of Florida for a method of combining the needles of the English yew with a synthetic to make taxol in the laboratory.[5] Furthermore, in June 1991, it was reported that the Escagenetics Corporation of California is now producing taxol in its laboratories using biotechnology.[6] Despite such information, the tall tale of the Pacific yew persists, and by the end of July 1991, a report in the *Wisconsin State Journal* relative to research planned to be carried out at the USDA Forest Products Laboratory in Madison, Wisconsin, made almost the same statements as those given above about the need for 30,000 to 40,000 Pacific yew trees to meet the demands of current cancer research. The article further stated that this new government-sponsored and -directed research was aimed at saving yew trees that are potentially threatened by the desire of the Bristol-Myers Squibb drug company to produce more taxol![7]

We now learn that Bristol-Myers has dropped its contract with Hauser Chemical Research, Inc., which formerly supplied it with yew bark.[8] Furthermore, new evidence now appears to show that "taxol from the Pacific yew is not a cure, it's not a panacea, it's not the penicillin we were looking for."[9] And so in the end, all we are left with is the question of how much damage was done to our forests in this frantic search for a nebulous miracle, fostered and stimulated by untested "truths."

This displeasing account of the extraction of taxol from yew bark has all the earmarks of King Leopold's gluttonous attempts to obtain latex for the production of natural rubber from the *Landolphia* vine in the Belgian Congo in the 1800's. It is yet another unfortunate example of how, instead of seeking an orderly and ecologically sound means of obtaining some desired natural product, too many find it easier and more profitable (in the short run) to trash nature with little consideration as to the end results.

We should pause here to ascertain whether anything of a similar nature is still occurring in tropical areas. According to Stephen Corry, director-general of Survival International, "Products that have long been available on the international market — in particular Brazil nuts — are now being marketed as a way to saving the rainforests and supporting indigenous peoples. These claims are highly misleading: much of the 'rainforest harvest' is purchased on the open market, often from unscrupulous dealers."[10] The article in *The Ecologist* from which this quote was taken was quickly attacked in the very next issue of this journal by T. Gordon Roddick, chairman of The Body Shop International PLC, as "a facile and inflammatory piece."[11] This exchange clearly demonstrates how contentious this matter of extractive industries has become. It also raises the question or concern as to what exactly the phrase "saving the rain forests" might mean, who might benefit the most from their "salvation" — and just what the true facts of the matter are.

Perhaps this issue is difficult for many to comprehend, given the lack of clear and factual information. For example, Norman Myers, a prolific author as well as a very determined individual dedicated to helping save tropical forests and environments is, I suggest, guilty (to borrow again from Wilde) of killing through hyperbole much of that which he claims he loves. In *The Primary Source: Tropical Forests and Our Future*,[12] he writes, with considerable overstatement and exaggeration, that tropical rain forests and their components (plants, animals, insects, etc.) should be considered as pharmaceutical factories. Factories? Even with only a slight personal knowledge of tropical rain forests one's imagination would be stretched to the limit to accept this. Not even Merck, the giant drug company — which a few years ago developed a well-publicized arrangement with the Instituto Nacional de Biodiversidad (INBIO) in Costa Rica in an attempt to achieve this very end[13]—has come close to this goal.

Myers goes on to state that "as the tribals disappear, with their long enduring life-styles, let us reflect that it is thanks to Indians of Latin American forests, together with the earlier forestland communities such as the Mayas, that we ever became aware of corn, potato, tomato, peanuts, cassava, avocado, guava, cashew-nut, vanilla, and sunflower, plus a host of drugs such as quinine, curare, mescaline, and cocaine."[14] He continues by painting a picture of such a wealth of drugs, cures, ointments, and byproducts that may be teased, extracted, or rendered from the plants of these regions that one is left to ponder how it is still possible that anyone anywhere could be sick today. The corollary which follows is that if so many of these marvelous drugs and potions have been produced and we still know so little about these ecosystems, untold numbers of additional cures must simply be waiting discovery. For this reason alone, Myers argues, what is left of these habitats must be kept pristine, if only to await the discovery of some new miracle drug. I certainly concur that conservation must be practiced in this area—but not for the reasons given. To continue to make such claims may well defeat the stated aim.

It should first be pointed out that corn, potatoes, tomatoes, peanuts, cashew nuts, and sunflowers neither came from nor grow best either in humid tropical Latin American forests or in Mexican forestland areas, but rather in upland, savanna, or dryland regions. As to the meaning of the word *host*, an ordinary dictionary's pertinent definitions are (1) army and (2) multitude. I would suggest that perhaps Myers may have been hard put to name many more than the drugs he listed; so, taking a page from modern advertising—when little more can be said about any product, the tired phrase "and much more" is trotted out for extra impact—he has resorted to exaggeration to strengthen his argument.

The truth, in all probability, is quite different than that presented. Human beings have been biting, sucking, smoking, drinking, and eating, in the manner of any inquisitive animal, just about anything and everything available in any and every environment, including jungles, for thousands of years. Our Paleolithic and even rather more modern ancestors could not have missed very much in their constant foraging, and in so doing naturally came up with a great number of important discoveries of poisonous, harmful, beneficial, hallucinogenic, analgesic, depressing, and stimulating substances, a great many of which we use today.[15] More recently, plant taxonomists, working carefully and systematically in conjunction with chemists, have come across a few more plants which were previously overlooked that have definitely been proven to be of real pharmaceutical value — not *perhaps*, not *maybe*. Thus, despite the fact that so much of what we might have hoped for (as in the case of taxol from yews and latex from *Landolphia*) has already been investigated and rejected, myths persist; too many are still convinced that miracles lie just around the corner and all that is required is a little patience and luck.

For example, in yet another article on this very subject in a recent issue of *Sierra*, Joseph Wallace is audacious enough to insinuate that "the botanical riches of the tropics *could* help solve some of the world's most pressing medical problems — *if* we can find out what's there before it all disappears" (emphasis added).[16] Even people who should know better continue to throw out highly dubious figures as to the number of life-forms that *could* provide humankind with untold benefit. A case in point is the series of television programs presented by *ABC Nightly News with Peter Jennings* concerning the bountiful riches of the tropical rain forest in Surinam.[17] I can only presume that the writers and producers of these specials must believe that those magical words "tropical rain forests" must conjure up in the minds of the viewers all manner of sorcery and healing associated with medicine men. My own experience in Surinam was that rural dwellers there would much rather be treated in a hospital by a doctor with medicines from modern pharmaceutical houses than use the touted "miracle drugs" from the forest. Since they are unable to afford the care they prefer, their only alternative is to seek help from some shaman.

So often have I been subjected to this type of television special, in which tantalizing cures are dangled before our eyes, that I've come to the conclusion it would be a far more dramatic story if solid evidence of success were presented rather than speculation. The proliferation of such phrases as "millions of dollars," "miraculous cures," and "riches from the rain forests which will soon save these from destruction" clearly identifies this approach as all too similar to that of the sly "snake oil" peddler from some traveling medicine show. And just as "snake oil," placebos, and incantations have been shown on occasion to be of some medicinal benefit, a bit of bark or root may, if one really believes it might, achieve the same success.

A much more dramatic story, of the sort that ABC News can do so well, would have been simply to tell the truth, rather than some jungle myth. At the time of the *Nightly News* show referred to, a number of scientific journals had already made known the situation in Surinam, as the general press would do later on.[18] This was summed up rather well by Nigel Sizer, who stated that "the world's largest unbroken stretch of tropical rainforest will be wiped out if Asian timber barons succeed in cutting billion-dollar deals with Surinam and Guyana, two of the Western Hemisphere's poorest countries."[19] If and when this takes place, what of the presumed cures and what of the shaman?

But let us return to Myers's argument. He speaks of tropical forests as being the source of a "cornucopia of foods." Actually it is most difficult to produce enough food crops to supply the needs of the burgeoning numbers of people now filling these environments. Except under special edaphic, or soil, conditions where such crops as paddy rice can be cultivated, humid jungles are one of the least attractive agricultural sites for the small landholder anywhere in the world. Furthermore, level and well-drained terrain, such as along fertile riverbanks, that would be propitious for successful farming ventures is limited. Land that is higher in elevation and often drier is usually more appropriate. Those who have worked and lived for long periods in such regions know that steady, unvarying meals of cassava, and perhaps rice and beans, hopefully supplemented with some tropical fruits and nuts, fish, or game, is a monotonous and not really too healthy a diet. Moreover, as populations swell throughout the humid tropics, increasing amounts of basic food necessities have to be imported. This dependence on outside food sources is exacerbated by the rapid disappearance of both game and fish because of overhunting and excessive fishing, leaving these environments in grave jeopardy. As Kent H. Redford carefully documents, this utilization of tropical jungles as a human food source is quickly leading to the serious ecological problem of "empty forests."[20] Such forests are categorized, in the words of Daniel Janzen, as the "living dead," since they now lack the critical life-forms needed for self-maintenance.[21] To the detriment of all, as this situation continues these regions are fast becoming completely environmentally degraded.

Then there are those who, demonstrating an unfortunate lack of any down-to-earth knowledge, imply that problems of this nature can easily be obviated by planting such miracle crops as the winged bean (*Psophocarpus tetragonolopus*), which are said to "rival soybeans in oil and protein content."[22] It has been my observation that in many regions of Southeast Asia, this plant has been used as a last-resort "starvation crop." It produces seeds that, according to Purseglove, are not found palatable by the indigenous people of Africa, India, and the West Indies.[23] In addition, winged beans grow on vines that must climb up stakes or over small bushes, and no one has even considered developing a method of harvesting them except by the laborious and traditional hand method. I will agree that the flowers and very tender young seedpods from this plant can be made rather tasty when prepared with butter, onions, peppers, and a variety of condiments by a competent and well-trained cook, but such culinary additives are completely unavailable to the ordinary inhabitant of these regions. It is interesting to note, in this connection, the number of earnest horticulturists, challenged by such a jungle myth, who try time and time again to establish and immortalize this vine as a crop by attempting, with a frightening lack of success, to promote its use as a solution to food deficiency in many tropical regions of the world. Even Norman Myers has taken to waxing almost poetic about the wonders of this plant.[24]

In an article titled "Research in 'Virgin' Amazon Uncovers Complex Farming," William K. Stevens has written another story of this genre. In this he points out how novel techniques let Indians harvest the jungle without destroying it.[25] On reading this piece, one is astounded less by the techniques themselves than by the fact that the smart crowd on Wall Street has not already beaten a path to the Indians' door; for the claim is made that utilization of this technology will bring to market "a broad range of export products that under ideal circumstances could bring billions of dollars into the debt-ridden economies of the Amazonian countries." *Billions* of dollars? The only tropical crop in South America I know of that comes close to — actually far exceeds — this figure is cocaine (*Erythroxylon coca*). Of course, there are enormous risks, not to mention legal problems, getting the leaves or extract thereof from this plant to the underground markets outside Latin America. Next in line might be cotton, for according to a recent article, by the year 2000 Fortaleza, in dry northeastern Brazil, will be exporting $100 million in textiles made of this fiber.[26] But this figure is far too small for Stevens's billions.

Nevertheless, anthropologists working out of Belém became so excited about these prospects that they made the claim that there are "thousands of ways of making the living forest more valuable than the destroyed forest." The truth of the matter is that there are very few successful ways to eke out what might be called an adequate and healthful living in this habitat. A careful review of the Belém commentary reveals no mention that the local inhabitants are probably existing on the most primitive subsistence level. They have no electricity, no schools, no hospitals, none of the creature comforts they all aspire to — nor apparently is there any hope for such things under this fabulous agricultural scheme.

To return to the point of contention, these myths unfortunately persist — and begin to fill the literature as "truth." Further evidence is given in a recent article on Professor E. O. Wilson of Harvard published in the *New York Times Sunday Magazine*. Now, no one would dispute that Dr. Wilson merits this sort of attention for all of his splendid efforts on behalf of biology, particularly his work on insects. The piece itself is a fairly straightforward one until, in an apparent attempt to make a telling point, the author inserts an entire paragraph devoted to how the tropics can be saved if we could develop economies based on new forest products. The article cites, in particular, "one plant with vast commercial potential, the winged bean of New Guinea, [which] has been called a one-species supermarket: its roots, seeds, leaves, stems and flowers are all edible."[27] Since ordinary lawn grass is edible as well, one can only wonder if the author ever took the time to sample any part of this "super" vine (*Psophocarpus* — previously mentioned) in any form or simply took as gospel, without further investigation, statements from a 15-year-old government publication. This foolishness certainly detracts from the story, and even worse, since this is an article about Dr. Wilson, it tangentially depreciates him as well.

In this manner jungle myths become established "facts," often attributed to those who have never lived in these locales. And these myths provide absolutely no benefit toward the conservation, maintenance, or protection of this ecosystem. They only create confusion, for on the one hand people are told how much is rapidly being destroyed, and on the other hand, they are lulled by fables of the "fear not, for the winged bean will save the rain forest" genre. I believe the only way to stop this sort of nonsense is to condemn those who continue to propagate this kind of misinformation to live in a jungle environment as the native inhabitants do, and exist for at least a week on a diet of nothing but winged beans.

Another example in this almost shameless (and endless) type of exposé is that of the rosy periwinkle (*Catharanthus rosea*). This plant is, of course, the source of the drug vincristine, which has been used for ages by those who lived in Madagascar and now assists many patients throughout the world who suffer from Hodgkin's disease and lymphoma. However, instead of this wonder drug–producing plant helping to preserve the tropical jungles of Madagascar, it has been the cause for the destruction of vast numbers of acres of this ecosystem. Indeed, it is now predicted that this once heavily forested island off the southeast coast of Africa (only slightly less than twice the size of Arizona) will have little or no forest cover left in another 50 years, and thus a greatly reduced habitat for its indigenous lemurs. This is chiefly due to the burgeoning of its population, now estimated to be at more than 12 million (or about four times that of Arizona), but also to the leveling of large areas of tropical dry forests by farmers there who have been induced to grow the rosy periwinkle (pharmaceutical factories?) to be used by Eli Lilly and Company as a precursor for a medicinal drug. In such a manner, we once more ostensibly kill that which we claim to love and then, as does any murderer, attempt to hide the evidence — using this plant to attempt to prove a false point. The tragedy is that the same result could possibly be achieved for less effort and greater conservation, as in the case of taxol from yew trees, by testing in a plant tissue laboratory or, as in the case of natural rubber, by developing a more efficient and ecologically sound plant-extraction industry.

Perhaps more germane is the recent story of the *sao la* goat of Vietnam. In 1992, this formerly undescribed mammal, completely new to international science, was discovered in the forests of that country. The publicity surrounding this find soon approached that generally saved only for rising film stars or athletic prodigies. Articles soon appeared in newspapers and such magazines as the *National Geographic*. This was quickly followed by the arrival of television crews from many countries, all jockeying for the best pictures — even offering considerable sums of money to local farmers if they could produce a live specimen for filming.

So, soon after simply learning of its existence, people now threaten this beast with extinction. This has come about, according to Philip Shenon, "not at the hands of loggers or animal predators, but because of the well-meaning frenzy whipped up by scientists, environmentalists and the press."[28] Is it inherent in us to cause the demise of those things we are supposed to love?

In place of the aimless "Searching for Eldorado" approach to medicine—the hope that in some wild place a plant will turn up with leaves or sap or fruit that can cure our ills—I would suggest further and more ingenious application of molecular biology through biotechnology. As Malcolm Gladwell points out in his review of Barry Werth's book *The Billion-Dollar Molecule*, scientists can now break down the different parts of a disease or virus, make three-dimensional models of these in a computer, and then figure out from this information how to design a drug to overcome or at least nullify the action of the unwanted molecules.[29]

A final example of the sort of tragedy that occurs when people try to save the jungles and forests of the world was that published by three excellent and dedicated botanists about the economic worth of a portion of the Amazon jungle. Because those involved have all performed admirably in their fields, it is somewhat difficult for me to chastise them for this particular report, but their dubious claim has now taken on such mythic proportions it must be addressed. To his credit, one of the authors, Alwyn Gentry, attempted to correct some of the defective impressions that had resulted before his recent death in a plane crash in Ecuador.

The article, "Valuation of an Amazonian Rainforest," was published in *Nature* in 1989. The authors made the argument that the "exploitation of non-wood resources would provide profits while conserving Amazonian forests." Figures on the annual yield and market value in Iquitos, Peru, of a number of forest products were compared to the "merchantable volume and stumpage value of the commercial timber tree [*sic*] in one hectare of forest at Mishana, Rio Nanay, Peru." This argument concluded by stating "that comparative economics may provide the most convincing justification for conservation and use of these important ecosystems."[30]

It is my contention that the data given in support of their argument are either incorrect or misleading, and that the authors, in yet another example of people desiring to protect this forest while actually doing it a disservice, promise more than can be delivered and hold out a false hope in the process. To prove my point, only their data presented relative to the extraction of nonwood forest products will be used.

To begin with, while this article states that "latex yields for wild *Hevea* were taken from the literature," a careful examination of the volume cited gives no such data. Indeed, the only reference by Polhamus to natural rubber yields was that of smallholders in Asia: a rate of 164 pounds per acre.[31] These figures are for plantation rubber probably on alternate-day tapping schedules of between 350 and 400 trees/ha. This would imply, at best, slightly less than half a pound of latex per tree per year. Additionally, these Far Eastern rubber plantings are known to be more productive than unselected jungle trees. While the principal species of rubber in the general Iquitos area is the Para rubber tree (*H. brasiliensis*), *H. guianensis*—which, as previously indicated, has long been known to be inferior to the Para rubber tree as a good producer of latex—is also present. Despite this, the data for latex production provided by the three investigators was given as a quite improbable 2.0 kg (4.4 lb) per tree. Furthermore, since the average price for top-quality rubber in New York during that time period was seldom higher than $0.50 per pound ($1.10/kg), it is questionable that these jungle gatherers—who probably do not tap the 24 scattered trees listed in this report on intense tapping schedules and who undoubtedly produce a low-quality, rather dirty and impure rubber—could receive $1.20 per kilogram for their product at Iquitos even at a subsidy price theoretically controlled by the Peruvian government in 1987.

The major income producer, of the 12 nonwood resources given, is *Aguaje* (*Mauritea flexuosa*). This palm is known as a source of oil and starch, wine, timber, cork, fiber for weaving and tying, and palm hearts and is locally referred to as the tree of life.[32] My experience, however, is that the principal means of harvesting the fruit (borne only on female trees) and the sole means of harvesting palm hearts is cutting these palm trees to the ground, which naturally kills them. Thus, while female palms may be a good source of income, they are disappearing at an alarming rate with all the seeds being sold and few or none left for replanting. The same may be said about the other high-income-producing palm referred to, the *ungurahui* (*Jessenia bataua*) which also has an excellent cabbage. This palm, of course, must also be felled in order to obtain the cabbage or palm heart.

With such destruction, where, one wonders, is the "convincing justification for conservation" referred to?

Actually, the data given in the *Nature* article, which certainly may be categorized as constituting a rather incomplete and inexact presentation of the facts, jeopardize the entire argument and put an interested public in a position of wondering just whom to believe. It is inconceivable that anyone could consider that harvests that require killing the source of the product to be sold would go on in perpetuity, as suggested by the authors as a keystone of their thesis. My chief concern is not so much about the original paper itself, for the general public seldom reads scientific journals, as that subsequent to its publication in *Nature* a spate of almost word-for-word repeats of the same data appeared in a variety of more readily available news and information sources ranging from the *New Scientist*[33] to the *New York Times*[34] (including the Stevens article referred to earlier), in *Environment*,[35] and in the journal *Trends in Ecology and Evolution* (TREE),[36] thereby guaranteeing a much wider audience. Many more who have seen or heard about such reports probably now believe what was presented could be true.

I am not alone in my concern relative to the mischief and damage that may have been caused by this article. Oliver Phillips also criticized this same paper in a letter to *Conservation Biology* by stating that "the controversy [over the "use it or lose it" approach to forest conservation—see Putz[37]] is indeed unnecessary, not least because it overlooks the present reality that much commercial and subsequent extraction from tropical forests—for fruits, medicines, latex, fiber, game, and timber—is non-sustainable."[38] Also commenting on the valuation of tropical rain forests, Richard Tremaine criticizes the data provided by M. J. Balick and R. Mendelsohn in their article "Assessing the Economic Value of Traditional Medicines from Tropical Rainforests." Tremaine believes that this argument contains a number of questionable economic assumptions. For this reason, he concludes that "for this to be effective, economic analysis must be conducted fully, accurately, and in such a manner that results and conclusions *can be validated*" (emphasis added).[39]

This tricky game of extrapolating from dubious and doubtful numbers can, of course, be continued almost endlessly. The total income from one hectare of forest is given in the *Nature* article as $697.79. The rule of thumb in a great deal of the tropics is that one person can attend to 2 hectares (approximately 5 acres) of land with the hand tools at his or her disposal. This presumably implies a yearly cash income of only $1,395.58. Using a figure of 250 working days a year (the remainder given over to hunting, fishing, and other nonharvesting duties), the average income works out to be $5.58 per day. Even taking into account that little need be spent on food, shelter, clothing, and other basic necessities (batteries, needles, bullets, salt) in a forest dwelling near Iquitos, this level of income can in no way be considered as satisfactory since it relegates the families involved to positions far below the poverty line. Michael Parfit, who addresses this point in greater depth in an article about life in the Brazilian rain forest, suggests that even for the most fortunate there, life is exceedingly grim.[40]

Anyone who has lived and worked for any length of time in such regions as those under discussion soon becomes aware that something very significant is missing in each of the arguments or statements made above concerning the wealth or potential bounty of the tropical rain forests. This is rather similar to the problem of the hound, in the Sherlock Holmes story, that didn't bark. On closer examination, it becomes obvious that this disturbing missing piece in the puzzle is that the authors, and many others like them, appear either frightened of or unable to deal with or unwilling to even mention the word *population* as it relates to numbers of human beings. Quite surprisingly, it is not to be found in the *Nature* article referred to above. While, to his credit, Myers is much more outspoken on this subject at the present time, he devoted only a brief mention (less than two pages) to the "future buildup of population numbers" and their potential impact on forest environments in his 1984 book.[41] His concern at that time relative to burgeoning populations was basically given over to the manner by which hordes of young people, migrating from urban settings, would soon decimate the rain forest environments essentially because they did not know how to subsist in such habitats without destroying them.

It is puzzling why so many who write about this part of the world are so leery of mentioning the obvious cause for the degradation of these environments: human populations in tropical areas are growing faster than in any other region. For it is these growing numbers of mostly poor, untrained invaders of the only land which is left to them who exert so much pressure on these ecosystems. How much better if those who wish to save tropical rain forests would put their efforts behind some form of population control rather than propagate utopian misinformation in an attempt to accomplish the same goal.

There are those, of course, led by the likes of Karl Sax, Paul and Anne Ehrlich, and Garrett Hardin, who have for some time attempted to bring before the public the one simple fact that the carrying capacity (the number of organisms — including human beings — that a given habitat can adequately support) not only of the rain forest environment but, indeed, of the entire world is limited and that we are pushing these limits to the extreme.[42] Which leads to a final point on this matter of jungle myths. To provide a balance to those tales and myths noted above, another story — I could even say parable or metaphor — is presented here. It may not represent a completely novel approach, but it is portrayed in a new context and by one who has spent considerable time living and working with Shipbo Indians in the Peruvian Amazon.

This relates to the thesis of Dr. Warren Hern, a physician and professor of anthropology at the University of Colorado, that the human species is fast becoming a global cancer, and its obviously burgeoning growth has all the marks of the so-called dedifferentiated cells in a malignant tumor. According to Dr. Hern, the principal reason forests and jungles are disappearing at such an alarming rate is uncontrolled human growth, and until this population is controlled, the destruction will go on in spite of any other new scheme.

When this idea was published in the journal *Population and Environment* in the fall of 1990,[43] it did not receive a favorable response from the academic community. Was this reaction due solely to disagreement with Dr. Hern's hypothesis or was it a form of denial suggesting that those who were not favorably impressed are still laboring under the influence of tall timber tales of one sort or another and see salvation only in yet-untried schemes?

What can be done to help overcome or even diminish this trend in world population increase? It should be obvious now that unless some form of positive, intelligent action is soon taken, the end result can only be the inevitable degradation of our environment.

7

EVERYBODY
PLANT A TREE

A SUITABLE RESPONSE to the dilemmas we have been discussing might be for everyone to get out and plant trees wherever and whenever possible. Actually, many would probably be happy to heed this call, for what makes the "environmentalist's dream," spoken of earlier, so appealing is very simply the idea of planting a great many trees. This may be especially true today, now that we are told over and over again that far more trees throughout the world are being cut or destroyed everywhere than are being planted or allowed to reseed themselves. To emphasize this point it should be noted that while Paul Bunyan, an important legendary folk hero, was extremely prodigious and prolific in his ability to fell forests, someone like John Chapman, better known as Johnny Appleseed, may be an even more important exemplar in our culture, due to his persistent planting of new ones everywhere he went. Indeed, tree-planting ceremonies have come to occupy a special place and significance in our culture. Thus the true purpose, the raison d'être, of the National Arbor Day Foundation is to assure that partaking in such an act will bring to mind a host of wonderful things that may soon accrue to humankind, whether the tree planted later lives or dies. An event of this nature is also supposed to engender the type of feeling which may bring a tear to the eye of the participant, especially when this act is coupled with a recitation of Joyce Kilmer's poem "Trees." However, there are those who insist this heartfelt emotion may have its roots in rather earlier human tradition and folklore ranging from the rites practiced by ancient Greeks in sacred sylvan groves, to the value placed on holy Hindu forests in India and Nepal, to the belief of indigenous peoples that trees in the Amazon basin harbor spirits, to the worship of Druids within the confines of special oak forests in what today are the British Isles.[1] There is even increasing evidence that the cradle of humanity lay in the branches of trees scattered throughout the African veld.[2]

It may have been due to a combination of such attitudes and emotions that President George Bush announced his "America the Beautiful" program during the State of the Union Message in early February 1990. As previously indicated, in this he outlined a proposal for planting a billion trees a year in the United States during each of the next ten years —10 billion in all. While this was, according to Philip Shabecoff, "the latest in a series of incentives by Mr. Bush to establish his credentials as an environmentally minded President,"[3] many have been left wondering whether it was indeed a serious proposal that, for some reason, the administration simply was unable to enact or perhaps a public relations scheme designed to keep outspoken environmentalists quiet for the moment.

The first question that might be asked, if this program had actually been implemented, is where such a number of saplings could be obtained. Andy Lipkis, founder of the group known as TreePeople of California, who began his project by securing seedlings from the California Forestry Division as well as private nurseries, has, after considerable and quite laudable work, finally been able to complete the planting of a million trees in the Los Angeles area. It has further been reported that he has actually been responsible for helping to plant more than 200 million trees in many different parts of the world during the past 20 years. We should acknowledge that this may be an impressive start, especially if we could be certain that thrifty and well-formed specimens of the ideal species for each different environment were used and adequately cared for following planting. At the same time, however, it must be pointed out that these efforts have actually involved but a fraction of the number of trees President Bush hoped to see planted in the United States *each year* for some time to come.

As originally proposed, the "America the Beautiful" project was budgeted to cost $175 million a year for a period of 10 years, or $1.75 billion overall. This program was also to have been managed by the U.S. Forest Service with as much volunteer input, from such organizations as the Boy Scouts and Garden Clubs of America, as possible. Furthermore, it was intended that private organizations be asked to assist in defraying the costs of this operation.

Obviously, the state and federal forest nurseries of each different locality to be served, after being given specific tasks (and naturally provided with the necessary funds), could be geared up to produce the seedlings required. But, one might ask, of what species, by whom would these trees be planted, and in what localities? For a variety of reasons, such questions, while important, are difficult to answer. And, of course, more questions would remain to be answered. What size tree is to be used? Will these be planted bare-root or with a burlap covering around the earth-enclosed roots? Who will do the planting—professionals or inexperienced volunteers? What follow-up care will be provided? Is the land to be planted level or hilly? Is it rocky? Is it cleared land, scrub forest, brush, or second growth? These are not foolish or trite queries to be asked regarding a program of such magnitude and cost. Let me elaborate.

During the decade of the 1980's, in order to beautify the area of the Grand Avenue Mall in the city of Milwaukee 6- to 10-foot broad-leafed trees of a number of different species (together with individual metal grills to protect each at street level) were planted at an average cost of $1,200 per tree. In a similar manner the landscaping of corporate headquarters, resorts, and on a grander scale, golf courses also require the establishment of a variety of very expensive trees, many of considerable size. The costs of these programs, all of which are planned to be recouped by some means in the near future, are really not a matter of immediate consideration. It is obviously not fair to compare such small, local programs with a project of the magnitude of that proposed by President Bush.

I therefore contacted a number of local nurseries in the state of Wisconsin and found that if one purchases not single trees but rather large numbers of them (for substantial savings), potted or balled three-year-old saplings, ready to plant, sell in the range of $25–$65 each, depending upon the species, or an average of $45. Even taking into account the economies of scale that might be gained with larger-scale tree purchases, such costs are prohibitive for a large-scale planting. Whether the trees were to come from private or state nurseries, we are talking in terms of a minimum of $35–$40 billion per year simply to supply the seedlings required for the "America the Beautiful" program, not a mere $175 million.

On looking further, I discovered that in order to obtain the material required for a large-scale planting program, state nurseries will provide, under contract, large numbers of plants at a much more reasonable cost—in the neighborhood of about $120 per thousand for 1- to 2-year-old, bare-root conifer seedlings, dug and ready to go. A billion trees at this price could come to only $120 million.

But what about other planting costs? A standard spacing of 900 trees to the acre for such conifers as red pine implies more than a million acres to be required for the billion trees. Without even beginning to take into consideration where this amount of real estate would come from nor what this might cost and how it would be paid for, simply using herbicides (a procedure known as chemical clearing) to prepare the planting areas would cost about $45 an acre on relatively level land. Thus, we must add another $50 million for this treatment. Hand planting costs about 8–10 cents per tree. Even using the lower figure it is obvious that we must factor in an additional $80 million just for this activity. The cost of a possible second chemical clearing or herbicide application, again at $45 per acre, must be added. While this herbicide application is a rather standard operating procedure, since there are generally no provisions for any type of follow-up care for such reforesting projects, everyone involved will certainly have to pray for rain. Without adequate soil moisture, the entire planting, which is now, by our estimates, at $300 million per year, will be a crashing failure. Furthermore, since no consideration has been given to such additional costs as transportation from the nursery to the field, it is easy to see that the proposed $175 million annual budget would be only about half the amount required each year for a 10-year period.

As but a single example of the difficulties to be encountered in such a tree-planting venture, I submit an editorial from the New York Times titled "Plant Trees. Then Protect Them." In this, it was noted that in the Olympic Forest in Los Angeles, where trees from all over the world had been planted amid considerable political fanfare but without significant community involvement, a large percentage have now died.[4] Did they so wither, one might ask, because they were not the proper species, because they had been incorrectly planted, or because they were not adequately attended to after planting? Barbara J. Eber-Schmidt, executive director of the New York City Tree Consortium, suggests an ominous number of pitfalls and problems related to keeping trees alive once they have been planted. She insists that one cannot just shove a seedling in the ground and then go away and leave it.[5]

This entire controversy did not simply disappear with the changing of the administration in Washington. Secretary of the Interior Bruce Babbitt, the present "environmental czar," is faced with even greater challenges in this regard particularly in a political environment in which everyone is determined to cut spending. Thus, we might have asked where funds for any environmental project the size and scope of the "America the Beautiful" program would come from. With promises for financial aid to Russia, Israel, Haiti, and many other foreign countries, not to mention crime prevention, possible implementation of an antiballistic-missile defense program, and a host of other important areas where money is presumed to be desperately needed, do we have enough to expend extra funds on new tree plantings—and still balance the budget? Taking this fiscal reality into consideration, does a tree-planting project of the magnitude proposed stand a chance of enactment? We might also ask whether this was really a serious plan of a theoretically responsible government in the first place, or was it simply a bit of rhetoric designed to gull the American people? The answer to these questions is critical, for if we cannot carry out such a program in our own country, are we admitting we cannot cope with the environmental deterioration now taking place all about us? Furthermore, for all our supposed wealth, technological competence, and fervent talk of protecting the environment, since we have not yet been able to initiate and carry out this particular program, how could we ever seriously take on the vast planting of rubber trees throughout the world as previously suggested?

Naturally, reforesting billions of trees is not an easy or simple venture. On a couple of recent trips to China where I was fortunate enough to travel quite a bit by car and train, I was able to observe the effects of the considerable tree-planting efforts in many regions of that country during the past 30 to 40 years. From what I was able to see, the overall effort appeared to be quite an achievement. However, it was easy to note that some species certainly did not do as well as others and that many trees along roadways, rivers, canals, and even village streets demonstrated a grave lack of care, as evidenced by their total absence or generally poor condition. My observations on this matter were quickly confirmed by foresters, botanists, and ecologists, both local and foreign, who informed me that in the desire to have as many trees planted in as short a time as possible, serious errors were made in species selection as well as follow-up care. We too, have made similar errors in tree-planting projects in the United States, as evidenced by our lavish and widespread planting of a single species—the American elm—the majority of which were later decimated by disease. This particular topic will be more thoroughly addressed later.

Planting trees is obviously a noble challenge in theory, and so easy to talk about—rather like condemning sin. But what often happens in practice? Mr. James W. Kinnear, the president and CEO of Texaco, in a letter to the *New York Times*, pats himself and Texaco on the back for enlisting "ordinary people" (sort of like Leona Helmsley's "little people"?) to participate in Global ReLeaf, a program of the American Forestry Association. According to Kinnear, his company even committed $1 million toward carrying out this effort in a few selected cities.[6] If the amount of money pledged were to be used *only* for the purchase of nursery stock, a total of 8,333,333 seedlings could be obtained at a rock-bottom price of $0.12 each for bare-root, 1- to 2-year-old conifers. Considerably fewer trees could be bought with this amount of money should the more desirable maples or oaks or other broad-leafed trees have been selected. If all the funds are spent on the seedlings (at the nursery, not at the planting site), what of transporting and actually planting the young trees on some plot of land? And who will pay for this? Presuming that volunteers will assume these and all other costs, including land preparation, establishment, and subsequent follow-up care, at currently recommended planting distances (900 trees per acre), the number of plants involved (if only conifers were to be used) would fill a total of about 9,259 acres. This area is about the size of 11 Central Parks (840 acres) in New York City. If broad-leafed trees were chosen, their smaller number would imply reforesting a plot only about five or six times the size of this park.

I have seen no references as to the outcome of this project, nor where any of the presumed plantings may have taken place. I can only assume that had this program been an outstanding success, a certain amount of publicity would, by now, have been provided. Furthermore, if this had been the case, this scheme of reforestation could have been recommended as a model or guide for future plantings.

In this connection, the majority of those with whom I have spoken on this subject, people generally quite knowledgeable about forestry and tree-planting matters, have heaved a collective sigh of relief that really so little indiscriminate and wasteful tree planting has actually been carried out. Their argument is that, despite quite enormous amounts of money spent, the majority of those responsible for the reforestation projects of such groups as the National Arbor Day Foundation, Global ReLeaf, CARE, Energy Releaf, the Agency for International Development (AID), and the tenuous "America the Beautiful" scheme do not know what they are doing. The repeated selection of incorrect species at improper planting distances and in unfavorable mixtures can only do more future harm than good. Ted Williams, for one, is far more cynical about and ruthless toward these groups than I. Writing in *Audubon*, he refers to them as environmental illiterates, for their bumbling, often quite detrimental efforts to perform what they would like to feel are worthwhile acts.[7]

The tragic irony is that tree planting is quite the proper thing to do. As a new study shows, planting 95,000 trees in the metropolitan area of Chicago would result in a new benefit of $38 million over a 30-year period. Included would be savings on air conditioning and heating, lessening of CO_2 emissions from power plants, and absorption of pollutants from the air itself.[8] A more recent article in the journal *Science* indicates that as much as a ton of carbon dioxide is absorbed each year by a hectare (2.471 acres) of Amazonian rain forest, thus providing a critical "carbon sink."[9] Unfortunately, we are rapidly going in the wrong direction in this region, cutting and burning faster than replanting.

As in the case of questionable advertising of environmentally safe or friendly products, too many individual people are now attempting to make a good thing for themselves or their particular institution by promoting a variety of tree-planting projects. These are now being conducted in the United States but particularly in foreign countries, more often than not on what is suggested as a proper scientific basis (trial plots, regular planting distances, measurements, and so on) with a variety of distinct tree species. I have visited too many such sites in African and Indian locales as well as in Central and South America and am generally quite disappointed with what I am shown.[10] Basically these tests are short-term, poorly designed projects usually aimed more at promoting those involved than at clarifying some silvicultural enigma. To establish some basis for credibility, most participants in such so-called investigations assert that the work has been planned with the aim of providing local farmers with knowledge about new planting schemes and the marked superiority of exotic trees over native species. Claims are also forthcoming that the results of this work will practically guarantee that the farmers who plant these relatively untested species will obtain excellent monetary returns for their efforts. From prior experience, I am aware that such projects rarely if ever achieve their stated goals, and generally the only benefit that accrues is the grants themselves, often provided by some major funding organization, to those directing the studies. In almost every case, the local people with whom I discussed what was being undertaken were quite unimpressed — except for those, or their families, who had some direct involvement in the study. After so many past failures of high-sounding governmental, international, or even private organizations, including the highly touted and quite unsuccessful Green Revolution,[11] most peasants are well aware that no quick-fix miracle is likely to bring them immediate help. A corollary to many of these tree-planting extravaganzas, which unfortunately tends to confuse the issue considerably, is that long before work has actually been completed and some final analysis made, data have already been published or seminars presented on how each of these trials has already practically achieved its long-range goals with a high measure of success. Longtime residents of rural areas, if they do become aware of such efforts, are seldom fooled by them.

Should there have been any easy solutions to the problems these reforestation schemes are purportedly designed to rectify, they would have long ago been adopted. Now, with current interest in matters pertaining to deforestation increasing all the time, there are obviously a number of examples of well-planned, long-term field studies presently being conducted in a number of different tropical areas. Some are attempts to modify and update forestry programs and studies that were originally initiated many years ago when European colonial powers simply tried to transfer proven silvicultural techniques from temperate areas to tropical ones. Unhappily, generally for ecological reasons, these programs were seldom successful, and the wreckage of many can now be seen from the Far East through Africa to such areas in the New World as Belize (formerly British Honduras), Guyana (formerly British Guiana), and the eastern Peruvian Andes. However, such new experimental projects as the Nepal-Australian Forestry Project (NAFP), the CELOS management scheme (begun, interestingly enough, by Dutch foresters in Surinam), and others[12] do show positive signs. In general, these reforestation programs require beginning not with bare ground or worn-out pastures to be replanted but rather with a forest of some kind — even low second-growth — which is then so managed as to improve and increase its stand of timber while selected specimens (trees that are either mature, dead, or of an undesirable species) are periodically removed for market. However, we must understand that everywhere the number of these bits and pieces of high-grade or secondary forests are decreasing all the time.

Then, of course, it should be noted that a certain small but perhaps growing number of farmers throughout the world, when they are financially able, do keep and properly maintain woodlots or have small tree farms on their land. To these they occasionally add new seedlings, or, better still, permit selected ones, which have sprouted naturally, to prosper and grow. Almost inevitably, the species utilized are well-known, native ones. The grass may be reported as being greener on the other side of the fence, but far too many mistakes have been made with exotics or out-of-place species to excite those who have neither the time nor the funds to gamble on unsubstantiated claims. The transfers, probably by some well-meaning souls, of two plant species from Australia, eucalyptus to California and melaleuca (bottle brush) to southern Florida, have resulted in environmental disasters as these species have attracted pests that have proved seemingly impossible to eradicate by any means.

It is naturally the large multinational corporations, such as Weyerhauser, Champion Paper, International Paper, and Georgia-Pacific, that should be, and in many cases actually are, actively and effectively engaged in tree-land farming. Some of this activity is even conducted in an ecologically appropriate manner. The greatest amount of reforestation, in such states as Georgia (which boasts of having more seedlings planted per year within its borders than any other state), is for the production of pulpwood rather than in the development and maintenance of natural forests. These short-lived trees, all planted in geometrically straight rows, do not a real forest make, despite the considerable erroneous comments to the contrary. This activity is what I deem to be true agro-forestry. In such cases, instead of attempting to combine agriculture and forestry, which is seldom a satisfactory or even economically sound mix, uniform stands of the same species of trees are planted in the manner of an agricultural farm crop to be harvested, en masse, followed quickly by the replanting of a succession of fast-growing trees. A high degree of economic success has even been achieved in tropical regions of Brazil with the establishment of thousands of acres of clonal plantings of quick-growing eucalyptus cuttings.[13] These have been, as in the case of the pulpwood-tree farms of Georgia, carefully selected to produce a similar absorbent pulpy product, much of it used to fill modern disposable diapers for both young and old. Some claim that this is an ecologically sound system, especially since all these trees will absorb large quantities of carbon dioxide. Unhappily, this argument is false[14] (as will be discussed at greater length in a later chapter), since young trees actually expel, by a significant amount, more of this gas than they absorb, and the disposable diapers that have turned children and old folks alike into ambulatory privies inevitably lead to an added solid-waste pollution problem.[15] Furthermore, the transpiration rate of these rapidly growing trees is tremendous, removing, as the leaves pass large volumes of moisture into the air, enormous quantities of water from the soil, often to its detriment.

It must be understood here that the corporations which oversee this type of forest management are not primarily interested in growing trees. Their chief interest, naturally, is in making money. For example, a recent advertisement by the Georgia-Pacific Corporation (two complete pages in *Forbes* magazine) did not once mention the words *trees, forests,* or *lumber,* but rather stressed the company's strong cash position.[16] Many might consider this somewhat misleading, since following Georgia-Pacific's recent purchase of the Great Northern Nekoosa Corporation for $4.5 billion, there may not really have been, at that time, such a great bundle of cash in the company coffers. It is not difficult to discover, if one takes time to search out the facts, that this same corporation actually reported a drop in its second-quarter earnings in 1991 from the previous year, with $29 million reported as a portion of this year's earnings actually the result of a decrease in capital through the sale of some of the company's timberland.

The truth is that the executives of such corporations may never see the harvests of trees they have been instrumental in planting, and so probably do not have as deep or serious a feeling of stewardship over their forests as might be hoped for. Even though we publicly insist that as a society we have a more noble attitude in this matter and speak of trees for our grandchildren, when pressed, many often confess that they are generally interested only in immediate results and hardly plan more than a couple of years into the future. Robert Heilbroner pointed to this seemingly universal human trait when he wrote of our "preference for present material enjoyments over future ones (which is why we won't lend a dollar today, even without risk, unless we can expect to get back more than a dollar tomorrow)."[17] This definitely suggests that if we are to think seriously about successfully planting billions of trees, including rubber or any other species, we must take into consideration a wide gamut of problems and difficulties which face us, especially if this is to take place in some foreign country where the extent of our hands-on control is diminished.

Those who are anxious to let everyone know how well we are doing in the matter of planting trees, including the American Forestry Association, insist that there are a greater number of trees being planted now than ever before. Perhaps so, but a large percentage of these are set out in long straight rows like corn and will be cut in 10 to 15 years for pulp. A total of 33.5 million of another type of tree (estimated at 8 percent of those planted annually just in Wisconsin) are sold each year when quite young and then after a couple of weeks' use are discarded — Christmas trees.[18] These items, which some consider a squandering of resources and others as their very bread and butter, having completed their short-term apparent usefulness, end up mostly being a burden on our waste disposal systems. After all, does there really exist what can be called an inexpensive yet practical use for a discarded Christmas tree?

Furthermore, the very generic name used not only is quite misleading but has become the source of a certain amount of rancor relating to the debate over the separation of church and state in many parts of the United States. These trees may be symbolic, but the custom does not have its roots in any Christian tradition. It was handed down, rather, from the pagan Norse celebration of the Festival of the Winter Solstice when evergreens were decked out with objects representing the fruits of summer, once the days began to lengthen in winter as the sun announced the return of spring. This whole performance has been skillfully incorporated into a Christmas tradition by those anxious to make a killing in sales at this time of year, on any item and by any means possible. Certainly, all must agree, these gaudy ornament-bedecked evergreen saplings have very little to do with anything relating to "peace on earth." And these two single examples — pulpwood and Christmas trees — demonstrate the difficulty we face in any quest for the permanent establishment of some of those forests and jungles that are now disappearing so rapidly.

Possibly the best means of accomplishing this goal is to surround an area with a high fence of barbed wire and keep everyone out. In time, if there are adequate seed sources in the immediate vicinity or in what is known as the soil seed bank, nature will take care of the matter itself. This approach is probably too simple a solution for our modern technologically oriented society to grasp; furthermore, it is often believed that in such cases time must be counted in terms of centuries.

That this is not necessarily the case was well demonstrated following the recent explosions of the volcano Mount St. Helens where, when left alone, nature far outperformed humankind in rehabilitating damaged areas. This is also basically the approach so strongly advocated by Bill McKibben, who writes on how the eastern part of the United States, after fairly large areas were cut and trashed, is returning to its original natural condition in "an explosion of green." [19] He is by no means so sanguine about how such a scheme might take place, nor does he go so far as to provide us with any specific guidelines as to how such might actually be accomplished.

Despite this sort of evidence, we tend to keep thinking about something of a production-oriented nature, such as planting any kind of tree anywhere. Fortunately, some are beginning to understand that this system of indiscriminate planting will not work and that we must look for something else — something closer to the natural "deep woods" system. A further complication for the many who enjoy woodland and forest environments is that, owing to our burgeoning populations, those national parks and forests that have been set aside for the enjoyment of all are becoming so crowded that some form of rationing or prior reservation is now required in many cases, and such requirements will only increase in the future as demand for these facilities grows. Soon, all that may be left for the many who would like to visit and spend some time in a wilderness area may be a completely artificial and very expensive theme park. Will we soon come to the point when our entire experience of the natural environment, with the exception of grain farms, cattle ranches, or the sterile and monotonous rows of pulpwood or Christmas trees, will consist of a few city parks, the scattered trees of suburbia, overcrowded national forests, and recreational centers filled with artificial plants and animals?

This bleak prospect calls to mind the thought left to us by Henry David Thoreau: "I went to the woods because I wished to live deliberately, to front only the essential facts of life, and see if I could not learn what it had to teach, and not, when I came to die, discover that I had not lived" ("Where I Lived, and What I Lived For," in *Walden*).

8

THE ROLE
OF DIVERSITY

IN FURTHER PURSUIT of a practical yet ecologically sound solution to the problem of future supplies of renewable raw materials, it
would be prudent to take a closer look at what caused the disasters brought
on by coffee rust, South American leaf blight, and Dutch elm disease. The
impact of these fungal attacks clearly points out a very important aspect inherent in the management of tree crops or forests everywhere but particularly in the tropics, where such things as weeds, insects, and pathogenic
microorganisms compete with, parasitize, or actually consume plants and
plant parts (and animals as well) throughout the entire year. As pointed out
by Daniel Janzen, cold climates effectively tend to cut down or even tem-
porarily eliminate similar instances of predation or competition in the
temperate regions, but obviously not in the tropics.[1] If we cannot effectively control such impediments or dangers to forests and trees, it will be
quite difficult to achieve our goals.

Let us begin then by questioning why the Ford Motor Company, which
attempted to establish large blocks of plantation rubber in the Amazon
during the 1920's and 1930's, had such severe and costly disease problems
while neither the rubber trees worked by the *seringueiros*, in the jungles
quite close by, nor the large areas of solid stands of rubber in Asia suffered
similar decimation and destruction.

In the first place, it must be remembered that when Wickham sent rubber seeds from Brazil to Kew Gardens near London, he sent nothing else.
SALB attacks only the leaves and flowers of *Hevea* species. The fungi that
cause SALB utilize these as their resource base, producing, as a waste product, a chemical almost identical to the hormone (abscisic acid) in plants
that, activated by some change in climate (winter or a dry period), causes
leaf fall in deciduous species. The same is true of coffee rust in that the organism *Hemileia vastatrix* utilizes, as its resource base, only the surface

layer of living coffee leaves and berries, but by so doing, through the very hormones produced as the result of this attack, eventually causes abscission and subsequent leaf fall and fruit drop. If the assault persists and leaves continue to fall, the trees will naturally die. This fungus (giving the appearance of a very small mushroom) is seldom if ever transmitted on dry coffee seeds or beans, which can usually be shipped about with impunity. When the transfer was made, during the 1800's, from Ethiopian forests to the East Indies, however, it was not dry seeds but rather entire coffee trees that were shipped, and in this manner the disease had a free ride.

SALB, indigenous to tropical America, never got to Asia, since only rubber seeds were transmitted by Wickham to Kew and from there only healthy, thrifty plants were sent on to Ceylon. Then, of course, until very recently, everyone was quite content with the performance of the so-called Far Eastern clones, and few felt it necessary to bring fresh genetic material from the Amazon to help improve on what they already had. Later, once SALB had been identified as the cause of so much damage in the Ford plantations near Santarém, no one who was associated with rubber in Asia was anxious to run the risk of transmitting this disease by attempting to import entire plants or even budwood from this region. In addition, a sufficiently large body of knowledge has now been developed concerning dangers of this nature that many quarantine and inspection stations have been established throughout the world to monitor and control the movement of plant and animal diseases. Indeed, budwood from recently selected rubber clones is presently being shipped from the Amazon basin to the Far East to be crossed, once this material has grown to flowering age, with the best material already at hand. The difference now is that all rubber budwood, from any locality, is carefully passed through such stations. This process of very thorough and frequent inspection, as well as special fungicidal treatments, has helped to prevent the transmittal of a variety of diseases. Nevertheless, owing to the enormous amount of material and goods, including both plants and animals, presently transported, often by air, this overall movement presents a constant and serious danger.[2]

That the seringueiros were and are now seldom troubled with the ravages of fungal diseases—such as Phytophthora palmivora, a pantropical plant malady that attacks a wide range of tropical plants including palms (hence its name)—is due to a principle of population biology which in its simplest form may be called the "needle in a haystack" strategy. This is not to say that fungal diseases have not established themselves in these jungles; they certainly have. Actually, following the logic of natural selection that everything which has evolved fulfills some particular role in our holistic universe, all pathogens execute essential functions in their particular environments. There are scientists who contend that "Disease is essential to ecological balance in a natural forest. Because most are heterotrophic microorganisms, pathogens help break down and release elements sequestered within trees and, by increasing mortality, they facilitate succession and help to maintain genetic, species, and age diversity."[3]

Furthermore, just as a serious outbreak, say of measles, according to the germ theory of disease, will occur only when a certain minimum number of children are brought together in close contact with each other, so, in a similar manner, SALB will not cause serious damage unless it is able to utilize a resource base of large, uniform, and readily available trees. Since such are not to be found in a highly diversified jungle setting, this fungus never has the chance to achieve a population explosion. The trees in a plantation setting, though, easily become such a resource base for this specific pathogen; therefore, SALB is able to develop rapidly to a lethal climax.

In the middle of the nineteenth century, the tropical plant explorer Alfred R. Wallace wrote a letter to Charles Darwin from a Southeast Asian hospital asking for comments on some novel ideas pertaining to what he referred to as natural selection. Wallace had formed this new theory from observations over a number of years in many parts of the tropical world. This letter, some believe, may have been the spark that Darwin needed to organize and complete his own thoughts on the same subject on which he had been working for an even longer period. The result was the presentation of a paper of joint authorship before the Royal Society of London on the then novel idea of natural selection. It was thus that a critical milestone in the development of evolutionary theory was brought before the general public. One of the keys to this principle was the importance of diversity. As Wallace wrote, concerning the virgin tropics: "If the traveller notices a particular species and wishes to find more like it, he may often turn his eyes in vain in every direction. Trees of varied forms, dimensions and colours are around him, but he rarely sees any one of them repeated. Time after time he goes towards a tree which looks like the one he seeks, but a closer examination proves it to be distinct. He may at length, perhaps, meet with a

second specimen half a mile off, or may fail altogether, till on another occasion he stumbles on one by accident."[4]

The English ecologist Paul Richards, who also included this same quo-
tation in his book *The Tropical Rain Forest*, goes on to say, "The richness of
the tree flora is indeed the most important characteristic of the rain forest
and on this many of its other features are directly dependent. Trees of different species are most commonly found mixed in fairly even proportions;
more rarely one or two species are much more abundant than the rest."[5]
With such a high degree of diversity and dispersal of distinct species, it is
no wonder that any specific organism (which is often also completely dependent on a single species of host plant) is unable to dominate large areas
of jungle forests. This natural strategy by which plants (and animals) ostensibly hide among their neighbors from some life-form that might do them
damage, is complemented by another artifice that Professor Lawrence
Slobodkin, of SUNY/Stony Brook, calls the behavior of the "prudent predator."[6] In this instance, if any particular organism can utilize but a single
food resource, and goes so far as to consume every bit of it, this voracious action is obviously tantamount to committing suicide. If, however, the predator is sufficiently prudent to merely debilitate by not building up its own
production too greatly in relation to its particular resource base, it can expect a longer and fuller parasitic life; this will be more likely to take place
when there is a high degree of species diversity. With rubber trees scattered
about and mixed with many other species, there is thus little chance for
fungi to establish a strong beachhead and thus do quite serious, to say nothing of lethal, damage to the parasitized tree.

Should, however, the environmental situation become so altered that
instead of there being only a very small number of *Hevea* trees scattered
throughout the Amazonian jungle, or but a few coffee trees dispersed in
the understory of some Abyssinian forest, there are thousands of these trees,
all planted in solid stands in the presence of their principal predatory microorganisms, the result usually implies disaster. With an apparently in-
exhaustible resource base of the food of choice, the rapacious organisms
quickly achieve the critical mass required for a population explosion, burgeoning rapidly beyond the area's carrying capacity, and thus decimating
the entire resource base. It does not take very much imagination to realize
that this biological principle is also at work in the case of another predator

(probably the most efficient and definitely one of the more imprudent of all) called *Homo sapiens*, which — in complete negation of its scientific name — is right now doing the very same thing to its own particular resource base — the earth itself. The clear implication is that unless we take it upon ourselves to seriously and more intelligently address the manner in which we misuse our environment, we may as a species be facing what soon could be a suicidal condition.[7]

We may point our fingers (as we so enjoy doing) at others for allowing such a stupid thing to happen and wonder how it was possible that those in the tropics couldn't have worked out this problem some time ago and taken care of the matter. But, of course, we must admit our similar mistake of flaunting these very same elementary and basic rules of biology throughout the length and breadth of our own land, as previously mentioned, by planting as many lanes, streets, avenues, and byways as possible with one single species of tree — *Ulmus americana*, or the American elm. Then, when the disease struck, we tried to dodge the issue, and any responsibility as well, by calling the fungus the Dutch elm disease. We have long ago learned that it is quite easy to place the blame for unfortunate matters on others, if only by the names we use — "Japanese beetle," "Mediterranean fruit fly," "Delhi belly," or "Asian flu." In any case, the rate at which elms began to die off soon equaled anything happening in the tropics. And this virulent and unsightly plague, afflicting what was practically our national tree, left vast areas bare of any shade. The cost of dealing with this problem was in the millions of dollars.

One might have thought that this painful lesson in our own country would have been sufficient to preclude other such mistakes. A recent survey has shown, however, that more than 90 percent of urban tree plantings in the northeastern part of the United States over the past few years have consisted of only four species — the sycamore, or plane tree, Austrian pine, green ash, and Norway maple.[8] (To someone's credit, little or no attempt has yet been made to replant elms.) Now, as many already are aware, one fungus has begun to decimate sycamores and another one is fast at work on the Austrian pines. It has even been recorded that the spread of the disease affecting sycamores was probably aided and abetted by the use of small chain saws and other pruning equipment of the urban foresters themselves.[9]

I have visited rubber plantations in Africa, Indonesia, Malaysia, South China, and Central and South America and in almost every instance, at least on well-managed farms, the principal method of dealing with disease and pest problems, in addition to the use of carefully selected trees, is by means of frequent applications of agricultural chemicals. Much the same could be said for coffee, citrus, banana, and African oil palm plantations as well as large-scale farms devoted to such mechanized crops as cotton and rice. And as these farms increase in size, so does the expense of dealing with pathogenic organisms, pests, and diseases. Some banana farms now require spraying by small plane or helicopter every other day to bring in a crop. The typical situation on many tropical cotton farms is that the farmer will perhaps make some money or at least break even the first couple of years but that from then on, until the operation is abandoned as being too costly, the only ones in agriculture who stand to gain are the fungicide or insecticide salespeople and their companies, the pilots of the spray planes, and the companies that make these special aircraft. Furthermore, farm workers everywhere are now becoming quite vocal about the manner in which these sprays are affecting not only the crops but the health of the laborers themselves.[10]

A guide to an innovative solution to this matter may be contained in recently developed ideas of population biology known as the MacArthur-Wilson theory of "Island Biogeography." This novel concept originally dealt with the immigration of plants and animals to isolated islands, at varying distances from the mainland, and involved research on the survival or extinction of the newcomers together with the influence or impact of these newly arrived immigrants on the lives and well-being of long-term residents.[11] This idea has now expanded the definition of "islands" to the point that an island need no longer be considered only as a discrete body of land surrounded by water but alternatively as a single plant, isolated in space from similar plants, or blocks of the same plant so isolated, by physical barriers or simply different types of vegetation. The ability of a fungus to migrate (by having the wind or some animal carry mature spores), from a plant that it is slowly debilitating to a another plant which can serve as a new resource base to perpetuate the fungal line so that it will not become extinct, is the focal point here. The farther apart the islands, the less subject they are to invasion.

We have already seen, however, that it is almost uneconomical to attempt to conduct a plantation type of operation on a commercial basis, even though many still try, by extracting latex from a scattering of dispersed rubber trees in a highly diversified jungle. To some this may sound like a wonderful environmental proposition, sort of the rural cottage-industry approach, where everyone does his or her own little thing, as written about by William Morris, at the height of the Industrial Revolution, in his book *News from Nowhere*.[12] This approach, on the surface, also sounds as though it were ecologically quite proper. But, as I tried to demonstrate previously, this sort of "save the planet" scheme has been shown to be extremely poor economics. Actually, the more highly concentrated the producing units, the easier it is to manage them and to extract from them a uniform product—more in keeping with the efficiency of Adam Smith's eighteenth-century pin factory or that of a beehive where groups of individuals do their one specific task. While these may often appear to be completely disorganized operations, the apparent bedlam—whether directed and coordinated by intelligent human management or, in the case of insects, by means of chemical control—is truly a harmonious blending of diverse actions for a common goal or benefit.[13] With proper ecology (and a lesser problem with disease and pests) but very low returns on one end of the spectrum and hard-core economics (fraught with biological dangers and high operating costs) on the other end, how can this dilemma be solved?

The answer, it would seem, is to locate that specific point between ideal ecology and maximum economic returns that will bring in the highest yields consistent with preserving the long-term environmental integrity of the locale.[14] In other words, this may be achieved through use of the "island" concept by which "islands" are viewed as consisting not of single rubber trees but rather of easily manageable blocks or strips of trees completely surrounded by plantings of other species that do not have diseases or insect predators in common with the *Hevea* species—or better yet, by the very jungle itself. In the latter case, the ideal would be to have plantings so laid out that the jungle exists as a continuous entity without any break in its form, for it has been well demonstrated that if this is not done, insects, small animals, and even birds will disappear from the environment. Without these, the true jungle itself, just as with the artificial forest that is a rubber plantation, will certainly become an "empty forest"— Kent Redford's concept previously alluded to.[15]

This scheme is similar to one advocated in a previous chapter that would allow cutting for lumber in only a portion of the national forests of Wisconsin, leaving some in true primeval "deep woods" conditions. Indeed, studies by Thomas Lovejoy of the Smithsonian Institution — initiated some time ago in a 10-square-mile area of the Amazonian rain forest in Brazil, and financed mainly by the World Wildlife Fund and the A. W. Mellon Foundation — have shown that small blocks (1, 10, or even 100 hectares) of jungle surrounded by pastures, farms, or degraded land may not, by any means, be considered true patches of jungle, but rather what is called edge or fringe — up to 70 percent in the case of the 100-hectare plots. These bits of former jungle, in turn, do not and cannot act or perform as true forest environments; therefore, they probably do not have the capability of future regeneration to a typical forest for this ecosystem. Nor are they also capable of serving as a proper home to a wide range of truly indispensable animal life on which these environments and eventually we ourselves depend.[16]

In this connection, Craig L. Shafer of the National Park Service, in analyzing the values and shortcomings of small reserves, concludes that these continue to fill a worthy niche in conservation strategies, especially when some of them are all that is left. He also suggests that small reserve viability should be improved by buffer zones, adequate usable corridors, and replication of habitat areas.[17]

These examples are presented not in order to delve more deeply into the principles of tropical ecology but rather to demonstrate how, to provide for minimal environmental disruption, extractive plantation industries might be designed in the future. While the exact configuration of each specific layout would have to be unique, there is a high degree of probability that, to optimize economic success, any program involving the establishment of large "island" blocks of tree crops must assure that these are interspersed, in the form of a matrix, within an area of contiguous jungle of a size approximately equal to that devoted to the tree crop. It is interesting to note that in a proposal on how to protect his variously sized plots in the Amazon jungle, Lovejoy suggested, in a sort of reversed thinking process to that just presented, that these areas might be surrounded by such a crop as rubber which would then act to buffer the edge or fringe of each.

Any way one looks at this, it is now easy to picture that instead of the projected block of 40,000 square miles of natural rubber plantings in simply one part of the tropics, what really is needed is at least double that amount, or approximately 80,000 square miles of land, scattered throughout the entire region. Half of the area would consist of high-grade, budgrafted rubber trees (by no means in one solid block but rather in separate efficient islands laid out so as to meet tapping requirements) and the remainder in "deep woods" forest or jungle, areas for workers' houses and gardens, and finally, land required for the plantation's nurseries and processing facilities.

But if a greater land area is now required as part of the option for the production of sufficient natural rubber to allow us to continue to drive on the tires to which we have grown accustomed, it appears that under the constraints of ecology, the entire matter may be far more complicated and demanding than originally suggested in the "environmentalist's dream."

One may wonder whether it is possible that such an issue should be taken seriously and, even more important, put into action. Yet, we have arrived at a condition that for the sake of our own future we must weigh, adhere to, and act on such principles — or else the earth's ecosystems will truly be in jeopardy and all of humankind with them.

9

IMPOSSIBLE DREAM
INTO INEVITABLE NIGHTMARE

A KEY ATTRIBUTE of the previously described impossible dream is the obvious and inescapable desire on the part of many for some wonderful event to soon take place that, without requiring much work on our part, will considerably brighten or improve our future. A growing number, everywhere, daily demonstrate this almost incurable character trait of something-for-nothing aspiration by praying to Lady Luck while wagering rather substantial sums, against incredible odds, on all manner of lotteries, sporting events, and gaming tables. Kenneth Clark couched this human peculiarity in more philosophic terms when he lamented our all still being victims of "the Fallacies of Hope,"[1] even though he may have been considering more profound and lofty aspirations than the rather ordinary, plebeian, quick-fix paths to success listed above.

Taking a cue from Clark, Professor Hugh Iltis, of the University of Wisconsin, a vociferous and able proponent for the intelligent management of our environment, lectures on the curses of "The Ecological Fallacies of Hope." These, he stresses, relate to a plethora of sanguine daydreams of life in the future that constantly ignore the ominous pressures of steadily growing numbers of human beings on the earth's available resources. He also insists that there are too many who expound on all the wonderful things that will soon take place as the result of some untested and improbable marvel of modern technology.[2] But the divinations of such oracles appear to be eagerly sought by others, who, striving for immediate satisfaction, ignore the many caveats along our collective path.

Two of the principal challenges facing us are the rapid increase in the conversion of unspoiled natural habitats to some form of monocultural land use, ranging from mechanized row agriculture to single-species tree farms, and the arduous, monotonous, and generally quite unappealing systems of labor commonly associated with monoculture — systems usually rife with the potential for a wide range of human abuses. Let us address each of these challenges separately.

Examples relating to the establishment of rubber plantations in the tropics of the world could be given to illustrate the problems and dire consequences associated with improper and excessive use of land; however, since the very same results with their accompanying abuse of the environment occur in temperate areas, more familiar to most of us, they will be presented first. Basically, these have to do with our misguided efforts to extract ever more resources from the land for our own often extravagant and thoughtless use, which have put in jeopardy not only a growing number of individual species but entire natural habitats as well.

According to William K. Stevens, "The concept of protecting whole ecosystems rather than single endangered species, which is being increasingly emphasized by conservationists, is embodied in a number of laws governing Federal lands and in several public-private conservation efforts." He goes on to state that this idea has been promoted by Interior Secretary Bruce Babbitt as the Clinton administration's central strategy for keeping species off the endangered list while accommodating private economic interests.[3]

This refers to the results of a study by Dr. Reed F. Noss, Dr. J. Michael Scott, and the late Dr. Edward T. LaRoe III for the Interior Department, which demonstrated that ecosystems that characterized and dominated whole regions of the United States, prior to the arrival of Europeans, have declined over more than 98 percent of their area and are considered critically endangered. Indeed, the Midwest prairie-savanna and the Eastern forest ecosystems, which may have covered as much as 40 percent of the entire country, are now seriously threatened.[4] The prairie-savanna has been almost completely destroyed, with only a few scattered pockets of original habitat remaining. This, of course, may be attributed almost exclusively to the conversion of these environments to row-crop agriculture. The Eastern forests have been lost to a combination of ecological mismanagement, such as fire suppression as well as the removal of much of the natural cover for conversion to single-species tree plantations, and mechanized agriculture.

And herein lies the growing dilemma. On the one hand, people everywhere need to be able to count on agricultural and forest production to provide our various societies with the food, shelter, and clothing required. It is now assumed that this is economically best achieved through the use of monocultural plantings aided by heavy inputs of agricultural chemicals. These latter must be increasingly utilized to achieve the desired results, as was previously spelled out in the discussion of diversity. In many cases, these efforts are also affected by a variety of politically engendered subsidies and financial benefits to the owners of such operations, which often tend to put a strain and toll not only on the land but on taxpayers' pockets as well.

Then, of course, it must be emphasized that croplands in the United States, already near their productive limit, are not going to keep up with a population that will double within 60 years. Additionally, it is estimated that about 120 million acres of cropland will be lost, in this same time period, because of such factors as urbanization and erosion.[5]

This activity naturally must be balanced by what is taking place on the other side of the coin, something most of us are either completely ignorant of or loath to think about. This general oversight is due to our propensity to believe that we are the masters of all nature and can do with it whatever we choose. Only in the latter half of the twentieth century have some of us slowly begun to learn that we are but a part of nature and that if we abuse it too often or too seriously the end results can only be a degradation of our own habitat.

To carry this argument a step further, it should be understood that temperate ecosystems are often not so complex as many of those in the tropics, suggesting that often-irreparable damage may be caused by converting these latter habitats to monocultural schemes of land use. This relates not only to the disease problems that have been noted previously but also to their potential environmental destruction. This would be due to the fact that modern-day "high-tech" land uses, even of tree plantations, are structurally and biologically less diverse than natural ecosystems in terms not only of a highly diminished flora but of an impoverished fauna as well. We should be concerned as to how long such degraded habitats can continue to supply us with the variety and quality of those things we need.

This is not to say that there has not also been some realistic advice on how we should face the future. A case in point is the book *Earth in the Balance* by Vice President Al Gore, written when he was a senator.[6] In this he points out, with the help of a star-studded cast of experts (except for the one who let through an incorrect story relative to the transfer of rubber from Brazil to Asia), the more serious problems now adversely affecting the earth's environment. Where I would take issue with his general thesis—

which is, all in all, a serious and unselfish proposal on how we must begin to deal with our habitat — is the manner by which he advocates "saving the Earth." It is not the third planet out from the sun that is in need of help, as I have earlier stressed, but rather the unique interwoven systems of living matter thereon that urgently need a respite from the vicious battering to which they are now being subjected.

Since we in the United States are guilty of consuming far more than our share of the world's resources and contributing a greater portion of the current global pollution, the question before us is whether, while so much desirous of having our earth be a glorious and trouble-free planet, we can really assume that such a dreamworld is a God-given right that we Americans are predestined to enjoy.

To illustrate the overall implications of this unfortunate mind-set more fully, let us return to our symbolic Para rubber tree. If someone were to decide today to go ahead with the development of a large-scale rubber tree–planting program, it would take a minimum of two years of good, hard work just to locate the land, obtain the financing, contract the personnel (both managers and workers), and begin to train them. Actually accomplishing this in the time span suggested would constitute an "economic miracle" but let's proceed anyway. Next on the agenda during this preparation phase would be obtaining the necessary seed (keeping in mind the limited time span for the annual harvest), and planting these in a carefully prepared nursery. A year later the seedling trees would be large enough to bud (providing that the problem of budwood was taken into consideration), and six months to a year later the trees could be transplanted to the field. Now comes a 3- to 4-year wait until the trunks of the trees are at least 48 centimeters in circumference, at which time they are large enough for tapping without damage to the trees themselves.

Although this sounds rather routine, it adds up to about 8 to 10 years of elapsed time before significant amounts of latex can be produced, if everything is done efficiently. That would put us just into the twenty-first century, or rather close to the target date for bringing a new plantation begun today into production. Will it occur to anyone to engage in such an operation? It is true that a few tire companies have rubber plantations, but in the case of the New World, most of these are in Brazil, where, by law, any company wishing to sell tires there must now demonstrate that it is also producing natural rubber there. With the exception of fairly large-scale new plantings in the vicinity of São José do Rio Prêto, Brazil, thousands of miles south of the Amazon,[7] there is little evidence, at present, of a genuine desire on the part of any tire company to establish new rubber plantations anywhere on a grand scale. In fact, some companies still in the business of growing rubber probably wish they were not, as is undoubtedly the case of the Japanese company Bridgestone relative to the plantation of its subsidiary the Firestone Tire and Rubber Company in Liberia, which had been completely nonproductive for some time owing to a serious revolution in that country.

Yet, one might ask, if someone does not begin such work at once, will it be too late? Even if we attempt to "do the right thing," not only in the case of rubber but with other natural substances as well, can we avoid serious problems and difficulties in the immediate future? The tragic series of confrontations in the Amazon basin that eventually led to the murder of Chico Mendes, among others, is basically one in which a rapidly increasing number of people, forced out of other, more impoverished lands, by trying to do anything possible to keep themselves and their families alive have exerted tremendous pressures on this very critical ecosystem. This movement resulted in clashes with the affluent and politically well-connected few whose aim has been to convert large areas of this region to cattle raising. This particular confrontation, between rapidly growing populations and poorly understood environments, may be looked upon as a significant modern premonitory omen. Today, one of the cries of the environmentalists is that tropical rain forests are being sold down the river for the sake of fast-food hamburgers — by no means always true, but it fits the Mendes case. This situation may also be used as an example of the parable by Garrett Hardin titled "The Tragedy of the Commons" in which everyone, for quite selfish reasons, by attempting to take more than a fair share, destroys and ruins the entire resource base under consideration.[8]

The 40 to 50 million acres (62,500–78,125 sq mi) of Amazonian rain forest that is reported to be vanishing each year is equal in area to about the size of North Dakota. While this is considerably more than the amount of land estimated in a previous chapter to be the area required for planting sufficient rubber for the world's immediate future needs, it is quite close to the amount calculated to be required for planting our future requirements of natural rubber plus the corridors and buffer zones of virgin or "deep woods" forests recommended for ecological reasons.

According to James Brooke, José Antonio Lutzenberger, Brazil's former special secretary for the environment, was "credited with having single-handedly reversed an international perception that the Brazilian government is indifferent to the fate of the Amazon rain forests."[9] However, perception may not match reality; others, like Stephan Schwartzman, of the Environmental Defense Fund in Washington, D.C., claim that "for all the Brazilian environmentalists have had to say there has been very little real change."[10] And even though Sr. Goldemberg insists that the average rate of deforestation from 1978 to 1989, in Brazil, has been only 21,800 square kilometers (8,400 sq mi) per year, or an area four times smaller than the 40–50 million acres per year mentioned above. One would wish to believe Goldemberg, and perhaps his figures are quite correct, but the larger estimate, which is found in the *World Resources 1990–1991 Report*, was based on satellite data gathered by the National Oceanic and Atmospheric Administration, according to the report's editor, Dr. Allen L. Hammond.[11] Whatever the actual numbers are, the area in question is a large one, and it should be understood that any mass deforestation and conflagration there is not merely the work of land-hungry cattle ranchers, dedicated arsonists, or careless smokers, but rather of thousands upon thousands of poor and landless people who are convinced they have no other alternative of making a living for themselves and their families than by clearing land to raise something on which simply to subsist. Indeed, this is the case in other regions as well, and it has been reported that fires from "slash-and-burn" areas in Sarawak are now so intense as to limit and even alter the flight patterns of commercial aircraft in this region, and the forest continues to burn and the smoke to billow.

Where, in the midst of worldwide economic hard times, will all the operating capital come from to put these and thousands of others to work so they can help improve the global economic picture? The dream, spoken of earlier, contemplated employing many in an ecologically sound scheme to increase the production of natural rubber that the world will obviously need in the near future. At the present time, however, adequate funds do not appear to be available on either a national or world level. One of the basic reasons for this current economic position of the United States is its trade deficits caused, in great part, by a seemingly insatiable demand for oil. This cost as well as the interest payments alone on our steadily growing national debt continue to hold us in check. If we look deeper into the matter, we would discover that sometime between 2005 and 2010 (barring any unfortunate and unplanned-for disaster in some major oil-producing area of the world) petroleum resources in the United States will be close to exhaustion. Years after the Persian Gulf War, which was basically fought to assure steady and reasonably priced supplies of this commodity, the situation in the Mideast is still highly unsettled, with Saddam Hussein still making bellicose threats. We might, perhaps, begin to overcome part of this problem by reducing consumption, even by means of increased taxation, but that is something the American public is loath to even begin to contemplate, as such an effort would certainly detract from the way of life to which we have become so accustomed — and which we seem to expect can continue without interruption into the future.

Thus, on closer examination, it is easy to see that the natural rubber planting scenario presented above might not proceed so smoothly as described. Actually, ignoring such far-fetched and costly schemes as the irrigation of more dryland areas, the only regions that may be considered for the production of natural rubber are in the more humid tropics. However, a cursory examination of the situation in these locales reveals that in Sri Lanka, for example, quite intense and bloody conflicts between Hindus and Tamils are taking place even within rubber plantations themselves. Civil strife is also common in the Philippine Islands, and while, on the surface, things may appear rather pacific in the most important rubber areas of all — the Malay Peninsula and Indonesia — a struggle between Muslim Malays and Indonesians against Chinese (who some say produce the major share of the latex), Hindus (immigrants from India as well as citizens of the Indonesian island of Bali), and the natives of Irian Jaya and Timor is constantly smoldering under the surface, ready to erupt at any moment. However else one may view them, most of these conflicts relate, in one way or another, to the increasing scarcity of land or the increasing pressure on this resource by growing numbers of people.

Moving over to Africa, equally disastrous situations are all too obvious — ranging from southern Sudan, where there has been a continual struggle between the brown Arab Muslims of the north and the black Christians in the south, on through Rwanda, Central Africa, Zaire, Angola, Nigeria, Ghana, and the Ivory Coast to Liberia and Sierra Leone. Rubber can be grown in all of these places, but Africa, which desperately needs some means of improving its employment picture as well as generating more agricultural income, is for the most part hardly even capable of maintaining basic food production. The major disincentive to long-range investment in this region and the root cause of social unrest and political instability is, of course, overpopulation, which can only become more serious as time goes on.

Bolivia, Peru, Ecuador, Colombia, Venezuela, Brazil, Surinam, Guyana, French Guiana, Central America, and Mexico all contain areas quite appropriate for the cultivation of rubber. While civil and political unrest in some of these areas could be a serious problem, few can presently be considered as very important rubber-producing nations. Of the 5.3 million metric tons of natural rubber now being produced on a worldwide basis, less than 30,000 pounds come from the Amazon basin (a minuscule fraction), as Karl Butler points out.[12] Furthermore, most of what is produced in the Amazon, as was previously indicated, is of low quality and does not provide much of a return for those who do the tapping; those Brazilian rubber plantations that are beginning to evidence a certain amount of high-tech plantation management are in the states of Bahia and São Paulo, both well outside the Amazon region. A similar situation is found in Central America and the Caribbean, where a significant amount of high-quality latex is produced only in Guatemala, owing to an excellent combination of climate, soils, and an environment almost completely free of SALB.[13] Despite serious political upheaval, recent attempts by French companies to plant more rubber on the Pacific lowlands there appear to show some promise.[14]

Turning to the second caveat mentioned, as Colin Tudge stated in an article on rubber written in 1981, few people in any of these countries aspire to become rubber tappers.[15] This may be due in part to the reputation gained by this industry over the past hundred years in many tropical areas of the world. Should one have to work for someone else to gather rubber, it is often in a position similar to that of an indentured servant. If people choose to work for themselves, they may run the risk Chico Mendes took and get shot for their efforts. The young are well aware of this and constantly seek work not on some plantation but rather in one of the many European or Japanese factories that have sprouted up like mushrooms all over the tropics wherever there is cheap labor. The main reason for this work preference, as well described by Tudge, is that on the plantation, out in the open, the "job is mind-blowingly tedious. Each tree must be tapped every other day, its cup emptied and its wound re-opened;

400 trees a day, 10 hours a day, 800 trees per tapper." And that's probably as far as a person can expect to get in life and the best to which one can look forward — an exceedingly grim prospect. For, as Adam Smith pointed out over 200 years ago, "the man whose whole life is spent in performing a few simple operations — generally becomes as stupid and ignorant as it is possible for a human creature to become. The torpor of his mind renders him, not only incapable of relishing or bearing a part in any rational conversation, but of conceiving any generous, noble, or tender sentiment."[16]

Discounting the problems related to agricultural hand labor, compared with other opportunities, rubber is not an agricultural commodity that might attract the ordinary investor. Let us take the case of Costa Rica, where during and for a short time after World War II a great deal of very sophisticated work was done on rubber, principally by the Regional Rubber Research Program of the USDA. Until recently Goodyear even had a fairly large and active plantation on the east coast there, and as many as 50 years ago some dozen small farms on which three-component trees had been established were scattered about the country. While interest rates for agricultural loans are somewhat less than the going rate of between 13 and 40 percent per annum for loans in general in Costa Rica now, these loans are extremely difficult to obtain, and few investors would think of encumbering themselves for a period of 8 to 10 years before even modest returns can be expected.

Although three-component trees still stand at some locations, only one farm continues to tap. The manager there told me that he can now only barely make ends meet in competition with the price of Guatemalan rubber. What he must pay his laborers in base salary, plus all social benefits, retirement, and housing with water and electricity is more than double what tappers would receive in Guatemala — and the price for rice and beans is about the same in both countries.

Michael Parfit, another who was intrigued by the recent polemic over rubber extraction in the Amazon, believes that the ranchers and hundreds of others who wish to utilize the land in these areas will not be stopped. In recounting his stay at the 5,500-hectare (13,600-acre) Michelin plantation on the Brazilian coast, north of Rio de Janeiro, Parfit states that a point is made there not to speak of the tappers as *seringueiros,* a term which is becoming somewhat degrading, but rather as *sangradores* — bleeders, of which there are 850 plus an additional 700 support people to produce 3,000 tons of high-quality rubber per year. By way of comparison Parfit believes that it would take at least 6,000 *seringueiros* working over their *estradas* along the Amazon to produce the same amount — but the rubber would by no means be of the same quality. The Michelin *sangradores* receive $75 a month (about $0.40 per hour) plus houses with running water and electricity for their efforts.[17] There is even a hospital and a much better social life there. But how much better this is than what the people like Chico Mendes receive is not the point. What is of importance to the present argument is rather how a family, even a small one, can attain the *joie de vivre* to which all aspire. A total of $75 a month for food and clothing (but little else) can hardly make anyone too enthusiastic about the future, especially anyone who is inundated with advertising propaganda and overwhelmed with movies or perhaps television, all of which constantly portray the wonderful life others are enjoying.

The bottom line is that, ecologically and economically speaking, getting into the business of producing natural rubber (as with most other operations that extract something from either the sea, the land, or below ground) is nothing to dream about, and the majority of those already involved believe the entire matter to be more of a nightmare than a dream.

Is this the end of the bad news, we might ask, or are there other unfortunate and detrimental aspects relating to the symbol of the Para rubber tree we should know about?

10

WHAT TO DO
WITH A USED TIRE

DESPITE THE EUPHORIA of planning to do the right thing by our environment, it must have been obvious that those suggested approaches and remedies previously described were not going to improve matters immediately in the way one may have hoped. To make things worse, as we are now gradually becoming aware, even our best efforts at "saving the planet" are rapidly being overtaken and overturned by a growing number of ecological disasters and misadventures. When we take time to study this predicament, the first of these undesirable environmental problems we usually notice is that as the very mass of humanity increases throughout the globe, so does our propensity to foul our nest. The disposal of the refuse we generate is getting to be a taxing, onerous, dangerous, and in such cases as emissions from the North River Sewage Plant on the island of Manhattan, odoriferous chore.[1] With each passing day we learn of yet another fountain of waste with which we must deal, and we all can quickly draw up a long list of our own particular grievances in this regard.

One concern of the general public is that, in the recent past, it has too often been dealt a bad hand regarding the disposal of refuse and rubbish. It is natural, therefore, that it looks at its cards with considerable suspicion when it comes to the manner by which getting rid of waste is administered. For example, we are only just now becoming aware that the Soviet Union dumped aging nuclear submarines with damaged reactors as well as more than 10,000 containers of atomic waste in the Barents and Kara Seas of the Arctic Ocean near the island of Novaya Zemlya.[2] These actions were tantamount to sweeping a lethal mess under the rug, and the global significance is frightening to say the least. Actually, these misdeeds became public knowledge only when we learned that the Republic of Russia is now asking for our assistance in bringing up this dangerous waste and burying it properly so that it will not continue to pose a threat. And while it is alarming enough to learn of Soviet environmental crimes, we must now face the additional shock that the federal government of the United States did basically the same thing (and was also not completely truthful and open about the matter) with nuclear waste from its nuclear weapons tests. Back in 1962, and under license from the Atomic Energy Commission, but without any public hearing on the matter, waste from a nuclear test site in Nevada was transported to and buried at Cape Thompson, Alaska. It is understandable that the citizens of this area, whose present cancer rate far exceeds the national average, are not particularly sanguine about the way the government attempts to gloss over the entire matter.[3]

But it is not simply large-scale government mishaps that haunt and plague us. The disaster following the *Exxon Valdez* oil spill in Prince William Sound off the coast of Alaska clearly demonstrates that private industry is quite capable of doing the same and of attempting to overcome ecological tragedy in a similar fashion. Another example, of a growing number which could be cited, but on a slightly smaller scale, is the Pigeon River, in western North Carolina, which used to flow clean and pure up to the town of Canton, but was turned by pollution from the Champion Paper Company plant there into a foamy, brown stream. A report by Michael Satchell on the behavior of this company shows that even after the people of this region began to take action to force Champion to do something about the pollution it caused, the company, ever mindful of its "bottom line," rather than take proper environmental action instead issued a steady stream of threats, false promises, bribes, and political pressure.[4] This performance caused many to wonder that this was actually taking place in the United States, where we would like to believe we all act under the Benthamite code of "the greatest good for the greatest number." As an aside, it may be of interest to note that, as in the case of Exxon, the Champion Paper Company recently indicated that it will establish a multimillion-dollar trust to settle a lawsuit relating to this situation in North Carolina.

A somewhat similar case involves asbestos, and the way certain large corporations have stalled and stonewalled every effort to show that this ingredient (an integral part of many of the products these companies formerly sold) might be detrimental to a person's health. They did this so well and for such a long time that the end result may now be that thousands of victims of continual exposure to asbestos are just plain out of luck so far as being recompensed for their pain and suffering; meanwhile, company ex-

ecutives and their lawyers (who obviously made a Mephistophelian contract somewhere along the line) are certainly not living under economic
duress — and are apparently also without remorse or feelings of guilt of any
kind — as a result of their actions.[5] This behavior typifies an unfortunate aspect of classical capitalism with which we are still extremely reluctant (or
not honest enough) to come to grips.

While we have obviously not yet arrived at a condition where the common good is of primary consideration, this matter is becoming increasingly difficult to ignore. Ostensibly, we claim to believe that Adam Smith's
"hidden hand"[6] will guide all of us to the best of all possible worlds. And
well it might, except that as our numbers grow, this miraculous hand becomes ever more tied by rules and regulations, most of which appear to favor not the common good but rather the interests of an ever shrinking and
more powerful few. We cannot continue to contaminate and defile our environment and then either ignore the matter or hope that someone else
will clean up the mess. This problem will eventually negatively affect everyone everywhere, rich and poor alike.

To return the focus of discussion to the symbol of rubber, of the multitude of examples that could be used, I have selected only those which per-
tain to what should be done with worn-out items made from this commodity, especially the mountains of tires that are cluttering our landscape.
Actually, we are now reaching the point where there is simply not enough
readily available real estate in many areas that can be utilized as landfills to
bury these discarded materials. Furthermore, if simply left in the open, tires
become an ideal breeding ground for mosquitoes[7] or a potential source for
ghastly fires that defy control and produce a dark, polluting smoke that can
pall the landscape for miles around, thus adding to the atmosphere's par-
ticulate count and volume of carbon dioxide.[8]

Since I first began to write on this matter, John McPhee published an
article in the *New Yorker* titled "Duty of Care" that addressed this same issue of what to do with used tires. His final point is that in England there is
a Duty of Care law which requires that before dumping anything, one
must obtain a waste-management license, since what happens in the disposal of trash and refuse of any kind must be identified. In the case of the
disposal of worn-out rubber tires, even the stores that sold them must be informed.[9] In answer to a question as to whether we have such a law in the
United States, McPhee's reply was a chilling "of course not." However, it

should be pointed out that, according to David Pandarad, the Georgia Senate unanimously approved a bill that supporters say would clamp down on the illegal dumping and burning of tires in makeshift incinerators and landfills across that state.[10]

But, while we appear to be plagued by yet another waste product that is becoming difficult to manage, a number of institutions and companies have begun research and development efforts, as is quite proper, to find the means to overcome or lessen this waste burden. For example, it has recently been discovered that old rubber tires can serve as ideal building blocks for mending disintegrating underwater ocean reefs or even constructing new ones. When placed below the surface and out of reach of damaging waves and tides, tires of any size and condition can easily be molded to the required shape and contour of a reef, and a wide variety of sea life takes to these as though they were designed for the purpose. In the same light, it has been demonstrated how used tires are effective in building levees and supports to bridges and dock foundations. The cost of transporting used tires to the required sites is, however, expensive, and reef building and levee construction, although important, do not appear to be matters of frequent enough occurrence.[11]

Since these specific uses may not make too much ecological sense, from an overall economic standpoint probably the best thing we can do is to recycle, thus mimicking the manner by which nature handles waste. Dead plants and animals, expelled gases, and organic rubbish of any kind have always been decomposed or reconstituted in earth, air, and water, to be returned and used again in a never-ending cycle. Following this lead, the most intelligent thing we can do with a worn-out tire is recap it. New materials and equipment now permit the rapid and thorough bonding of a specially prepared strip of rubber polymer to the bald treads of an old tire with complete assurance as to the long wear and safety of the newly resurfaced tire, particularly if speed laws are adhered to. These retreads even give the appearance of new tires. However, in our increasingly prodigal society, rather than recycling used materials, the battle cry still seems to be "pitch it" (whether *it* be a newspaper, empty wine bottle, beer can, or other accumulated junk). It is usually easier simply to purchase a new set of tires, and leave the garage with the responsibility of disposing of the old ones.

There is a movement in many developing countries of the world toward being a bit more environmentally astute in such matters. Madison, the capital of Wisconsin, together with its suburbs, has listed in the Yellow Pages of the phone book two firms that will recap tires. By comparison, San José, Costa Rica, with more or less the same number of people (but a lower total number of vehicles of all kinds), has four times this many retread centers, and each of them is much larger and busier. In truth, though, this activity is probably not so much environmentally or ecologically motivated as it is brought on by economic necessity. It is much cheaper to pay for a retread than to purchase a new tire.

But we cannot continue to recap or retread tires indefinitely, and there are far too many used tires on hand now (estimated between 2.5 and 3 billion in the United States alone) simply to convert them into swings or other items for use in school play yards, or bumpers on the sides of ships and loading docks. Of course, as we should be well aware, tires are very efficient sources of heat, and using them for this purpose is one of the most common schemes by which they are disposed of. This varies from the burning of thousands of tires on cold winter nights in Florida to protect citrus orchards from freezing to their being employed as hydrocarbon fuel for combustion in high-tech installations such as those of the Oxford Energy Company in Connecticut and California, where the heat generated by burning tires is converted into electrical energy.[12]

Unfortunately, in the case of both of these plants, the electricity produced costs about five times what this utility would have to spend to generate the same number of kilowatts from steam plants fired by natural gas. Part of the difficulty, according to Barnaby J. Feder, has to do with the expense incurred in separating the rubber itself from all the foreign elements that have been blended in to make the tires safer, more durable, and sufficiently technically advanced to keep up with the competition. This basically involves the unbinding and segregation of such inputs as sulfur (which Charles Goodyear found so critical more than 150 years ago), zinc, nitrous oxides, carbon black, and of course, nylon, rayon, or steel. While each of these products can be sold for reuse, the means thus far employed to separate them have not made the entire process a cost-effective one.[13] Then, of course, there is the matter of the large quantity of atmospheric pollution and carbon dioxide generated in the process.

In this regard, according to Jonathan P. Hicks, American Tire Reclamation (a subsidiary of the privately held Rao Wholesale Tire Centers Inc. of Detroit) has developed a system for extracting oil as well as carbon black from waste tires for reuse. A pilot company in Arkansas has also demonstrated that it is possible to reduce tires to oil which may then be used for heating, with a minimum outpouring of pollutants.[14] The Texaco Oil Company and Phoenix Technologies of Jacksonville, Florida, are also apparently tackling the problem of converting used tires to heating oil with some success.[15] Unique Tire Recycling of British Columbia plans to adopt the same sort of scheme of reducing 900,000 tires a year into crude oil, steel, and carbon black.[16] In each case, the cost of the final products appears to constitute the major drawback. Admirable as these efforts appear on the surface, they will hardly put a dent in the stockpile of 3 billion tires now in waste dumps nor in the approximately 250 million used tires added to this stockpile in North America each year.

Since one of the current issues facing the present administration in Washington is how to bring our deteriorating transportation system back to a safer and more efficient level, one would think that an ideal solution would be to convert old tires to some type of material that could be used to resurface our decaying highways.[17] Too often we see on roads, newly blacktopped with asphalt, signs warning "Slippery When Wet." Rubber on rubber not only suggests a smoother ride, but would last longer and provide a much surer grip at all times and in any kind of weather. This is exactly the approach taken by the Rubber Asphalt Producers Group of Phoenix, Arizona. While technically successful, embodying the favorable characteristics listed above, the resulting product, despite what it might provide in terms of safer driving conditions, is at present still too expensive to put to general use.[18]

But the basic question which arises in each of these cases is, expensive to whom? Each of the companies mentioned above insists that with extra funds for technological studies on improving efficiency, its end products would soon become cost-effective. Few investors, however, appear eager to bear the expense of possibly improving the proficiency of any of these establishments. Nor does it seem likely that anywhere within the present or forthcoming federal budgets there will be found any of the funds required for such development. Either this is not the right time or else we as a nation are not in the proper mood for an approach of this nature, since any such outlay of funds would seem to require some form of increased taxation. Given, however, the prospect of overcoming many serious waste dilemmas and perhaps even reconstituting mountains of trash and refuse for our bene-fit, one may wonder where money might come from should such activities be given the high priority they perhaps merit.

Is it inevitable that, as previously stated, the end products of modern tech-nology will generally leave us with some poisonous or disagreeable form of waste or pollution? There are, for example, growing concerns today that the agricultural chemicals (insecticides, herbicides, and fungicides) that are claimed to aid in a bountiful production of foodstuffs may also be re-sponsible for certain cancers or a lowering of the human male sperm count on a worldwide basis. If true, one logical inference is that as we strive to provide more goods and services to increasing numbers of people, in an effort to keep the economy growing, we are, at the same time, so altering our environment as to hinder its capacity to function in our favor. It is debat-able, certainly, whether or to what extent technology can provide the means to overcome these waste problems as well. The prime difficulty to be faced here is that of economic inertia and, probably more important, greed. While a variety of ingenious and worthwhile schemes have been proposed to deal with waste disposal by ecologically approved methods, such proj-ects are unfortunately too often opposed by an army of those who adopt any and every means possible to keep them from taking place. In the case at hand, the powerful opposition comes from those conventional road-paving companies that use traditional cement-asphalt mixtures to repair damaged or worn-out highways and whose owners have developed such a remarkable symbiosis with the officials of state and federal transportation departments that these latter continue to approve the use of these hardly optimum road coverings rather than attempt to utilize a more technologi-cally improved system.

Sooner or later, this Gordian knot must be cut, or untied, for eventually we must turn to some form of recycling. In this connection, it has been suggested that if only 25 percent of the nation's annual need for highway resurfacing were to use rubber asphalt, millions of used tires, which would otherwise be scrapped and thus constitute a growing waste problem, could be consumed.

Since this mountain of used tires, which inevitably results from a prod-uct so vital to the entire world, continues to grow, it would appear prudent to begin to employ some environmentally satisfactory method of recycling our rubber products. This is especially true if these tires are in part fabricated from such a nonrenewable source as petroleum. Continuing to ignore this matter will amount to but another example of our lemminglike rush toward an increasingly unpleasant or even threatening lifestyle, which is certainly not what we have hoped and dreamt it might be.

Are there any signs that we are intelligently confronting these and other challenges of a similar nature, or are we determined to continue down the slippery slope toward environmental degradation?

11

ARE WE CAPABLE
OF DOING THE RIGHT THING?

EVEN ASSUMING THAT all of the land required for the economically viable production of natural rubber could be easily obtained, planting and maintaining these quite considerable areas in the humid tropics to meet potential rubber demand would imply a large-scale, complicated forestry operation. K. G. McIndoe provides a detailed account of the manner by which the Firestone plantations were established in Liberia, on the west coast of Africa, over 80 years ago and clearly points out the tremendous amount of work and effort required.[1] Despite new technological innovations that have been adopted since that time, this is still not a simple task, and adding the extra input of the essential environmental buffer still makes the entire effort a most challenging one.

Furthermore, it must be understood that obtaining, planning, planting, and managing the thousands of square miles of rubber as well as the natural ecological zones envisaged would not take place in one single locality but would have to complement those areas throughout the world's tropics where rubber has already been established. Producing plantations of this crop are now to be found in regions ranging from the Philippines on through South China, the Malay Peninsula, and Indonesia, to Sri Lanka and South India, to the more humid areas of West Africa, and finally across the Atlantic to Brazil, Colombia, Bolivia, and Peru, and northwest into Central America and southern Mexico.

After taking into account the silvicultural problems to be encountered in such an undertaking, it should be obvious that this novel approach to forest plantation management would have to depend on how skillfully a highly diversified set of social, cultural, and political situations are administered as well. As mentioned in the previous chapter, we have not always appeared capable of dealing with the numerous environmental problems confronting us; for this reason, before delving into the possibility of a massive planting effort in distant lands, all with sociopolitical systems distinct from our own, we should again examine our nation's track record in developing, managing, and preserving forests, range, and agricultural land together with wildlife areas. Are there signs of promise and hope to be found in the manner by which we supervise and carry out these operations, usually of a much less complicated nature, within our own borders, and over an extended period?

For reasons not easy to explain, Americans have an enormous propensity to try to obtain as much as possible of whatever it is we want in the shortest possible time; coupled with this behavior is the equally profligate squandering of what we have just obtained, all of which generally leaves both our neighbors and our offspring to fend for themselves. It has been suggested that a prime cause for our current economic doldrums is that we have not, as yet, adopted a strong tradition of stewardship or saving for long-term goals. Nor have we faced up to the sociopolitical problems that inevitably seem to arise when little consideration is given to the matter of a more equitable income distribution.

To be honest, it is only too apparent that humans everywhere exhibit avarice, especially when they have the upper hand and think they can "get away with it." In reflecting on such matters, Robert Heilbroner writes that Adam Smith believed the goals of the capitalists he was attempting to describe were often deceptive and oppressive. Heilbroner continued by saying that "nowadays, even the staunchest supporters of Smith's version agree that the effects of private economic effort are not always in the public interest."[2]

An examination of our dealings with complex situations of almost any kind (including the challenge of environmental protection) provides ample evidence of this streak of avaricious behavior, often of a deceptive nature, even among those who outwardly claim to be honest and devout citizens. Any number of examples come to mind, but the one to be used here was chosen since it has all of the earmarks of a Chico Mendes type confrontation: a defender of the common good menaced in his efforts by a small, wealthy, and powerful clique. This particular case is that of Donald Oman, district ranger of the U.S. Forest Service in the Sawtooth National Forest in Idaho. The story, reported in the *Rocky Mountain News* as well as in a number of other journals,[3] relates to the manner by which Ranger Oman, in attempting to carry out his official duties, encountered a formidable range of roadblocks. His life was threatened by cattle ranchers. He was asked by his superiors (with the obvious implication that the bureaucrats in the Service caved in to outside pressure) to request transfer to another post — sweetened with the promise of a promotion if he were to do so.

What the conflict comes down to is whether the Forest Service — a federal agency that is under increasing attack from many sides, often for very good reason — will protect our public lands for the benefit of the majority, as Ranger Oman has been attempting to do, or whether it will provide certain cattle ranchers with grazing rights at excessively low rates ($1.97 per animal per month in the early 1990's, or approximately a fifth of the going rate on private lands at that time) and turn its collective head as these ranchers abuse the privilege granted them. According to Don Oman, too many ranchers are seriously jeopardizing the public range by overgrazing to the point of the complete destruction of environmentally fragile areas. He has thoroughly provoked many large-scale cattle and sheepherders by insisting they keep within the limits of their contracts so far as numbers of animals per unit area is concerned. As reported by Timothy Egan, Winslow Whitley, the owner of one of the largest herds in this region, estimated he would make a profit of about $250 per cow using only public lands (in a manner he chooses, not necessarily in conformity with Forest Service regulations), which, with his herd of 1,563 animals, could garner him just under $400,000 a year.[4]

But Whitley is not the only one who is selfishly (and under our present system, probably also quite legally — for some reason difficult for many to understand) taking more than his proper share from the public domain, and this unfortunate scheme of land use has been going on for such a long time that the wealthy, who seem to have developed an intriguing network with the Forest Service, believe that they should have things pretty much their own way. The figures provided by Egan show that the Forest Service, after spending $34.5 million on its range-management program in this particular area, took in a grand total of only $10.9 million in grazing fees. The difference between these two sums represents a serious loss of the public funds under the fiscal trust and responsibility of this governmental organization. Whitley's gain, therefore, was a loss not only to the environment but to the taxpayer as well. Depending on how one chooses to view the situation, this is a case either of questionable Forest Service policy generally or of excessive federal largesse to Whitley in particular.

However, as always seems to be the case, there is another side of the coin.

Many in government, as well as private ranchers, claim that instead of public lands being ruined by cattle ranching, these are generally in good condition and actually improving with time.[5] Some even allege that, taking everything into consideration, costs to ranchers on either private or public land are quite similar. These statements are at once challenged, and there is no doubt that this argument will continue well on into the future.

There is, in addition, one predominant environmental factor that will inescapably make this entire confrontation over land use a hypothetical one—water.[6] Serious difficulties relating to drought have occurred many times in human history, and many believe that, with only a slight climatic nudge, it could take place again, particularly in the desert portions of the western part of the United States. Even recent heavy rain and snow in the western mountains will not overcome this problem. And this dominating and overriding factor of the availability of water on a utilitarian basis must always be taken into consideration especially when continuous and growing pressure is placed on the resources of this region. Thus, it is not simply a question of overcutting or overgrazing but a matter of future depletion of water for the entire region as well.[7]

Beginning with Gifford Pinchot, who was the chief of the Forest Service during the administration of President Theodore Roosevelt, and going through a long list of capable, honest, and dedicated employees, such as Aldo Leopold, up to the present case of Don Oman, the principal goals of the Service were conservationist in nature. The main charge of this government agency has been to see to it that all public lands were so managed and administered as to provide multiple uses for the greatest number of citizens. However, primarily because of a lack of scrutiny as well as accountability, the cancer of bureaucracy set in early. By 1960 flagrant misguidance and abuse of implied stewardship of the commonweal so overshadowed any good performed that the U.S. Congress was obliged to pass what is now known as the MUSY (Multiple Use Sustained Yield) Act. This legislation specified exactly what the Forest Service was to do, with an emphasis on the multiple-use aspect of its charter—grazing, forestry, recreation, conservation—so that no single, privileged group would benefit exclusively from the public domain.

This congressional effort to rectify a growing problem, however, apparently had so little corrective effect on the performance of the Service that elected officials passed another bill in 1976, called the National Forest Management Act, or NFMA, written in an attempt to once again bring the Forest Service into line. Results to date would hardly warm the heart of a conservationist, or even an average taxpaying citizen. The entrenched bureaucracy of the Service continues to do pretty much as it chooses, knowing that some of its more contentious policy decisions (or lapses) will either be backed by loggers and cattle ranchers or be protected by local congressional representatives and senators — many of whom have a keen ear to the demands of those constituents who make major contributions to their campaigns and who, incidentally, just happen to be the very same ones who make consumptive use of public lands. There is just too much smoke raised in the many examples and stories about how old so-and-so got a lucrative consulting job with some branch of the lumber industry the minute he retired from the Forest Service not to believe there is a fire somewhere. That the Forest Service has built and maintains an expansive network of roads almost exclusively for the benefit of logging companies and at a tremendous expense not to these corporations but to the U.S. taxpayer should be a matter of considerable public interest and concern.

Timothy Egan has more recently pointed out that Interior Secretary Babbitt is now facing a perhaps even stronger and more determined group fighting to prevent increases in grazing fees and block new steps to protect national forests. While pleas are made to help "old cowboys" maintain the survival of a vanishing way of life, Egan points out that the top 500 holders of grazing permits include, for example, the Metropolitan Life Insurance Company, the Mormon Church, a Japanese conglomerate, and some of the wealthiest families in the nation.[8] Indeed, the lead editorial in the 31 October 1993 issue of the New York Times, titled "Bruce Babbitt's Landscape, at Risk," further emphasizes this controversy. Moreover, it also indicates that when the $1.86 monthly charge for each cow-calf unit was raised in New Mexico to $3.45, there was no evidence that even the smallest ranchers were forced from public lands.[9]

In February 1995 the Interior Department announced changes in its grazing policy that did not raise fees for ranchers but would, it was claimed, improve rangeland management. This move has not gladdened the hearts of most environmental advocates, for they believe this policy can only lead to greater environmental deterioration. While there still appears to be some hope within the Bureau of Land Management that higher fees will be forthcoming, present policy is to leave it to Congress to set fee levels.

This merely tends to substantiate the too often overlooked economic principle that wealth inevitably flows from the poor to the rich. The money made, in this case, by the affluent and well-positioned few from the *public domain* actually amounts to a direct subsidy. Perhaps the American people did not realize what was being done in their name and at their expense, or were unable to do anything about it, but this public domain — "the Commons" as described by Garrett Hardin[10] — is gradually being ruined by those few who are taking more than their share. Would this also be the result in tropical regions, where there certainly is little in the way of anything approaching a Forest Service, if a large-scale rubber program were to be initiated?

A recent editorial in the *New York Times* titled "Preaching to Brazil from Hawaii" stresses the point that we would be less sanctimonious if we took better care of our own tropical forests in Hawaii and Puerto Rico rather than constantly pointing the finger of blame at Brazil. It concludes that "to preach respect for nature to Brazil, Americans need to practice it more assiduously in their own forests."[11] In this regard, probably one of the most important rain forests with which the United States should be concerned is not in Brazil but rather in the Pacific Northwest — the ancient forests to which I previously alluded. It is inescapable that the public is the all-around loser and that the futures not only of spotted owls and jobs for loggers (who may soon all have less forest to cut) but also of entire ecosystems are in jeopardy.

It is not just a matter of the excessive amount of money spent on road building by the Forest Service for the almost exclusive use of timber companies to extract lumber from national forests — to the point that the roads cost far more than revenues from sales of timber and direct grants provided by the federal government. The real problem is not simply the currently damaging cutting techniques nor profligately wasteful handling of the logs once they arrive at the mills. Nor is it simply a question of jobs for those felling the forests or working in the mills. It is not only that clear-cutting and road building are the cause of landslides, floods, washouts, erosion, siltation, and the disappearance of habitat so important for regrowth, or that salmon and other fish so important to the region are disappearing,[12] or that a very large percentage of the lumber cut is sent directly to Japan where it is processed for "value-added" economic benefit to that country. More than all these negative consequences of the disastrous policies of the U.S. Forest Service, what is perhaps most devastating of all is that in the pursuit of short-term gain we may be at the point of eliminating forever the possibility of future generations making use of a unique ecosystem.

There are, naturally, other frightening aspects of this controversy. For example, in a desperate attempt to combat what many perceive as wholesale pillage of public resources, one of the most radical of environmental organizations — Earth First! — which used to engage in such acts as driving railroad spikes into timber trees so that these would destroy (at some considerable danger to the operator) loggers' chain saws,[13] has now moderated somewhat its unabashed illegal activities. However, according to Christopher Manes, the author of *Green Rage: Radical Environmentalism and the Unmaking of Civilization,* civil disobedience and destruction of property is completely vindicated in defense of a wilderness that is being destroyed by disobedience to our country's laws.[14] Which leaves one to ponder whether the ends justify the means regardless of which side is being considered.

It has been suggested that these types of confrontations might easily be dispensed with if we simply let private industry take control. After all, one of the prime tenets of capitalism is that operating in an open market will lead to the best possible solution for everyone. A rudimentary check on what is actually happening here reveals that the principal logging and lumber companies have discovered that managing their privately owned forest tracts on the best possible sustained-yield basis produces a return of only somewhere between 4 and 5 percent per annum. Since these companies are, as previously stated, in the lumber business for one reason only — to make money — and since returns at this level are much less than would accrue if company funds were simply invested in government bonds, for example, they believe they must change their operating plans to achieve greater immediate income from the forests they own.

For those who follow such matters, it is becoming increasingly obvious that these large timber organizations have opted to attempt to get higher current returns on investment by clear-cutting their own forests, trusting that, while these lands gradually reestablish forest cover, these same corporations can obtain what lumber they need from public lands at current giveaway prices. Perhaps in the future (and this naturally will be someone else's problem) timber companies can go back to their own lands and once again cut their own timber—who knows? These corporations obviously do not seem to have much concern as to whether the Forest Service will be able to adequately and properly reforest so that there will always be enough lumber to meet future public demand and need. Their present scheme of management seems geared to provide them with the required cash income in the immediate future—which is as far ahead as they are looking.

Some 50 years ago, Bernard DeVoto was carrying out his own crusade relative to the very topics mentioned above, from his "easy chair" at *Harper's* magazine. Since then, many others, culminating for me with Wallace Stegner,[15] have continued to address these themes in a persistent and knowledgeable manner. I am particularly attracted to Stegner, who, besides being an excellent writer, obviously knows the problems firsthand, having actually lived in this region; he even confesses to having been part of the problem when he was young. The strong evidence presented in these several reports forces me to the unfortunate conclusion that we do not demonstrate a serious capacity for doing the right thing and, even worse, are apparently not much troubled by this fact.

The question must be asked: if this attitude is true relative to our own natural resources, how might we perform if we were given the opportunity of developing, maintaining, and operating rubber plantations in developing countries of the humid tropics? The picture that immediately comes to my mind is that given by Vicki Baum in *The Weeping Wood* of the life led by the *seringueiro* Ambrosío and how he suffered under the tyrant "El Boliviano," who was the worst beast among the bestial *jefes* of the Peruvian Amazonian Company.[16] We may shrug off such a suggestion and claim that we would not possibly be so cruel and oppressive to the people who would work the plantations today.

In this connection, one should ask about the root causes that led to the shutdown of overall operations at the world's single largest rubber plantation and processing factory since the late 1980's. The 200-square-mile farm of approximately 8 million rubber trees of the Firestone Synthetic Rubber and Latex Company (now a subsidiary of the Japanese Bridgestone/Firestone Corporation) in Liberia at one time employed some 8,500 workers.

They, together with their families and relatives, made up a total of between 75,000 and 80,000 people.[17] Not only is this country now in shambles but neighboring ones are suffering as well. African specialist Fred Hayward has indicated that refugees fleeing from Liberia into such countries as Sierra Leone to the north add to the tremendous burden that this latter poor nation has to bear—through no fault of its own.[18] In addition, the task of helping to maintain and supply the U.S. forces stationed off Liberia's coast has fallen on the shoulders of Sierra Leone with no recompense and little thanks. Under this considerable political and economic pressure, coupled with a weak economy of its own, this latter country has also just suffered a very damaging coup.[19]

Was this catastrophe Firestone's fault? Many believe the company could have done more but was fearful that perhaps Charles Taylor, one of the major strongmen in Liberia, might win (he did—sort of) and leave them completely out in the cold. So they stayed out of the struggle and were left out in the cold anyway. Could our State Department be held accountable, even partially, for what has taken place in this part of the world? The end result of this dismal chapter in the history of a country the founding and development of which the United States was deeply involved with, and the recent history of which many now feel basically smacks of neocolonialism, can certainly not be a matter of any national pride. Political unrest of this nature, coupled with our "out of sight, out of mind" attitude, has helped aggravate tropical deforestation in Liberia—to the tune of about 110,000 acres (or very close to the size of Cook County, which mostly comprises the city of Chicago) *each day*.

Should the world require increasing amounts of natural rubber in the near future, the crucial question is whether Americans, or anyone else, have demonstrated a capacity for improving the dismal political and economic situations existing in many places throughout the humid tropics. With Timor, Rwanda, Burundi, Somalia, Zaire, Bolivia, Burma (Myanmar), Nigeria, and the Sudan (to name but a few countries) demonstrating how instability and lawlessness are fast becoming the standard in most of the tropics, one might think that such improvements would receive widespread support; to begin with, the majority of people in these regions obviously yearn for the stable infrastructure required for long-term tree-crop operations. However, present indications are that providing assistance in developing a well-planned, pantropical scheme for producing the world's future rubber needs will be exceedingly difficult, if not impossible, given our poor record in conducting projects of this nature. Part of the tragedy is that such a project seemed so neat and simple when first outlined as an environmentalist's dream.

In the past, when we reached such difficult roadblocks or confrontations, it always seemed that someone was able to come up with a solution — usually of a technical nature. Is there a possibility that some such breakthrough may be in our future?

12

HIGH-TECH
TO THE RESCUE?

BASED ON THE history of outstanding scientific and technological success during the last two hundred years, it is the strong conviction of
many that we should turn again to this sort of applied engineering approach to overcome or mitigate a spate of problems now confronting us.
After all, this has clearly been a most auspicious route for surmounting ad-
versity and achieving sought-after goals in the past. It certainly was the
path by which the United States gained its position of world dominance
during and after World War II. Throughout that particular period, it was
science and technology that provided the best means of producing, in a
very brief time span, not only most of the rubber we needed, but all the
guns, planes, ships, and bombs required as well.

However, before we close the book on this one and make the decision
to devote all our time, energy, and efforts in this direction, it would be wise
to examine the situation a bit more thoroughly, for a headlong rush into
some promising engineering operation is not without its own specific problems and difficulties — as the Ford Motor Company learned the hard way,
with its attempts to establish rubber plantations in Brazil earlier in the
1900's. Even from the beginnings of the age of scientific enlightenment, a
series of obstacles blocking what were hoped to be the answers to many of
humankind's dilemmas gradually became evident — barriers not unlike the
hindrances to our vaunted technological progress that are, unhappily, be-
setting us today.

Take, for example, the case of England. Beginning with the reign of
Queen Elizabeth I, vast areas of the world fell under British hegemony,
resulting in an era of global dominance, as evoked by the statement that
"the sun never set on the British Empire." Conquest of new territories was
soon followed by a flurry of trade and commerce between these colonies
and the mother country. However, due to a rise of piracy on the high seas,

coupled with the disruption resulting from a series of wars among European nations, England was forced to build a larger Royal Navy in order that Britannia could truly "rule the waves" and thus more effectively protect its colonies and commerce. Consequently, rising demand both for more and larger naval vessels and for merchant craft fueled production of such commodities as iron, copper, glass, and lead, which were required in the construction of these ships.

To supply this vast shipbuilding industry, forest resources as well were consumed in ever-increasing quantities; at the same time, timber (often in the form of charcoal) was the basic source of energy and heat for industrial and residential use. As forests were depleted to supply these growing demands, some of the more astute observers became disturbed over the alarming rate at which woodland resources were disappearing. A description of the decimation of forests, not only in England but later, as demand grew, in Ireland as well, together with an accounting of what many people thought of all of this reckless activity, is rather thoroughly and very entertainingly provided in John Perlin's book *A Forest Journey*.[1] In fact, so much of the forest on the British Isles was cut for these different purposes that in order to meet its needs in the seventeenth and eighteenth centuries, England was forced to import cordwood from as far away as Russia. Even before this time, the Royal Navy made certain that it had proprietary rights over all North American conifers within its colonial domains in order to have a constant supply of spars and masts for its ships, since such large trees had all but disappeared from England. In a manner similar to that by which Spain had earlier consumed practically all its own forest resources from its possessions in the Americas to build its famous and ill-fated Armada, England soon began to commandeer from its New World colonies sizable amounts of oak and other tree species required for the building and repair of its ever-growing numbers of large oceangoing vessels.

Once again, as had previously happened so many times in the history of humankind, a nation was faced with the grim prospect of completely running out of an essential resource—and once again, fortune smiled. This time, the solution lay in the discovery that coal, a substance which England has in great abundance, could substitute very well for, indeed was often superior to, the best charcoal then produced. Now, instead of importing logs and timber from far away, all that was required was to simply dig this dirty, black mineral out of the ground in many different localities in the

British Isles for use as a substitute for wood. What was additionally fortuitous was that coal, because it did not require any of the labor and effort needed to build the kilns used in converting wood to charcoal, could immediately stoke the furnaces for the production of iron and steel and soon replaced the lumber formerly used for this purpose.

However, in the process of extracting coal, often from deep in the earth, it became immediately evident that a serious obstacle to further mining efforts would have to be conquered if this mineral was ever to become a truly viable substitute for wood. Put simply, the deeper mine shafts penetrated into the earth, the more prone they were to flooding. A great deal of time and effort were devoted to surmounting this barrier. Necessity had once again become the mother of invention, yielding one of the most important and novel forms of technology ever developed. It was all spelled out in a popular English children's nursery rhyme, which goes something like this:

> Little Jimmy Watt watched the cover of a pot,
> Dancing up and down like a dandy,
> Then he went and learned a trade,
> And the first steam engine made,
> The whole world found it very handy.

"Handy" is hardly an adequate description. Once this machine — whose invention is attributed to the Scotsman James Watt (1736–1819), and which, incidentally, used coal as its energy source — was coupled with a pump, this apparatus could draw water out of even the deepest shafts, making the mining of coal a most promising enterprise. And, once people saw what could be done with such steam-powered devices, it was not long before these machines were providing power for factories and mills, and then for locomotives and ships, freeing the latter from the vagaries of wind.[2]

In each case, considerable trial and error naturally was involved relative to the best design for the most efficient machine. Illustrative of some of the difficulties faced is that for a long time it was believed that regardless of the efficiency of design, steam engines would not be able to drive ships across such a large body of water as the Atlantic. The argument was, of course, that any vessel so outfitted would be required to carry so much coal, to be used to heat the steam boilers, as to leave little room for either cargo or passengers.

In order to improve the capacity of engines as the need for more power arose, a series of laws were eventually elaborated to chart the potential efficiency of each one proposed as well as to describe its limits. Probably the individual most prolific in this work was the Frenchman Nicolas Leonard Sadi Carnot (1796–1832); steam engines and their cycles still bear his name, just as the standard unit of power—the watt—was named after the inventor of the steam engine. As all of these studies necessarily related to such physical factors as heat and friction, the final results were soon known as the laws of thermodynamics, and even today, these continue to be the basis of those engineering and technological efforts related to the use of power in some form. The First Law deals with the conservation of energy, which is generally a rather easy concept to understand. A simple example is that when the chemical energy in a battery is converted to electric energy that then operates a motor (mechanical energy), the total amount of energy in the system remains the same, with the understanding that, inevitably, some is converted not to mechanical or electrical energy but rather, through friction, into heat energy. It is the Second Law which states that because of such losses (into heat energy) as just described, perpetual motion is impossible, and thus introduces the concept of entropy with its accompanying diffusion of heat and gradual slowing down of all movement coupled with an increase in disorder or chaos, which is generally less well understood.

It is somewhat disconcerting that so little attention is paid to the understanding of something so important to all who live in this scientific and technological world of ours. It is this lack of basic comprehension that causes so much confusion with regard to the benefits, and limits, of science. To paraphrase Lester Thurow, we all live in a zero-sum world,[3] not solely from an economic standpoint but from many physical and natural ones as well. Even the act of breathing causes an expenditure of energy on each individual's part. And all energy in one way or another (with some minor exceptions, such as that derived from natural atomic breakdown) has its origin in the energy of the sun. Coal, peat, oil, waterfalls, wind, forests, crops, and grasslands have all received energy, on which we humans are so thoroughly reliant, by means of photosynthesis, evaporation, transpiration, and convection, which are all impossible without the input from the sun's heat and light. According to the First Law of Thermodynamics, the obvious corollary is that each time a portion of this energy is utilized, there must be a corresponding recompense, adjustment, or payment made in some form. Thus, the warmth we receive from each pound of coal we burn implies the irreplaceable dissipation and loss of energy, accompanied by an increase in foul, grimy smoke; emissions of a variety of gases, including both carbon monoxide and carbon dioxide; and of course, a residue of ash, which together with the smoke and gases emitted is the basis of the growing pollution we will, rather sooner than later, be forced to do something about.

The new industrial technologies previously mentioned provided those who had them a tremendous amount of political as well as raw economic power. With these technological innovations, European nations soon dominated a great deal of the rest of the world, in one way or another.[4] The United States, too, did not tarry in availing itself of this same knowledge and these same machines to consolidate its control over the native inhabitants and the very large section of North America it usurped from them. Japan quickly followed Europe's lead in becoming a strong technological nation, though not without its own ventures into brutal imperial subjugation of other Asian peoples by means of modern military technology.

It was a similar application of technology that permitted the construction of the Panama Canal, built all of the dams and hydroelectric plants of the TVA, provided almost all who wanted them with inexpensive vehicles that could take them anywhere, and made the phenomenon of urban Los Angeles possible, with its incredible system of pipes, canals, and aqueducts that bring water to this fundamentally desert locale.[5] And now we take all these marvels of modern technology so completely for granted that with water now becoming an increasingly critical and overused resource in many parts of California, plans are being drawn up to ascertain whether this commodity could not be brought in from sources still farther away — even Alaska. If technology achieved solutions and breakthroughs in the past, it can, we reason, provide us with the means of doing this again.

Symbolic of the industrialization of the 1800's and early 1900's was the tall factory chimney from which billowed masses of colored smoke. Indeed, pictures of manufacturing complexes of that period always portrayed such an image, and no proper view of a train or steamship, particularly such monsters as dreadnoughts, was complete without the standard emissions of steam and clouds of dark vapors pouring from the smokestacks. These scenes, now prized by developing nations as a symbol of their efforts to play catch-up, have generally been replaced, in the more affluent regions, by buildings of glass, aluminum, and steel in clean, park-like settings. Smoke-billowing locomotives have all but disappeared from our landscape, although they are still widely utilized in many of the less-developed countries, and cars, trucks, and planes, which do not appear to expel any exhaust (though, of course, they do), have largely taken over. Grungy coal miners and assembly line workers often exhibiting the image of Charlie Chaplin as portrayed in the movie *Modern Times* have also been replaced by sanitized workers, all scrubbed and clothed as though ready for an operating room, bending over complicated pieces of electronic equipment on bright, clean assembly lines where the computer chip is king. We are slowly but obviously relegating many of the truly onerous, repetitive, dirty, and low-paying jobs to what has been called the "Third World," complaining all the while about loss of employment at home. And the people who live there who have lower levels of expectation for what is generally considered as "the good life" may look upon this filthy, often unhealthy form of employment as perhaps a step forward, despite the choking smoke, eye-stinging haze, foul smells, and mounting deposits of waste.[6]

Regardless of trends in this direction, First World societies have by no means converted wholesale to such clean energy sources as sun, wind, and water power. Coal and gas-powered power plants, and to a certain extent atomic energy plants as well, together with their high-voltage-carrying power lines,[7] are still with us, as are oil refineries, chemical factories, pulp mills, and a long list of other major sources of pollutants. However, we are beginning to acknowledge that these energy sources are not the best solution for our needs, and the fact that they continue to produce potentially harmful waste products has only slowly begun to claim the public's attention. Two of the solutions by those who manage these forms of technology are the "out of sight, out of mind" strategy and trading of pollution vouchers with companies that do not pollute as much. At the same time, those in charge of such arrangements do anything they can to buck the tide of resentment as well as any laws designed to force them to make changes to lessen pollution, compliance with which may cause some immediate damage to the almost sacrosanct "bottom line."

This matter was given considerable publicity and brought to a head when President Bush agreed to permit industrial companies in the United States to increase emissions of polluting gases without notifying the public. Actually, as reported by Keith Schneider, this was the result of a flap between Vice President Quayle and EPA Administrator William K. Reilly over the implementation of the 1990 Clean Air Act. A number of executives from heavy industry companies had argued before Vice President Quayle's Council on Competitiveness that the law's regulations were too costly, and the council then acted, apparently on their behalf, and to the detriment of Reilly's stand that an increase in toxic air pollution clearly not only violated the law but also impaired the overall environment.[8] Today, with their *Contract with America*,[9] Republicans appear anxious to do away with even more regulations of this kind.

The reasons behind deregulation often include the argument that, if unshackled, businesses will develop and apply new technologies that will create a civilization where all these difficulties will be quickly done away with. Newt Gingrich, the Speaker of the House, was so enthusiastic about this glorious prospect that he even signed his name to the foreword of the book *Creating a New Civilization*, by Alvin and Heidi Toffler, another optimistic scenario for the future.[10]

Not everyone has bought the argument,[11] however, and a close examination shows that the Second Law as well as problems of waste and pollution are barely mentioned. In a recent article, in the *New Yorker* magazine, titled "Marxism: The Sequel—There's Something Oddly Familiar about Mr. Gingrich's Ideology," Hendrick Hertzberg points out, "The tone of what can fairly be called Tofflerism-Gingrichism is uncannily like that of Marxism-Leninism." He continues to note the parallels between the two, culminating with the statement that in both "history is relentless, progressive, and ultimately irresistible" and that both have an almost identical "strong and similar worship of technology."[12] All of which leaves one with serious doubts about the kind of future we face, since the Marxist-Leninist philosophy by no means has the appeal it once had. Can we count on a similar Toffler-Gingrich approach of a technological pathway as the best guide for the future?

In this entire matter of the inevitable creation of a new civilization through a withering of the state (read federal government) and what amounts to practically a worship of technology, little or no mention is made of either the constraints of increasing population or the impact of pollution. This ignores the types of pollution previously mentioned as well as the increase of such other forms as noise pollution. There is, naturally, a certain amount of opposition to and complaint about the noise from jet engines on the part of those whose homes are at the end of busy airport runways, but in general there is little outcry concerning the high-volume noise from lawnmowers, tree chippers, leaf blowers, vacuums, garbage-removal, and street-cleaning trucks that often inundates many urban settings. One might even detect that many rather enjoy this hubbub, as it implies that things are normal, under control, and moving along well. A further difficulty is that, in addition to producing tympanic-membrane-bursting spurts of noise, a power mower, snowmobile, or chain saw will also pollute the atmosphere more than will a single car.

The changes in modern life that make us ever more dependent upon some form of concentrated energy, with its accompanying waste and pollution, are gradually being recognized as among the principal drawbacks to modern technology. Those who can afford it try to stay away from mining operations, transmission cables, power plants, and industrial factories, opting rather for clean, air-conditioned homes, apartments, and offices—with their tidy green spaces outside and their pleasant paintings of bucolic scenes inside. And no modern office is complete without proliferating numbers of computers, fax machines, fancy multibuttoned telephones, and copying machines all within easy reach.

Those who were never exposed to the once staggering pollution and poverty of our own steel belt (often called rust belt) can easily get an idea of what this was like from the pictures now coming out of Eastern Europe[13] and many other localities such as India and China. These images, plus descriptions by those who have visited such regions of the mentally and physically retarded, sick, and dying children whose demise is directly attributable to pollution, make abundantly clear this unfortunate aspect of what some call technological advance. When this contamination is coupled with the dangerous and backbreaking work involved in extracting coal and oil, it is easy to see why many advocated the use of "clean" atomic power as a better alternative. This epitome of technologically oriented energy production is, we have come to learn in the era of Three Mile Island and Chernobyl, not only extremely dangerous but also fraught with frustration, particularly as regards the attempt to locate areas in which to confidently and safely dispose of atomic waste.[14]

Acid rain and polluting gases from factories, exhausts from gasoline- or diesel-burning engines, spent atomic rods from power plants, and other wastes daily raise questions that individuals as well as local and national governments find difficult to solve. Add to these not only the smoke from fires (whether of natural or of human origin) burning large areas of forests and jungles but also the enormous amount produced simply from the combustion of any kind of organic material in the process of preparing food by a large majority of us, and it is easy to see that we face a monster of a technological problem. Moreover, taking into account the recurrent volcanic eruptions throughout the world, we are forced to realize that even nature adds considerably to atmospheric pollution.

But while everyone naturally waits for someone else, or some new technology, to solve the problem, especially if the solution is thought likely to cause personal economic hardship, few are eager to become directly involved unless or until some institution, such as the government, forces them to. But let us not forget how governments have been frequently unable to demonstrate a truly clear and firm position, usually either ignoring such matters or coming down on the side of the well-entrenched few.

For the poor, who constitute the majority of the world, one of the only means of obtaining food is by clearing unused (now often marginal or overused) land and planting some crop. The Europeans who colonized North America in the 1600's and 1700's did the very same thing, cutting down a good deal of the New World forests in the process. This approach has generally been considered as wasteful and destructive. Proposed technological solutions, from Thomas Jefferson's advocacy of utilizing lime as a means of helping restore soil fertility to the present-day recommendations of the promoters of agribusiness and Green Revolution technology of applying not only lime but fertilizers, fungicides, nematocides, insecticides, and herbicides as well, have not always met with the approval of those who plead for a more organic answer. These approaches have been shown to be increasingly wasteful and even more ruinous of the land, and the runoff of these chemicals pollutes nearby streams, rivers, lakes, and other waterways.

This particular style of farming has made modern agriculture completely dependent on petroleum. Oil is one of the principal raw materials in the production of most agricultural chemicals and the prime energy source for all aspects of mechanized farming. According to Albert A. Bartlett of the University of Colorado, "Modern agriculture is using land to convert petroleum to food."[15] David Pimentel of Cornell University has calculated that approximately 265 gallons of oil equivalent are required to produce a hectare (2.471 acres) of food (ranging between 2,240 to 3,360 pounds) in the United States and Europe.[16] This oil-based agriculture, which is the very basis of the attempt to sustain surging numbers of people throughout the globe, is also transforming the earth's environment through the depletion of valuable, often finite resources and the increased destruction of vital ecosystems.

The best solution to these wasteful and damaging methods of utilizing energy is clearly some form of population control. Obviously, unless something is done soon to constrain the proliferation of people, the problem can only worsen. Unfortunately, those directly involved in formulating policy relative to this dilemma, or even peripherally involved in simply reporting on such matters, demonstrate an appalling fear of discussing or even mentioning this rational option. Several religious and cultural factors contribute to the population crisis: the importance of purdah in Muslim countries;[17] the strict, conservative approach of the Catholic Church to sexual matters;[18] age-old traditions in such densely populated countries as China to produce large families,[19] in spite of Communist policies regarding small family size and forced abortions; and a prevalent fundamentalist belief that the command of Genesis — "be fruitful and multiply" — is still applicable today.[20] We can only wonder how future generations will assess the role of those who preached and advocated profligate procreation.

It has been demonstrated that humans now appropriate, consume, or waste nearly 40 percent of all of the globe's potential terrestrial net primary productivity.[21] Since we constitute, even at almost 6 billion strong, only a small percentage of the total amount of living matter on the earth, it is increasingly obvious that we are taking far more than our share, and in so doing are very probably causing the extinction of, or at the very least jeopardizing, a vast number of life-forms through our indiscriminate and thoughtless acts of overconsumption.

Aldo Leopold was one of the first to point out this difficulty when he wrote in the foreword to his *Sand County Almanac*: "We abuse land because we regard it as a commodity belonging to us. When we see land as a community to which we belong, we may begin to use it with love and respect. There is no other way for land to survive the impact of mechanized man, nor for us to reap from it the esthetic harvest it is capable, under science, of contributing to culture."[22]

Let us take another look at the option of technology. The recent excitement over "cold fusion" offers an instructive starting point. Hopes were raised in 1991 following the hasty announcement of the achievement of "fusion in a jar" as a successful demonstration of a method that held the promise of making the clean energy we clearly so much desire available to all and at little cost.[23] But, as we now know, such expectations soon were dashed after further and more extensive testing, performed by what now appear to have been more competent and careful investigators, demonstrated errors which indicated that vast amounts of energy could not be produced in this fashion.

Following this came the news that the Joint European Torus (JET) team had made a breakthrough in the attempt to harness nuclear fusion. They claimed to have achieved, under experimental conditions, a very brief yield of a million watts of energy in a controlled nuclear reaction.[24] Beneath the encouraging headlines, however, the truth of the matter, once again, is that even given unlimited financial backing to proceed as quickly as possible, the most optimistic prediction is that the day when the world can benefit from this knowledge is still far off—probably not until sometime beyond the year 2050. This raises the question as to whether, the way things are going now, we can ever get there. Already, JET is reportedly appealing for $5 billion to continue with its technological development. Where will this money come from?

Late in 1993, the announcement was made by Princeton University that its Tokamak Fusion Test Reactor released up to 5.3 million watts of power for a brief instant.[25] Those familiar with this work have acknowledged that the use of such power to generate electricity is billions of dollars and decades away and that the reactors would have to be shut down and torn apart every six months to remove the weakened walls made radioactive by the neutrons produced.

Another technological hope is that hydrogen gas can be widely used to produce energy. Hydrogen is already being used for very expensive and special purposes—mainly connected with fueling space shuttles.[26] However, a major difficulty to be encountered for a wider use of this gas, as pointed out by chemistry professor P. G. Wolynes, is that the Second Law of Thermodynamics precludes the inexpensive production of hydrogen utilizing current methods.[27] In so informing us, Wolynes assumes the role of Cassandra. (The mythological daughter of Priam and Hecuba, Cassandra so attracted Apollo that he gave her the gift of prophetic power. When later thwarted, however, Apollo decreed that her prophecies would never be believed.) And so despite such formidable caveats as those of Wolynes, many people are beginning to point to some of the exotic schemes just mentioned as possible touchstones for a bountiful energy future.

The anxiety of many, and the chief point of contention here, is that as modern technology increasingly utilizes energy in the form of coal, gas, or petroleum these fossil fuels disappear forever but the pestilential waste from such use remains.[28] Although many claim we have sufficient fossil fuel reserves to last for years, this dubious hope is of little consolation for the young people of the world, or for those who take the needs of the world's future population into consideration.

There is no doubt that technology has provided many people with a life today that not even kings and emperors of the past could even have dreamed. But this in no way lessens the burden or downside of technology as we know it. For example, in the very process of producing synthetic rubber, according to P. E. Hurley,[29] temperatures ranging up to 1,000° F are required. This clearly demonstrates how costly this technological process is, not just from an economic standpoint but from a conservation one as well, for the energy needed to generate such temperatures comes from a nonrenewable source. When this energy source is gone, it is gone forever—and with it the technology dependent on it. In addition, it should be again emphasized that the pollution from this process is enormous and perhaps quite detrimental to the health of plant workers as well as those who live nearby.[30] One of the major sources of noxious waste in Eastern Europe, Russia, and China, in fact, has been synthetic rubber factories! Now comes word from Odessa, Texas, of the 1,300 people who are bringing a $27 million class action suit against the General Tire Company there for the smell and pollution coming from its synthetic rubber–processing plant.[31]

These serious and unfortunate drawbacks, of which we are becoming increasingly and unhappily aware, must somehow be overcome before we can really consider that we are approaching our hoped-for goals. Can such be done, or will we become so buried in technologically initiated waste and strapped by diminishing fiscal resources that this can never be achieved?

13

ROLL

OUT THE BARREL

ONCE AGAIN USING our chosen symbol in order to unify the overall argument, let us examine what would happen should we make the decision to go all-out and take the path of technology to solve the problem of producing all of our future rubber needs. Since this scheme would require using petroleum as one of the major building blocks, before that question can be answered, we ought first to investigate a bit more thoroughly the availability of this raw material and the costs involved in its extraction, processing, and distribution. Are there currently ample reserves and supplies of this fossil fuel and will this be the case over the long haul?

Too many of us have for too long either forgotten or ignored the unpleasant consequences of the Arab oil embargo in the early 1970's—with the result that we somehow have pushed out of our minds that there is a finite amount of petroleum. The true facts about the supply of this important resource in no way support our collective case of denial. In September 1989, Richard A. Kerr predicted, in an article titled "Oil and Gas Estimates Plummet," that if the United States continued to import 50 percent of its petroleum needs, our domestic supply would last but another 32 years—until the year 2021.[1] About a year later, basing his calculations on the estimates by famed petroleum geologist M. King Hubbert, who advised in 1969 that Americans were consuming petroleum at an exponential rate of 7 percent per year,[2] Daniel B. Hawkins of the University of Alaska concluded that our own supply of this raw material will be exhausted not in 32 but rather in only 16 years.[3] That would put the date for the disappearance of our stores of petroleum at about the year 2006. In the same issue of the journal *Science*, Robert L. Hirsch, vice president for research and technical services of the ARCO Oil and Gas Company, basically substantiated the figures given by Hawkins; Hirsch then went on to paint a much more ominous scenario, prior to, yet anticipating some disaster such as the recent Persian Gulf War. He suggested that at a price of $22 a barrel the 1989 import level of just under 50 percent of demand represented a drain of $64 billion on the U.S. economy.[4] More recently, Cutler J. Cleveland, from his analysis concerning crude oil reserves in the lower 48 states, suggested that proven oil reserves in this region will decrease sharply and that the expansion of exploration in the Gulf of Mexico would not alter significantly the overall decline in yield per effort (YPE) for the entire nation, excluding Alaska and Hawaii.[5]

There are now projections that by the year 2000, the United States may be importing 56 percent of its oil, with about a quarter of that coming from the Persian Gulf. For the world as a whole, demand for petroleum is expected to grow 11.7 percent by that year, from the current level of approximately 68 million barrels a day up to an estimated 76 million barrels.[6] The difficulty involved in reaching these estimates is that this demand may put too serious a strain on the entire petroleum production picture. The reason, very simply, is that it is now becoming increasingly expensive to pump more oil.

I am obviously not overly enthusiastic about the manner by which the energy policy of the United States has been handled during the past few decades. Why, I might ask, didn't we listen to these warnings? Why did it take, seemingly, Saddam Hussein's aggressive moves to force us to face reality? Why have we spurned, for so long, efforts to promote energy saving? Why, one might even ask, in the recent debates over the raising of speed limits, was gas saving not a persuasive enough argument for keeping them lower? A classic example of this attitude was the manner by which the personnel of the Reagan administration, soon after taking charge in Washington, dismantled President Carter's symbolic system of solar cells from the roof of the White House and mocked his efforts to stress the investigation of alternate energy sources. One might have thought Carter's strategy should, instead of being abandoned, have been continued as a bipartisan effort of high priority.

But to return to the subject of raw materials, Hirsch had earlier predicted the possibility of at least a 60–70 percent dependence on foreign oil by the year 2000.[7] Since this appears now to be inevitable, two new questions come urgently to mind: Where are we going to get the kind of money required during the ominously critical economic period which we now face? How can 260 million Americans (less than 5 percent of the entire world's population) justify demanding such a large percentage of one of the world's increasingly limited resources, when everyone else wants this as well?

Discounting for the moment whether through higher taxes or some other means we might come up with the funds required to continue purchasing what we desire, another factor, even more prejudicial to our future, should be considered here. An unsigned editorial, relative to the regard by which our country is held by foreigners, appeared in 1990 in the British journal *The Economist*. The commentary stated, "If you stop the average European, Japanese, Latin American or, for full effect, Canadian in the street and ask him what he thinks about America, you are as likely to hear as much contempt as praise."[8] The implication is that it is going to take some rather difficult maneuvering to ignore this unflattering opinion while continuing to be so dependent on all manner of foreign imports as we strive to maintain our so-called but difficult to define American way of life.

The previous figures on oil consumption were all predicated on a price of $22 a barrel. A much more accurate picture of the true value of this commodity was presented in the *New York Times* op-ed pages by Alan Tonelson and Andrew K. Hurd of the Economic Strategy Institute. According to Tonelson and Hurd, if we were to include such real costs (often glossed over or ignored) as the billions of dollars in (mostly military) foreign aid doled out to Israel, Egypt, Pakistan, and other countries in an attempt to maintain the tricky balance of power in Southwest Asia and the Persian Gulf region, plus the even higher amounts the United States has spent (and continues to spend) on its troops in the area, the true price of a barrel of oil would be in the neighborhood of $80.[9] Once we insert this higher and much more realistic figure into our calculations and somehow include the various nonpecuniary factors, it should become immediately obvious that we must reckon on a number of rather serious difficulties. Principal among these is that not only petroleum itself but everything made from this resource also will cost more in the future. And we must begin to adopt this more realistic accounting in all our future economic projections.

As recently as the early 1990's, and due principally to breakdowns in OPEC policy coupled with a reluctance on the part of the major producers (e.g., Saudi Arabia) to hold back on production, the price fell to the $16–$18-per-barrel range.[10] More recently, by the early summer of 1996, for example, while the price for Saudi Arabia Light is still in the $17–$18 range, prices for West Texas Intermediate have gone up to $20–$22 and may go higher with greater demand. This anomaly appears to have had little to do with how much more difficult and expensive it has become to bring in new supplies, or with how many physical, environmental, and political obstacles to production there are.[11] Despite new technology, and increased efforts, the search for new reserves has proven to be most elusive.[12] There is no doubt that new finds, such as those in various parts of what used to be the Soviet Union[13] as well as those in the deep waters of the Gulf of Mexico,[14] will continue to be made, but at the same time, to be completely realistic, reserves are being depleted rapidly and the very process of extracting petroleum is becoming increasingly costly — and not just in dollars and cents.

In the petroleum-extracting business there appears to be an increasingly contemptuous attitude toward the lives and welfare of many of the native people who live in those regions now being tapped. Of the growing number of cases that could be cited, two will suffice.

As described by Joe Kane, the almost blatant disdain with which the Huaorani people in Amazonian Ecuador have been brought to the brink of extinction as a society by the damage inflicted not only on the members of this tribe but on the environment itself by "The Company" (Texaco) is most disturbing. This is especially true in the case of the devastating oil spills from Texaco's pipeline that are being deliberately caused.[15]

The other example concerns an equally brutal, almost savage trashing of the land in Nigeria that the Ogoni people call their homeland by the Shell Oil Company. This matter was brought to worldwide attention when the author and environmentalist Ken Saro-Wiwa, among others, was recently hanged by Nigeria's military dictatorship.[16] In addition to having their environment devastated, the Ogoni received no recompense — all payments for the oil extracted basically being left with the military regime in power. So for his efforts against environmental damage and a fairer share of the country's immense oil wealth for those regions from which it is extracted, and despite the protests of many nations, Saro-Wiwa lost his life. It is interesting to note that after this unfortunate episode, Shell made a public statement that it would not change its oil policy (apparently including its polluting scheme of extraction) in Nigeria.

Both of these examples simply add to the concern, first stated, that the question to be answered now is probably not whether global environmental collapse will occur, but rather how soon this will take place.

Kevin Phillips has brought to our attention, with his book *The Politics of Rich and Poor*, that in our own country, thanks to political and economic policies that seem inevitably to favor the rich, the wealthiest fifth of our citizens increased their share of the national income in the 1980's from 41.6 percent to 44 percent while the take-home pay of everyone else declined.[17] Indeed, we now learn that slightly more than 15 percent of us are presently living under the 1992 official poverty level of $14,763 per family of four.[18] Lower- and middle-class families, often now with two parents working to make ends meet, earn, in terms of constant dollars, about the same as did similar families (but with only one wage earner) when Eisenhower was president. Furthermore, few from these groups are truly aware of what happened to them. The argument may also be made that this is closely analogous to what is occurring in the world as a whole, where such wealthy nations as the United States have evolved a high standard of living often at the expense of those living in developing countries.

As previously pointed out, wealth everywhere tends to flow from the poor to the rich. Now with leaders like Saddam Hussein (who appears to have had a rather good hand dealt to him by the U.S.-led coalition even after its grossly overhyped glorious victory) pointing this out to large numbers of the humble and poor, the United States is finding this an embarrassing matter that is increasingly difficult to hide or ignore. Although Saddam appears to face a host of problems, and while the people of Iraq suffer, he continues to thumb his nose at the West. What is often overlooked in this saber-rattling posture is that he now sits on a much greater reserve of oil for the future than does the United States. Furthermore, a great deal of his apparently skillful propaganda is carried out under the mantle of Arab brotherhood and Sunni Islam, which has wide appeal in areas of Southeast Asia, Africa, and the oil-rich Middle East.

This overall concern relative to petroleum availability is occurring against the background of a long-standing debate between optimists and pessimists relative to the future availability of certain key resources. This confrontation and the apparent ascendancy of the optimists has been clearly pointed out by Garrett Hardin in the chapter "The Ambivalent Triumph of Optimism" in his *Living within the Limits*. Hardin describes how it "pays" to be an optimist, since optimists are the ones who supply only good news, that is, the sort of future everyone hopes and yearns for. On the other hand, pessimists are almost always cast in the role of pariahs since they usually predict only gloom and doom.[19] In terms of the present argument, it is obvious that we should turn to neither of these increasingly polarized positions for the guidance we seek, but rather to that provided by another group: the realists. The only logical position to take is to not buy into snake-oil or pie-in-the-sky or gloom-and-doom scenarios but rather to face the perhaps more difficult alternative — the facts. This is a complex and trying task partly because it almost automatically implies that the positions of both optimists and pessimists must always be chastised and deprecated. (It should be mentioned that Hardin uses the date 2059 as the probable point in time that we will have all but exhausted the world's petroleum supply.)

Before proceeding further, perhaps it might be wise to look at this matter from a different perspective. Instead of frantically searching for and fighting over oil deposits, should we not calmly and rationally contemplate the possibilities of utilizing alternate energy sources? Every bit of energy which can be obtained from a source other than petroleum or conserved altogether implies a lengthening of the period of oil's availability for energy use. Power companies all over the United States have come to the conclusion that it is less expensive and more efficient, as well as prudent in regard to the issue of resources, especially fossil fuel scarcity, to encourage their customers to adopt such energy savers as double-paned windows than to build more power plants, especially those run on nuclear energy.

A wide range of distinctly renewable energy sources have long been promoted and include methane and methanol from trees, ethanol from corn and sugarcane, waterfalls, winds and ocean currents, the tides, geothermal reservoirs[20] and, naturally, the very sun itself. Each one has its drawbacks or handicaps; otherwise they might be in greater use at present. For example, to maintain or even increase yields of corn and sugarcane for the production of ethanol and methanol will require judicious and ample applications or inputs of agricultural chemicals including fertilizers, herbicides, nematocides, insecticides, and fungicides, most of which are petroleum based. At the present, manufacture of ethanol is counterproductive, since it requires more energy and cash output than is generated — making this gasoline substitute not a very suitable one to use.[21] The geothermal generating plants of California are at the point of running down from lack of steam. Although some progress is being made in the direction of a more ample utilization of the sun's energy, nothing yet comes close to the optimistic projections which Farrington Daniels made three decades ago.[22]

Thus, perhaps the most obvious possibility or plan as relates to scarce sources of energy is simply to become more energy efficient.[23] The United States, in comparison with other countries, is atrociously wasteful in terms of energy use. Amory B. Lovins and L. Hunter Lovins, the founder and president, respectively, of the Rocky Mountain Institute, have long been enthusiastic advocates and promoters of alternate energy sources and claim that technology is presently available by which the United States could cut oil use by one-eighth, thus effectively ending the nation's petroleum dependency on the Persian Gulf region. They also believe that using a carrot of "free-bates"—a combination of fees and rebates to penalize new car buyers for choosing cars that fall below the fuel-efficiency minimums and reward them for purchasing those that go beyond—is far more effective in the long run than taxation or hidden subsidies to oil companies, which amount to the same thing so far as the general public is concerned.[24] In this connection, Harold M. Hubbard, of Resources for the Future, stresses that "bringing market prices in line with energy's hidden burdens will be one of the great challenges of the coming decades."[25] Finally, Richard Heede and Robert Bishop, writing in the magazine *Sierra*, point out that even the adoption of the Bush administration's National Energy Strategy (NES), which was intended to reverse a steady decline in domestic oil production, cannot possibly bring this about.[26] Furthermore, were the entire Arctic National Wildlife Refuge to be turned over to oil companies to do with as they wished, the total amount of oil that could be extracted under a best-case scenario would hardly make a percentage point's difference. Even according to oil company estimates such a move has less than a 50-50 chance of success, unfortunately implying, based on prior oil company performance (even excluding the still ongoing scandal surrounding the disgraceful episode of the tanker *Exxon Valdez*), serious detriment to the ecology of the region.

According to Heede and Bishop, the United States is the most densely petroleum-drilled region in the world. The number of dry wells the drilling of which was heavily subsidized by unknowing taxpayers is monumental. Those wells that did produce oil, also partially paid for by taxpayers who receive little in the way of gratitude to say nothing of monetary recompense for these efforts, are rapidly being depleted. While this clearly suggests that the goals of the NES are both economically and geologically improbable, and if put into practice would cause the nation's energy bill to skyrocket, the cry of the oil companies is to have the general public once more pay economic and now ecological homage as well to the false god of petroleum self-sufficiency.

However, in order to satiate Americans' demands and projected needs, even if continued reliance on cheap imported oil were possible, U.S. policies and Americans' expectations would be wide of the mark. In the first place, as pointed out by Peter Passell, "Washington does have an oil policy. The only catch, it seems, is that the policy is made in Houston and Riyadh." [27] The obvious aim in both power centers is certainly not related to any Benthamite "greatest good to the greatest number" production and distribution of inexpensive petroleum products but rather is focused on how to manipulate this commodity to achieve the greatest financial return to those who control the source. This is, after all, what is involved in the strategy of power and glory so well described by Daniel Yergin in his book *The Prize: The Epic Quest for Oil, Money, and Power*.[28] Following the turbulent events of the Persian Gulf War, Kuwait is now, at considerable cost and to the surprise of many, practically back to its prewar oil production figures. Other nearby nations such as Iran, while not so fortunate, since they have neither the funds nor the technical capability to increase their output, are, however, rapidly moving in this same direction. And as each oil-producing country begins to demonstrate a policy of prodigal extraction, we once more enter the cycle of believing there will always be an endless supply of cheap oil. This myth is further substantiated in the manner by which those who derive tremendous incomes from control of this resource increase their opulent and grand-scale expenditures. The description by Mary Anne Weaver of the manner by which Arab royalty annually splurges incredibly vast sums in the deserts of Pakistan in pursuit of the endangered houbara bustard (the flesh of which is reported to be an aphrodisiac) is but a single example of this lavish behavior.[29]

But this renaissance of bountiful oil production is by no means occurring everywhere. The Commonwealth of Independent States, the constituent republics of which possess combined larger oil reserves than any country, is presently in an economic and political free-fall. Even taking into account the proposed joint ventures with capitalist oil producers, the nations of the former Soviet Union, which now export all of the oil required by what were the Communist bloc nations, still have this enormously critical problem of even maintaining production with old and inefficient equipment. According to Leslie H. Gelb, lack of initiative to assist, in some manner, this crumbling empire with regard to its petroleum production is frittering away precious time. It was predicted in 1991 that, unless something is done soon, oil output from this region will decline from the 11.5 million barrels produced daily in 1990 to possibly only 9 million by the year 2000.[30] This does not take into account the recent oil spill in northern Siberia, which is reported to be far more serious than the *Exxon Valdez* fiasco.[31] Net exports of oil continued to fall to almost zero by 1994, leaving the Baltic states in a most serious condition. When this came to pass, it forced this group of nations and ethnic groups to begin making daily imports from other producing areas, which are expected to increase to at least 2 million barrels by the end of the twentieth century. What sources will provide this difference, and how will this change in distribution affect the future global oil picture?

Regardless of how much new drilling may take place anywhere in the years ahead, the numbers indicate that the world is slowly, steadily, and irrevocably running out of oil.[32] No amount of wishing, propagandizing, or working new or deeper fields can help us dodge this bullet. Undaunted by such information, many still promote the idea that something will soon turn up to negate this fact, and false hopes of this nature are continually being paraded before our eyes. One of the latest such dreams is relative to the discovery that a vast deposit of methane lies under the bottom of the earth's oceans, the idea being that once technology is brought to bear this can be used as a new and immense energy source.[33] However, we should probably concede that this and other such discoveries as the fact that an Amazonian shrub (*Euphorbia tirucalli*) might be processed so as to produce a substance or fuel that could possibly power a diesel motor are wishful thinking of the "fallacy of hope" category. While Nobel Laureate Melvin Calvin demonstrated the potential of this plant (in the same family as Para rubber) some time ago,[34] little has been done to continue such studies. Why? In any of these cases, the question relates to just how long a time frame would be required to develop new and untested products and where funds for such research and engineering might come from. It would require an ample start-up period to develop the necessary machinery and equipment, coupled with a great deal of financing, to develop economically useful products of this nature. As already pointed out, because of similar constraints we have not yet met the challenge of how properly to utilize, from an environmental standpoint, our growing mountains of worn-out tires. Are we prepared to look for new energy sources? If we admit we face serious difficulties so far as future oil supplies are concerned and begin work on new technologies immediately, is it already too late?

It is certainly true that oil companies have recently made remarkable engineering improvements in their striving for greater productivity. These include more rapid and deeper drilling of new wells and novel techniques that permit a more complete extraction of petroleum from older wells. After spending vast sums in attempting to extract oil from the enormous deposits of so-called tar sands in our western states and Canada, many were forced to come to the conclusion that it was doubtful whether any of the oil companies involved could ever economically obtain crude oil from such fields. However, from nothing a little longer than two decades ago, oil sands output in Canada has jumped to 390,000 barrels a day — and now represents a quarter of Canada's total crude output.[35] But at what cost?

Despite such positive signs, the hard question before us is, if we do not begin immediately to shift to alternative energy sources, save on oil consumption perhaps through increased taxation, and utilize public transportation to the utmost, will it be too late in the game by the time we actually get around to making these tough decisions? Overshadowing this doubt was the fact that by 1991 the world was producing oil very near the limits of capacity, according to Daniel Yergin, implying that there was and still is little margin for error. And the "error" Yergin refers to "could arise from a combination of political change and capacity limits in the Middle East, declining U.S. production, falling Soviet oil exports and rising demand resulting from economic recovery."[36]

Given this rather frightening and pessimistic overview relative to petroleum, we should take another look at the central symbol of this essay, rubber. How much oil will be required, and at what costs, in the production of rubber products, chiefly tires? We must first understand that the majority of tire companies are presently undergoing serious financial difficulties. The largest, Michelin, a French company with a 22 percent share of the global tire market, began to cut at least 16,000 jobs by the end of 1992.[37] This included the complete shutdown of such operations as the Uniroyal-Goodrich Tire Company factory in Eau Claire, Wisconsin (both former U.S. firms are now subsidiaries of Michelin). While this closing was blamed locally on weakness in the U.S. economy, it could also have been due to the costs involved in attempting to upgrade and modernize old processing plants. According to Jonathan P. Hicks, Goodyear, next in the industry with a 20 percent market share, "is working to overcome low demand and intense price competition, [and] said it would lay off up to 600 workers at two American plants and one in Canada." Bridgestone, the Japanese company with 17 percent of the market, saw its earnings fall by over half when it took over the Firestone Tire and Rubber Company in 1988. Continental (Germany—8 percent), with its acquisition of General Tire of Akron; Pirelli (Italy—7 percent), which recently acquired Armstrong Tire; and Sumitomo (Japan—7 percent) have all faced similar problems. In attempting to discover the cause for this demise in tire company operations, Hicks quotes Horst Urban, chief executive of Continental, who stated, "The tire market is going down everywhere in the world because of heavy cost problems, overcapacity, and major losses."[38]

Although tire producers insist that natural rubber has many outstanding traits—including such characteristics as high tack, greater green-stock strength, and lower heat buildup—the tread life of synthetic tires appears to have been significantly improved as the result of technological innovations culminating in what are known as highly polymerized polybutadiene synthetic rubbers. At first it was thought that, because of such innovations, with longer-lasting tires, demand for synthetic rubber would be slow at best. Some also suggested there would be an accompanying decrease in world synthetic production. There is, instead, an increase in demand causing a shortage in supplies.[39]

The economic problems that the major tire companies are now having, despite an upturn in car sales in the United States during 1994, are thus not necessarily due solely to the current serious worldwide recession (from which the nation is apparently beginning to escape), which many still feel will be with us for some time. Much of the industry's demise must be attributed to poor management decisions, many of which appear to be related to overstaffing, as is quite evident in other manufacturing and service organizations. There was also a recent and obviously greedy flurry on the part of a few large corporations to gobble up more than they could properly digest, and these were forced to sell off holdings or retrench. It is no longer true that car manufacturers lament the fact that sales are depressed and that many people either cannot afford or are putting off the purchase of vehicles (each with five tires). Current figures indicate that the U.S. car and truck population is still experiencing strong growth and, with an improving economic picture in America, will continue to do so. In spite of a less promising economic outlook in other industries, this trend is also taking place throughout the world where the dream of many is to own their personal vehicles. For example, Thomas Friedman writes that when "more of China's 1.2 billion people start trading their bicycles for Toyotas the world will witness the gas-guzzle of all gas-guzzlers."[40] He might also have mentioned that these cars will all have larger tires than bicycles do — and more of them. And this must definitely be considered as a harbinger of things to come so far as future demand for rubber is concerned.

Finally, in attempting to place a correct value on the petroleum products we now use, we must revisit the issue of pollution. Possibly the most difficult problem to be dealt with in the matter of modern technology is when to make the decision to dispense with inefficient and pollution-causing factories and processing plants, especially those engaged in the manufacture of synthetic rubber. Barry Commoner, director of the Center for the Biology of Natural Systems at Queens College, believes that this probably cannot be done in a free-market society where constant pressure is brought to bear on our elected officials to leave things as they are. His argument is that our only answer is to abandon technologies that create pollution.[41] Officials of the EPA expected their automobile exhaust controls would reduce annual carbon monoxide emissions by 80 percent and nitrogen oxides by 70 percent between 1975 and 1985; the actual figures show that the former was reduced by only 19 percent and the latter by 4 percent. However, at the same time, it must be admitted that some environmentally correct decisions are capable of being successfully carried out. For example, emissions of lead have decreased by 94 percent because that pollutant was completely eliminated from the gasoline production process. In the final analysis, though, the costs of pollution and the wastes involved not only in the refining of petroleum but also in the processing of synthetics, including rubber, must now be considered or we run the certain risk of jeopardizing our atmosphere either by poisoning it, heating it up, or degrading it in some manner.

An additional piece of economic data to add to the conundrum facing us in the synthetic vs. natural debate is that during the years 1994–1995, while the price of petroleum dropped from a range of $19–$21 down to

$14–16 per barrel on the New York market, the price of natural rubber increased from $0.43–$0.45 a pound to $0.92–$0.94 on the same market in the early days of 1995. This represents a 120 percent increase during that short time span. While the price of rubber dropped dramatically during the summer of 1995, it returned almost to its earlier highs and is still considerably more than it was earlier this decade. One might have thought that with lower oil prices the cost of synthetic rubber would have been lowered sufficiently to drag the value of natural rubber down with it. But this definitely did not occur, as previously pointed out in the case of a rise in the price of automobile tires. From the standpoint of classical economics, such a dramatic surge in price clearly indicates either a rise in demand or an equally noticeable fall in supply. In either case, the implication can only be that we are facing a growing and serious shortage of this product.

All of this should cause us to consider carefully any other viable alternatives or new technologies that may exist, for a way to intelligently utilize our diminishing resources in a world increasingly cluttered by a voracious populace.

14

THE PARA RUBBER
TREE AND GLOBAL ECOLOGY

IT HAS BEEN suggested by T. M. Lewinsohn that latex is a wide-spread defense in plants against natural enemies.[1] In more or less the same vein, David E. Dussourd reports that "the idea that plants produce latex as a defense against enemies was suggested almost a century ago by the German biologist Hans Kniep. While some shared his views, others discounted the notion, citing the numerous herbivores that relish latex-bearing plants. We now know that Kniep was correct."[2] Do these two rather sweeping generalizations imply that the sole purpose of latex in plants is to discourage predation by a variety of herbivores?

As previously stated, the latexes of certain plants do contain poisons. The most obvious case is that of the opium poppy *Papaver somniferum*, the source of opium, morphine, and heroin. It is also true that the latexes of milkweeds (*Asclepias* spp.), which are found chiefly in temperate areas, and which were the principal example used by Dussourd to support his statements, do contain substances (cardiac glycosides) that are toxic to some insects. However, it should be noted here that Monarch butterflies are closely associated with these plants, laying eggs on them as well as feeding on their latex, in part to obtain this sustenance as the basis for their own chemical defense.[3]

In contrast to the above, James Bonner and Arthur W. Galston have written, "The suggestion that latex might serve to protect the plant against attacks from herbivorous animals . . . has been disproved by Tobler." They then go on to mention references to snails, camels, and insects—all of which do damage to latex-bearing plants.[4] According to Polhamus, termites, leaf-cutting ants, giant snails, and two species of slugs are attracted to the leaves, roots, and bark of *Hevea* trees to such an extent as to present serious plantation management problems.[5] In Central America, I have observed that pocket gophers are quite capable of destroying entire rows of plantation rubber trees by consuming their roots for food. Furthermore, although latex is present in large quantities in the roots, trunk, and branches of Para rubber trees, it is hardly found in the leaves. From this, one is left to wonder, if the role of latex is to serve only to discourage attack, why it is not present in the foliage — that part of the plant generally most sought after by herbivores.

To pursue this matter a bit further, it is well known that in the Mulberry family, from some species of which rubber is extracted, a latex is produced which has actually been used by humans as a substitute for milk. The English naturalist H. W. Bates, when on the Amazon during the nineteenth century, wrote of enjoying the latex of the Cow-tree (*Massaranduba, Minusops excelsa*) in his coffee, although he cautioned against drinking too much of this substance.[6] More recently, Paul Allen has written, regarding another species of Cow-tree (*Palo de vaca, Brosimum utile*), "All parts of the plant produce an abundant, creamy latex, which is sweet and of pleasant flavor, particularly when first taken from the tree. The fresh milk has been tried in coffee and can scarcely be distinguished from good cream, while chilled it can be whipped and flavored with sugar and vanilla extract and served to unsuspecting humans."[7]

It also has been known for some time, as was pointed out to me by Eldon Newcomb of the University of Wisconsin, that small, single-celled flagellates live in the latex of various species of the Euphorbiaceae, closely resembling the manner by which the malaria-causing *Plasmodium* live in human red blood cells. One species of flagellate actually exists within the laticifers of the milkweed.[8] Dr. Lynn Margulis of the University of Massachusetts at Amherst, a recognized specialist in the field of microorganisms, is unaware of whether those flagellates that live in latex play any specific role, such as in isoprene metabolism, in the plants they inhabit, but believes that they must have a key function of some kind.[9] From a Darwinian perspective, why else would they be there? Finally, it must be noted that a great number of plant disease organisms utilize Para rubber trees as a resource base, including, in addition to South American Leaf Blight, those that cause dieback and rot not only to leaves but also to bark, roots, and even the tapping panel.[10]

A quick review here should permit us to recall that, in 1879, the Frenchman G. Bouchardat, by heating rubber to a high temperature, obtained isoprene and that three years later the Englishman W. A. Tilden synthesized isoprene from turpentine. This synthesis suggested that isoprene might be an important constituent of living plant matter. It is now known that this chemical is abundantly present in latex. The important points to consider here are what exactly is latex, and what are its functions?[11] This is certainly not a uniform product and varies in composition from plant to plant and species to species. Bonner and Galston indicate that in *Hevea* rubber, the major component of latex is water. The quantity of this medium depends, naturally, on the season of the year. Next in importance are the very long, branched chains of anywhere from 3,000 to 6,000 units of isoprene. It should be stressed here that it is the enormous quantity of isoprene to be found in a wide variety of living material that suggests it must play some very important, though yet to be fully understood, role in global environments.

These isoprene chains are mixed not only with water but also with amino acids, sugars, starches, sterols, organic acids, salts and other organic molecules; the quantity and composition of the isoprene is relative to the particular plant itself as well as its environment. Indeed, it is this hodgepodge of substances in natural rubber latex that when converted into condoms and examination gloves form a barrier to, and inhibit the passage of, the AIDS virus.[12] The composition of this conglomerate, which has so far proved impossible to duplicate synthetically, also varies from plant to plant. It is also known that certain people are allergic to latex and are thus unable to use latex gloves or condoms.[13] In terms of the present discussion the basic question that remains is just what is the purpose or function of isoprene, which makes up such a high percentage of plant latex?

Today, with increasing frequency, the news media focus our attention on such perturbing subjects as acid rain, depletion of the ozone layer, and global warming.[14] It is curious, however, that seldom within this wealth of information on what is taking place within the earth's atmosphere is the word "isoprene" ever mentioned. Chlorofluorocarbons (CFC's), carbon dioxide, methane, pollutants from tailpipe emissions, smoke from fires of any kind, even dust and gases from volcanic eruptions are all listed as being prime culprits — but isoprene, almost never. James Lovelock, originator of the Gaian hypothesis, informed me that this oversight may be due to the fact that many still consider the significance or importance of a gas as measured by its abundance in the atmosphere.[15] While isoprene is emitted by both plants and animals (including humans[16]) in a volume equal to that of methane, or about a million tons per year (+/− 500,000 tons), CFC's and dimethyl sulfide are present in the atmosphere in minuscule amounts of only parts per trillion. However, these latter two gases are viewed as being some of the more serious disturbers of a reasonable atmospheric balance,[17] while isoprene is practically ignored.

This lack of understanding on the part of not only the general public but far too many atmospheric scientists as well, while both curious and serious, may be due to the difficulty encountered in detecting isoprene. Once isoprene is emitted from either plants or animals, it combines readily and rapidly with a number of chemicals, including ozone and both the nitrate and hydroxyl radicals, and thus even sophisticated instruments may miss it. Yet isoprene emissions have recently been carefully recorded, and the sheer volume of this gas, not to mention the implications regarding the chemical reactions that take place, once isoprene enters the atmosphere, is enormous.

Methane — a simple, stable, and long-lasting compound, with no potentially energy-producing double bonds in its chemical makeup — has long been known to be one of the principal contributors to the greenhouse effect, if only because it is capable of absorbing infrared rays; indeed, increasing publicity has been given to this. Isoprene, on the other hand, does not absorb infrared rays (and thus, by definition cannot be considered a greenhouse gas), but with two double bonds, which indicate potentially high levels of chemical activity, isoprene does have the capacity for altering the composition of the atmosphere. That something of this nature is constantly occurring is evidenced by the fact that, while methane has an atmospheric life of approximately 10 years, isoprene's lifetime is only 0.003 years — implying that about one day after being emitted isoprene will no longer be detectable, having combined with some other compound or element in the air.

At this point, let us investigate a bit more thoroughly the implications of Lovelock's Gaian hypothesis. Very simply, this idea is that the entire earth operates and functions holistically as would a single organism or, as Lewis Thomas has suggested, even a single cell.[18] What Lovelock proposed was that the planet Earth — resembling basically almost an ancient Greek conglomerate of earth (rocks and soil), air (atmosphere with its complement of gases, winds, and clouds), fire (the sun's energy), and water (seas, lakes, oceans, and rivers) — evolved with living matter (once life began) as a single, tightly intertwined system in which each entity acts with all others as a self-regulating, cybernetic whole. While it is difficult to find references in the scientific literature to the possible role of such a major component of our natural environment as isoprene, Lovelock indicates that the very presence and almost immediate impact of isoprene once emitted into the atmosphere must be of considerable significance, for selection pressure could not favor the wasteful production of this substance. In other words, there is definitely reason and purpose for its very existence. What is this?

While it was perhaps "biologically correct" to deprecate the Gaian hypothesis during the 1970's and early 1980's, more and more scientists across distinct disciplines are now beginning to investigate what might be called Gaian questions. For example, some are now stressing the manner by which, through a recycling process among the constituent elements of earth, air, water, and living matter, the amounts of carbon dioxide in the atmosphere have remained almost constant for centuries.[19]

Now, however, it has become quite evident that there is an increase in the amount of this gas in the atmosphere. This increase is presumed to be due principally to humans' growing use of fossil fuels and burning of organic matter in clearing land, cooking, and heating, as well as to respiration, chiefly of young and actively growing plants.[20] Thus, a new polemic has arisen concerning the importance and impact of changes in the varying amounts of carbon dioxide, methane, nitrous oxide (chiefly from motor vehicle exhaust), and ozone in the atmosphere. James E. Hansen of NASA and Stephen H. Schneider of the National Center for Atmospheric Research tend to be positioned at one end of the spectrum while others, such as Richard S. Lindzen of MIT, present differing and sometimes contradictory views.[21] At the same time, the often inconclusive information available is used by still others, also with a dichotomy of opinions, in determining exactly what form or manner of political decisions to make in this regard. One side advocates that little or no change in emissions should be made now, as these will be economically too expensive or damaging to our manufacturing systems. On the other side are those who insist that if we do not take immediate steps to control our waste and pollution, and if we continue our abuse of nature, we may pass a threshold point when damage to the world's ecosystem would become irreversible and irreparable.

In this debate, however, an additional fact has yet to be given the emphasis it demands. A recent report indicates that scientists may have overestimated worldwide emissions of methane by about 25 percent and that global warming may not be so serious as previously estimated.[22] It is my belief that the data on the amount of methane, just alluded to, may have been quite correct but that those attempting to make sense out of it are missing something from their equations, because they either were unable to measure it or ignored its presence — that is, they never took into consideration the impact of isoprene in the atmosphere.

In 1962, Polhamus stated that "no one has demonstrated why a plant makes rubber and it does not appear to be a food reserve. Strong evidence indicates that rubber is an end product that is not reused in the metabolism of the plant."[23] Later, in 1989, C. C. Webster and W. J. Baulkwill, reviewing theories concerning the role of latex in plants, concluded that "as none of the . . . hypotheses has been proven, the function of latex and rubber in the plant remains unknown."[24]

Over 35 years ago, after leaving the directorship of the Missouri Botanical Gardens in St. Louis, Fritz Went, an outstanding pioneer plant physiologist, set out in search of what he spoke of as "the blue haze."[25] This haze is so evident in Virginia, for example, that a mountain range, the Blue Ridge, was named after this phenomenon. I well remember Dr. Went pointing out such a display to me as he analyzed the atmosphere around and above tropical forests in Costa Rica some years ago. I find it most puzzling that since then, with all the attention being paid to acid rain, ozone depletion, global warming, and atmospheric problems in general, so little has been done to follow up Went's initial lead.

Of those few researchers who are presently engaged in this matter, Reinhold A. Rasmussen of Washington State University, Thomas Sharkey, Francesco Loreto, and their associates at the University of Wisconsin, and Russell K. Monson and Ray Fall of the University of Colorado have demonstrated the considerable amounts of isoprene that are generated during the process of photosynthesis.[26] Data presented by Sharkey and Eric Singsaas strongly suggests that one function of isoprene in certain plants may be to serve as a cooling mechanism during the process of photosynthesis,[27] and perhaps this may help to explain why so much of this gas has been detected over Amazonian rain forests.

That this gas is emitted by a wide variety of both plants and animals is no longer in doubt, and this research clearly substantiates Went's original belief in its importance in the overall atmospheric feedback process. Once isoprene is seriously taken into account, instead of there being 25 percent less carbon (in the form of methane) in the atmosphere, it is obvious there should be a great deal more carbon (in some form) than previously thought; or did the two carbon atoms in each isoprene molecule simply disappear once this compound was emitted into the atmosphere? This should be of considerable concern to those attempting to analyze ozone depletion and global warming. It also suggests that those policymakers who opt for a do-nothing or wait-a-while stance should at least recognize the wisdom of preparing immediately some sort of strong backup position. Is there any such proposal, properly and intelligently designed, ready for execution if the need arises, for the United States?

We should bear in mind that the functions of isoprene are undoubtedly not simply to run riot like some loose cannon on the deck of a galleon in battle at sea but have some natural role or purpose in the environment. According to Darwinian theory, its presence in plants and animals must be the result of natural selection. From this it follows that isoprene must play a significant role in the overall interplay of the earth's environment, for natural selection would not favor the production of a wasteful or damaging compound. It must also be noted that, to date, no one has yet come up with a satisfactory explanation as to what exactly the major function of latex might be. What is known is that in addition to animals, 40 different plant families produce this substance, one of the most prodigious being the Euphorbiaceae, in which the genus *Hevea* is paramount.

An added point of interest about isoprene, according to Francesco Loreto, is that the amount of this gas expelled by a 15-year-old oak tree, while it is photosynthesizing, is approximately equal to the amount given off by about 100 people.[28] So far as the oak is concerned, this process occurs naturally only when the sun is out, and only during that time of year when the tree is covered with leaves. The amount produced by a human is the same throughout the year, for it is exhaled day and night. In round numbers, then, we could estimate that an oak tree gives off about the same amount of isoprene as 25 people would emit on a yearly basis. Again using round numbers, the present human population of 5.6 billion people — in addition to the enormous volumes of carbon dioxide and methane gases that we also emit as the result of natural, normal body functions — will exhale an amount of isoprene equal to that given off by 162,500,000 oak trees. At the recommended density of planting for rubber this would be equal to almost 812,500 acres. And as the human population increases, so will its contribution to isoprene levels. It is easy to see that the sheer quantity of human beings alone could cause a serious problem of additional atmospheric carbon. Where, we should ask, in all of our many calculations has this fact been taken into consideration?

In addition to the role suggested by Sharkey and Singsaas, isoprene probably does not serve as a food reserve, such as that found in the tubers of a potato. It is doubtful that it acts simply as an energy source for single-celled microorganisms. While some of the components of latex in which isoprene may be found are known to be poisonous, isoprene itself is not. However, it might very well operate in some manner as a global storage system or a sink for carbon. Simple calculations based on the figures given in Chapter 4 indicate that the amount of isoprene (estimated on a dry-weight basis) extracted in the latex from rubber trees is in the trillions of pounds. This does not take into consideration what is left in rubber trees, nor in all of those millions of plants from milkweed, dandelions, and ornamental *Ficus* plants to untapped rubber trees, which probably contain equal or greater amounts of isoprene-bearing latex than that extracted to produce natural rubber.

Additionally, while not derived directly from isoprene, all of the naturally occurring terpenes contain isoprene as their backbone, so to speak. These substances include essential oils, balsams, resins, camphors, carotenes, and vitamins A and E, popularly known in today's advertisements as "antioxidants." It is these which presumably sweep noxious "radicals" (both nitrites and hydroxyls) out of our systems. However, there is considerable debate as to what really is going on in the formation, chemical combining, emission, and action in humans, other organisms, and the atmosphere itself of these different chemicals.[29]

There is obviously an increasing concern relative to the impact of the quantity of carbon dioxide on the overall atmospheric picture coupled with worry as to the consequences for human life, perhaps not so much for us as for our children. In his book *Global Ecology* Colin Tudge states, "Steps are being considered worldwide to curb carbon dioxide and CFC emissions, but the hope of reducing the greenhouse effect seems fairly forlorn."[30] The omission of isoprene in such a statement is disturbing, for isoprene not only will react under certain circumstances to destroy ozone but also will contribute to the amount of carbon dioxide in the air.[31] Tudge completes this section of his book by stating that "taken all in all, . . . [the greenhouse effect] must be seen as the greatest of all the pending threats to present day life."[32]

The fervent hope of those who are aware of problems and dangers associated with the greenhouse effect is that somehow this deficiency may soon be corrected not only in a manner that brightens our future but in an economically sound way as well. In order to dodge criticism of the rapacious manner in which Alaska treats its forests in general and the Tongass National Forest in particular, Senator Frank H. Murkowski claimed that the "U.S. forest harvest is nothing like the tropics."[33] Such childish finger-pointing can only make one ashamed of our supposed leaders. G. M. Woodwell, director of the Woods Hole Research Center, indicated that deforestation everywhere is releasing billions of tons of carbon dioxide into the atmosphere and that simply replanting trees will not correct this problem. In this connection, Woodwell reminds us that a true forest is more than simply the trees therein and that carbon is bound up even in the organic matter in the soil.[34] This is yet another plea for a "deep woods" approach that would take into consideration all the substances found in a forest.

Because of the existence of a methyl group in the chemical configuration of isoprene, during its combination with other compounds, radicals, or elements, only naturally occurring compounds result. Butadiene, the principal building block for most synthetic rubber, on the other hand, has no such methyl group. As pointed out to me by Thomas Sharkey of the University of Wisconsin, upon decomposition, butadiene, because of the lack of a methyl group in its makeup, can only produce compounds that are toxic; the implication is that butadiene is unable to form byproducts that could be considered as friendly to the environment.[35] This is yet one more reason not to place too much old-fashioned trust in technology to lead us to a brighter future in which there will be less environmental degradation.

One final note on isoprene. In the overall picture of the recycling of atmospheric gases and wastes, as so well spelled out by such investigators as Eugene P. Odum and his associates at the University of Georgia, a complicated interplay of many different factors is at work.[36] From the present point of interest these include the traps or sinks for carbon dioxide in the benthic depths of oceans as well as in the enormous amounts of algae in the waters of the continental shelves. Carbonate rocks, all living matter, sea shells, and bones must also be included in this category. The difficulty we face is that the global recycling balance, which once operated with only minor disturbances, is gradually going out of sync, especially because of the excessive use of fossil fuels, with a gradual lessening of a capacity to absorb or store carbon; this decreased capacity is caused chiefly by pollution, destruction of the algal life in continental shelves, and worldwide deforestation.

Until we better understand the complex carbon picture, greater consideration should be given to the increased establishment of all manner of plant life. If by such large-scale planting greater numbers of jobs would be created, so much the better, for until humanity can truly come to grips with its population explosion, which it must do if we as a species hope to continue to exist, people will have to find employment. Hopefully, this enhanced economic gain would not be coupled, as so often has happened in the past, with another surge in human numbers, for this would only make for a no-win situation.

It should now be obvious that, despite its having many aspects of a bad dream, the entire matter of planting thousands of acres of trees of any kind (including rubber) does appear to be an idea worth giving very serious thought to — and soon. This is especially so when such plantings are established together with an equal area of contiguous and undisturbed natural vegetation. Furthermore, all these trees when 15 years and older tend to store carbon as opposed to those, such as eucalyptus and pine, planted to be cut while still young (5–15 years) for pulp or as Christmas trees, which give off more carbon dioxide than they store. Can a major planting of rubber trees be carried out not only in different parts of the humid tropics but throughout the globe? This is the challenge which must be faced in the immediate future.

Finally, I would insist that there are only two sure methods of controlling or containing global environmental degradation: through population control and correctly applied technology. This assertion may appear to contradict my previous emphasis on the deficiencies of technology. But there is more than one form of technology, and in this case, what is required is not one based on engineering, but rather, an appropriate technology based on the principles of ecology that would make direct use of the sun's energy and thus create little in the way of waste and pollution.

It has been suggested that the reason the eminent scientist and philosopher Ludwig Boltzmann committed suicide was that he was unable to rationalize and understand the dichotomy between, on the one hand, the implication of the eventual decay of the universe into a completely chaotic state due to entropy and, on the other, the ideas implied by Darwin and Wallace in their theory of evolution by means of natural selection as to how this decay is apparently overcome. More than 100 years ago, while attempting to analyze the processes of entropy, Boltzmann wrote, "Plants spread their immense surface of leaves and force the sun's energy, before it falls to the earth's temperature, to perform, in ways yet unexplored certain chemical syntheses of which no one in our laboratories has so far the least idea."[37]

15

"MAN'S
INHUMANITY TO MAN"

IN REVIEWING THE many different facets and aspects of how the Para rubber tree serves to symbolize our life and times, we will now examine more thoroughly the implications of the tragedy surrounding the murder of the rubber tapper Francisco (Chico) Mendes in Brazil. This cowardly, repugnant act has had a lingering and quite significant impact on the movement to preserve and protect the earth's environment.

> *Man's inhumanity to man*
> *Makes countless thousands mourn.*[1]

Sr. Mendes, the leader of the *seringueiros* in that part of the Amazon basin and posthumously a recognized key player in the worldwide environmental struggle, exemplifies those—the fishermen, miners, loggers, and others—who are engaged in the business of extracting something of value from nature. As earlier pointed out, Mendes was by no means the only one killed during this confrontation between cattle ranchers and extractors of forest products, but because of his unique position, his death serves to highlight one of the most important and intractable factors we must come to grips with relative to our imminent future prospects. For it is quite possible that unpleasant and disturbing confrontations of this type will increase as our numbers swell.

Such savage and viciously inhumane behavior is sadly quite common throughout every society in the world today—though certainly not new. One need only view or listen to the first few minutes of the local evening news almost anywhere. With few exceptions, these broadcasts are given over to a litany of the rape, arson, fraud, murder, and mayhem that has taken place recently in the immediate vicinity, quickly followed by similar descriptions on a national and international scale. We have become so inundated with such reporting that few stop anymore to consider what the root causes of such behavior might be. Are we the only species that engages in such brutal actions in response to life's difficulties?

René Dubos has stated that in "many species, the numbers of animals increase continuously from year to year until a maximum population density is reached; then suddenly an enormous mortality descends. This phenomenon, known as a 'population crash,' has long been assumed to be caused by epidemics corresponding to those which were so destructive in the course of human history, for example, plague or yellow fever." To further substantiate this point, Dubos wrote about how "lemmings periodically experience an irresistible 'collective urge' either to commit suicide or to search for their ancestral home on the lost Atlantic Continent and consequently they march unswervingly into the sea." He continues by quoting observations on massive migrations of these small rodents to their collective demise.[2]

C. J. Krebs of the University of British Colombia, an ardent observer of the behavior of lemmings, claims that no such collective and mass suicidal behavior has ever occurred among them nor does this sort of phenomenon take place now. He has even publicly stated that he will pay a considerable sum of money for a photograph of anything depicting what Dubos described above. Overpopulation may be a problem, but Krebs believes it is solved by these animals in an entirely different manner. He states that lemmings are nasty and brutal (apparently equaling human beings in this regard) but that instead of committing mass suicide in periods of high population growth, adults take to a vicious and savage killing of the young of other lemmings, probably in an attempt to afford a greater opportunity for their own offspring in the future.[3]

Rolf Peterson describes a similar situation when a high-density wolf population on Isle Royal in Lake Superior began to decimate the moose population there. With a crash in the numbers of moose on this somewhat isolated island, the predators began to kill each other in what is spoken of as interpack warfare until only a few from the different wolf packs were left.[4] There is no such word as *inwolf* in our vocabulary, but in increasingly frequent use today is the term *inhumane*—depicting a cruel and savage person, lacking in pity and kindness. Such behavior is not inconsistent with the manner by which Iraqis have long carried out a concerted effort to decimate the Kurds, who have for centuries lived in the same general area.

And are the recent wars that have taken place on the island of Timor in Indonesia,[5] in Bosnia, and in Rwanda any different?

Holocaust, Gulag, the Rape of Nanking, the "dirty war" in Argentina[6]—such words or phrases bring to mind similar acts of barbarism representative of this tragic flaw in our psychic makeup. One facile way of explaining this deplorable but apparently universal aspect of the human condition comes under the rubric "the survival of the fittest,"[7] where nature is red in fang and claw. It easily follows from this that "might makes right." Those more powerful, in one way or another, than their neighbors inevitably seem to evidence this brutal form of conduct. Attempts are often made to hide, obscure, or deny brutality of this nature, or else these acts are accompanied by excuses or rationalizations. Differences in race, religious persuasion, sex, and wealth provide some of the principal reasons given for instigating such actions. The meager and halting attempts to establish some kind of level playing field in this regard have been, even in our so-called civilized world of today, ineffective and frustrating at best. Devastation and slaughter of human beings cannot help but continue unless something is done to rectify this situation. Exacerbating this dilemma, and overwhelming our poor efforts to overcome it, is the fact that the wealthy, and thus more powerful, get richer faster with every passing day.[8] Thus, until there is somehow a more equitable global distribution of wealth, we can probably expect ongoing or increasing social upheaval. Economists from the time of Adam Smith have addressed this reality, but with few, if any, workable guidelines or suggestions.

What is clearly needed now is not another analysis of this acquired or inherited avaricious characteristic of human beings but first an admission that it certainly exists. Once this step is taken, we can begin with a more "manure-on-the-boots" approach as to what actions might help assure a better future for all. Unfortunately, time seems to be against us here, for as Lester Thurow has pointed out, in connection with what has been happening in the United States (it could just as well be the entire world), "We are presently experiencing a surge in inequality with international competition and feminization of poverty distorting the distribution of income."[9] Behind such ominous and unwelcome pronouncements is a recognition that modern scientific technology—the keystone for optimists—for all its apparent efficiency, seems incapable of providing any immediate solutions. In fact, most new technological innovations imply one or more of the following: an overabundance of waste and pollution, an overlord/subservient relationship between individuals, a full and happy life for only a small minority coupled with a dreary, plodding, desperate level of existence for the majority. In addition, as pointed out by Robert Wright, the increasingly oppressive environment for the swelling numbers of inner-city youth everywhere, from Cairo to Chicago, stimulates a "biology of violence" that makes victims of its young people.[10]

I have on occasion been taken to task for my insistence that these manifold evils are a problem — and that they have plagued us throughout the entire history of humanity. For example, Professor Iltis has long attempted to convert me to the idea that we humans are perhaps programmed to have a special affinity to nature itself.[11] According to Paul Ehrlich in his review of *Biophilia: The Human Bond with Other Species*, E. O. Wilson adopted and further expanded this idea originally expressed by Iltis, Loucks, and Andrews; in *Biophilia*, Wilson contends that we humans have an "innate tendency to focus on life and lifelike processes" and that in this manner we tend "to explore and affiliate with life."[12]

I concur that there has always been an apparent attempt in every culture to ameliorate or at least to curb the brutal aspect of human nature through adherence to the teaching and sayings of philosophers and religious leaders. However, even as we are inundated with talk of the importance of some form of religious belief, either too few now care to truly listen or the message is growing weaker, since human beings do not appear to be, in any manner, becoming kinder and gentler anywhere. Thus, I must reiterate that I am not speaking now of a love of pets, a fondness for visiting national parks, the joys of bird watching, or a multitude of other evidences of our desire to bond with other species. While biophilia may exist in a goodly number of human beings, particularly as it relates to any individual's love of or appreciation for some aspect of our natural surroundings, each day I am convinced that this emotion has little to do with most people's feelings toward other members of our own species, especially if they are slightly different in some respect from ourselves.

Richard Harwood writes of "Death in the 20th Century" and in so doing quotes from many astute observers of the current human condition. All are particularly pessimistic, with philosopher Isaiah Berlin stating that the twentieth century is the most terrible in Western history and Nobel Laureate William Golding insisting that this century has been the most violent in history.[13]

Many centuries ago, Plato addressed this same situation when he argued that in an acquisitive society there is bound to be an increasing exploitation of the poor by the rich coupled with a growing degree of social maladjustment and disunity as a consequence. He painted a picture of a growing oppression fueled by an intensifying bitterness, ending in revolution.[14]

One might ask why we haven't experienced a complete collapse, the result of some form of social or political revolution. To some degree, we must acknowledge that such revolutions have in fact taken place ever since the time of Plato. However, until recently, there were too few humans scattered about to achieve the critical mass required for such a global disaster. We have now arrived at the point where an enormous and upwardly spiraling population coupled with a correspondingly shrinking carrying capacity could easily lead to the chaos of deadly social upheavals — a truly frightening prospect of the future.

Definitions of carrying capacity are too often couched only in human terms — that is, how many people a particular area or ecosystem can provide for or sustain without irreversibly reducing its capacity to support at least equal numbers in the future.[15] Since the emphasis is focused almost exclusively on the welfare of human beings, to the neglect of all else, the true seriousness of the situation is often overlooked or negated. Sooner or later, we must come to the realization that we must protect and sustain all forms of life that are in some manner holistically bound together.

EPILOGUE

To ROUND OUT and complete the overall argument, while still utilizing the Para rubber tree as the symbolic keystone, the importance of a phenomenon known as a "threshold event" or "threshold point" will be described. In the process of tapping a rubber tree, latex, contained in the laticifers located just under the bark, flows from the wound in liquid form. This white, gooey substance will soon react to its new environment by beginning to congeal in a manner similar to that evidenced by other fresh organic fluids that contain protein molecules, such as blood or the white of an egg. As all should know, once an egg, in or out of its shell, is placed in boiling water or otherwise heated, shaken, or agitated, its white, viscous albumen is converted into a rubbery solid, which can never be restored to its original liquid form by any means. In a similar manner, latex will also rapidly and irreversibly coagulate into a hard mass on being subjected to agitation, or on exposure to acids, heat, or smoke.

Both latex and egg white are liquid up to a threshold point, but once that mark is passed they are forever and irreparably altered. What must be understood is that this kind of occurrence is not unique. Some of our most vital environmental components, such as the ozone layer in the upper atmosphere, may rapidly be approaching similarly critical boundaries.[1] If the threshold point is exceeded, as may happen if excessive amounts of anthropogenic pollutants continue to be added to the atmosphere, that vital portion of the earth's habitat could be seriously altered, probably resulting in some form of ecological devastation.

Calamities on an even grander scale, such as stellar novas, are reported to be quite common occurrences throughout the universe.[2] The classic example, for many, of a somewhat similar galactic episode took place some 65 million years ago, when an extraordinary catastrophe (enormous destruction and long periods of darkness) was presumably caused by the impact of a meteor on our planet. One of the principal, and now commonly known, results of this cataclysm was that the longest-lived of all animal families, ranging from individuals of very small size to some of the largest ever to have inhabited the Earth, and certainly the most dominant form of life at that time — the dinosaurs — became extinct. A key aspect of such an event, which all should clearly understand, is that once stable and critical boundaries have been crossed in some manner, there is no opportunity for making excuses and turning back for another try; the affected entity or system will be so inexorably changed that no one, not even the rich and powerful, would be able to bring things back again to prethreshold conditions.

A more commonplace, yet still striking, example of the irreversible consequences of crossing a threshold point is the transmission of HIV from one person to another. The method of exchange — whether through sexual contact, the use of infected needles to inject such drugs as heroin or cocaine, or even the accidental administration of tainted blood — makes no difference here. The effect is the same: once someone is infected, a threshold point is crossed, and the newly affected person will carry the virus until he or she dies from AIDS, for there is apparently nothing yet that can be done to reverse this devastation.

While this extremely serious social as well as health problem has reached epidemic proportions, and is now spreading faster among women than men on a worldwide basis, there was, according to Alan Riding, considerable skepticism that the recent Paris meeting in late 1994 to support a UN plan to combat AIDS would be successful.[3] It would appear that the issue is effectively being spurned and put out of mind by those who are unaffected directly.

Another example of what might be considered a "threshold event" is that which has been taking place with increasing frequency and intensity in the region near Antarctica. It has been reported that many of the citizens of the world's southernmost city, Punta Arenas, situated on the Straits of Magellan in Chile, are grateful for the advice of Bedrich Magas, a professor of electrical engineering there, regarding the best means by which to protect themselves from ultraviolet rays. Due to its proximity to that region just below the annual opening of the ozone layer, which was originally observed only over Antarctica but is now spreading farther north each year, this city is subjected to increasingly unsafe levels of ultraviolet radiation.[4]

Others, however, claim the recommendations of Sr. Magas have no scientific basis and that these rays are damaging only to the tourism sector of the economy. They insist that there is no need to alarm anyone until such time as more hard scientific data are forthcoming.

Granted, there may be nothing we can do to prevent the occurrence of massive galactic episodes, but almost everyone, it would seem, except in very rare instances, has the power to avoid crossing such threshold points as contracting the HIV virus or succumbing to melanomas caused by continual exposure to intense ultraviolet rays. Why, if this is true, do the resulting maladies not only continue to exist but tend to be increasing? Why is it that, once having been informed of the danger of specific actions or the need to take some particular precaution, we continue to ignore, even belittle such warnings? One answer, of course, is that basically no one welcomes unpleasant news in any form, and all would much prefer to listen, instead, to something of a more optimistic nature about the future. While this is obviously an ostrichlike approach to life, involving some degree of denial, even the more astute among us yearns to see a silver lining in the storm clouds on the horizon.

The political economist Robert Heilbroner describes how some of the more sagacious economists of the first half of the century, including John Maynard Keynes, Joseph Schumpeter, Wassily Leontief, Adolph Berle, Gardiner Means, and John Kenneth Galbraith, in their analyses of the present economic situation, generally began by agreeing that growth through capitalism, despite periodic slumps and bursts, appeared to be on a more or less continual upward curve. Heilbroner even suggested that "Keynes saw ahead nothing less than Adam Smith's heralded land of universal plenty."[5] Interestingly, all of this optimistic economic analysis was taking place during a time of terribly destructive world wars and global economic crises. It must be pointed out, however, that in the end the most universal consensus of this group was that (a) although this economic system had indeed raised a good number of us to a standard of living exceeding what most before had even dreamed of, (b) this could not continue, and (c) in less than half a century, the traditional fabric of capitalism would be completely destroyed. In fact, Schumpeter, summarizing the feelings of these economists, stated in reply to a question as to whether capitalism could survive. "No, I do not think it can."

It is not so much a question of whether capitalism would wither and die or whether socialism would replace it; indeed, the economic system first described by Adam Smith is hardly recognizable today. Originally, one of the key facets of this system was that competition in the market benefited the consumer. Today the individual purchaser of goods and services is as much ignored by the producers as the voter is by the politician, who, once in power, tends to act like a lord and no longer a public servant. In both cases, every effort is made not only to bend the needs and desires of the consumer/voter to favor the producer/politician but also, at the same time, to cause or induce the former to feel pleased with, or at least acquiesce in, what is taking place.

We often look to Voltaire as one who recognized humans' gullibility and complaisance when he proposed in *Candide* that even in the face of such major calamities as devastating volcanic eruptions, there was always a Dr. Pangloss somewhere among us who would insist, in an almost blasé fashion, that "all is for the best in this best of all possible worlds."[6] Voltaire was, of course, quite correct, and even today there seems always to be someone who will attempt to follow in the steps of his eternally optimistic protagonist. Unfortunately, these later mimics usually perform this role to promote themselves, rather than to assist or inform others, although doomsayers are often self-promoters as well.

In the early 1970's, for example, John Maddox, perhaps basing his thoughts on the early pronouncements of the very economists just mentioned, took to task, in his book *The Doomsday Syndrome*, such people as Paul Ehrlich, Barry Commoner, and "other prophets of ecological disaster" for predicting the many dangers that lay ahead for humankind. Among the various statements Maddox made to discount a number of people as "Doomsdayers" was that there was no need to worry about such problems as famine in the future since, owing to modern scientifically based agriculture, there would be no possibility of such occurring during the next several generations.[7]

It is unfortunate and disturbing that this scientist, until recently the editor of the journal *Nature*, could have made such an error in predicting future events. In this connection, I wonder how he deals with this matter now, for he surely must be aware that millions of people have indeed starved to death, particularly in Asia and Africa, as the result of serious famine, since the time of his predictions. He may have recanted on this point, but if so, I am unaware of it.

In the very next decade, it was a gentleman named Julian Simon who decided to award himself this Panglossian mantle. He was even audacious enough to insist that we were then being subjected to an oversupply of false, bad news about the earth's resources, population, and environment[8] — thus clearly fitting Brecht's definition of an optimist as a person who has not yet *heard* the bad news. And just as with Maddox in the previous decade, Simon, too, had and has his followers — those content to listen to him rather than to a growing group of scientists and investigators who by no means adhere to Simon's philosophy of optimism, indeed completely oppose it. The last time I heard Simon speak on these matters, which was about 10 years after he had first proposed this point of view, the feeling that came to me was one of pity for him and those who still think as he does, for the manner in which they have exposed their ignorance.

Now, in the decade of the 1990's, the latest example of someone who has decided he can have his cake and eat it too is a journalist named Gregg Easterbrook,[9] who cunningly walks the fence by decrying, on the one hand, the manner by which environmentalists argue their case while agreeing, on the other hand, with only that which is both politically correct and of an optimistic outlook on such matters. Unfortunately, in this entire debate, he demonstrates a lack of knowledge about this subject, and his arguments evidence confusion and perplexity. While he did mention the problem of disease as a clear and present problem for humankind in the future, this is by no means a new or startling discovery. Easterbrook's presentation would have been sounder had he simply acknowledged that many others had previously called attention to this matter, instead of attempting to claim it as his own. Since disease was one of the blocks to population increase proposed by Malthus,[10] it leaves one to ponder whether Easterbrook had ever read Malthus, or, if he had, understood the implication of one of the principal Malthusian impediments to population increase — the ravage of disease. Strangely, since this matter of disease was one of his major points, Easterbrook did not even cite Malthus nor others who have more recently pointed out how such epidemics as AIDS and now, once again, tuberculosis are causing such serious and increasing devastation to human populations throughout the world.[11]

Easterbrook's one clear aim seems to have been to make a name for himself as yet another champion for "this best of all possible worlds." He so obviously wants the glory of having been the one to slay the dragon of a gloomy future, one wonders how he must feel after reading what others have said about his book. For example, a review by Peter Raven, director of the Missouri Botanical Garden, states, "But Gregg Easterbrook concealing his know-nothingness under the guise of 'ecorealism' offers a much more effective poison pill to those who are either poorly informed about the areas he treats so superficially or those who are simply anxious to forget about them as rapidly as possible. As the world's productive systems slowly disintegrate, he, like his more bellicose colleagues, must take a share of the responsibility for the false counsel that he offers here to his fellow passengers on the down escalator." [12]

The few who take the time to seriously and honestly analyze the host of predicaments in which we now find ourselves certainly do not demonstrate such sanguine attitudes and instead appear to be quite pessimistic about our future. [13] The majority, on the other hand, who apparently do not understand or are unconcerned with the implications of what is taking place, evidence little anxiety with the big picture, since they are far too preoccupied with their mundane, daily struggle to scrounge a living in the face of ever-decreasing resources. This limitation of individual choice and freedom is, naturally, exacerbated by a skyrocketing growth in human population. It is also affected by modern technology, which, in a relatively short period of time, has ostensibly reduced the amount of space between people. As a result, enormous numbers are now being driven by a variety of pressures to abandon their traditional homelands and migrate and penetrate into every possible nook and cranny of the Earth, looking for a better life — or, at least, a less dismal and oppressive one. Is this surge of refugees and emigrants a premonitory indication that we are fast approaching another threshold point? [14]

These disturbing changes, by whatever name, are now the cause of serious disruptions and hardships not only to human beings everywhere, but also to our different sociopolitical systems and, of greater importance, to the earth's natural environment itself. The almost contemptuous attitude displayed by far too many optimists is accentuated by the crass manner by which we treat the very habitat that sustains us. Referring to a rather similar situation, Bob Herbert of the *New York Times* calls us "a nation of nitwits" and points out that if ignorance is bliss, we in the United States must be a deliriously happy lot.[15]

Three distinct views of our ignorant and selfish behavior toward nature appear in the Winter 1996 issue of the *Amicus Journal*. The first, by Donella Meadows, suggests that "some members of Congress think we should sell off National Parks to balance the budget. We owners had better wake up." In the second, Karl Hess, Jr., and Johanna Wald aver that we are in the process of eating our land away and that "thanks to the wisdom of federal policy, the use to which western public lands are put favors the one thing Americans want least from them: subsidized cows." Finally, Will Nixon points out how the Arctic Wildlife Refuge, which may be headed for additional oil exploration and its possible detriment to wildlife there, also protects people.[16] In a similar vein, and with a sense of urgency mixed with a touch of despondency, Thomas E. Lovejoy states, elsewhere, "The real challenge is how we as biologists can create a sense of urgency about biological diversity, climatic change, and human population growth."[17]

Simply on a nationwide scale, just in the United States, these matters will undoubtedly and unfortunately provide the basis for continuing confrontation. For example, as Stephen Engelberg points out, lawyers from Georgia-Pacific, one of the world's largest wood products companies, have been closeted with Republican staff members in the Senate Office Building in an effort to rewrite current environmental laws for the benefit not of the nation but of this industry and especially this one particular company.[18] One may well wonder why these lawmakers, having obviously abandoned their role as public servants, were not sensible enough in this endeavor to have also sought the help of professional foresters who are not exclusively from the private sector.

This form of behavior over the short run has caused a wide range of people — from Stanford ecologist Paul Ehrlich to Eduard Shevardnadze, former foreign secretary of the Soviet Union, two of the more astute analysts of the current dilemmas we are in — to be pessimistic about what they observe going on around them.[19] Some even believe that ours could be one of the many species headed for extinction. These assertions, which echo the anxiety of the Union of Concerned Scientists referred to in the

Preface, suggest that the light at the end of the tunnel is not evidence of our approach to a bountiful Eden but rather the headlight of a locomotive barreling down the track in our direction. This general concern, coupled with the consensus of a number of the economists mentioned above, is summed up even more strongly by Robert Heilbroner, who wrote, "If then, by the question 'is there hope for man?', we ask whether it is possible to meet the challenges of the future without the payment of a fearful price, the answer must be: no, there is no such hope."[20]

One would think that it should now be quite obvious that we face a grim future, even based only on what is taking place today in many regions where growing numbers are seeking, even demanding, a more equitable share of the public weal, urged on by a complete sense of despair and frustration. Some, we are becoming aware, have decided to wait no longer and are taking matters into their own hands. What is most worrisome is that, thanks in part to modern technology itself, a growing number of these individuals and factions in different parts of the world now possess many of the deadly tools with which to accomplish their aims by engaging in terrorism, with little or no compunction. The intensity of these social breakdowns increases with population growth, and a principal and major victim in each case is the natural environment.

Many ridicule these concerns about overpopulation and suggest that, on the contrary, greater numbers of people will be the key to stimulating demand for more sophisticated and efficient schemes for the communication of information and ideas as well as the production and transfer of goods and services. Larger human populations would, they argue, so improve the world's standard of living that it could afford any form of science and technology required to deal with any problem, including environmental challenges. For example, in 1987, when she was chairman of the World Commission on Environment and Development as well as prime minister of Norway, Gro Harlem Brundtland stated: "The commission found no absolute limits to growth. Limits are indeed imposed by the impact of present technologies and social organization on the biosphere, but we have the ingenuity to change."[21] This same person, it should be pointed out, announced to the entire world only five years later that despite being a signatory to the International Whaling Commission, Norway would negate its promise and begin hunting whales again, since food was becoming a limited commodity in her country.[22] Of course, to a certain degree it may be argued that this approach in itself demonstrates a form of ingenuity — but probably not the kind of which one might be proud.

Because of the uncertainty that faces us, we are left with a monumental number of decisions as to what to do next. One approach to the matter, as suggested by Jesse H. Ausubel, director of studies for the Carnegie Commission on Science, Technology and Government, is that since we may be worrying too much about what may happen in the future, we should hold off for the moment. In his analysis of the conflict between technology and people, which is aggravated by such factors as increases in greenhouse-gas concentrations in the atmosphere, Ausubel utilized EPA data to advocate waiting until we have more and sounder data on which to make decisions. The scenario he uses further indicates that by waiting we will also have a stronger economy, including per capita incomes of $150,000 or more in the United States and $35,600 on a global basis by the year 2100, which would provide us with the necessary funds to rectify any problem that might face us at that time.[23]

With the world still mired in a morass of problems and difficulties, which a great many self-styled prophets erroneously predicted (hoped?) would by now have long since been behind us, can we seriously base our future on pipe dreams such as Ausubel's? While he is neither a professional economist nor an ecologist, his argument, presented in a serious journal and including eight separate hypotheses, encompasses a great deal from both disciplines. In this, the overall presentation has a strong ring of what Wassily Leontief, a Nobel laureate in economics, speaks of as "academic economics." In an analysis of articles published during two different time periods in the *American Economic Review*, Professor Leontief points out that over 50 percent of the papers were based on mathematical models that had no data to substantiate them. This is not a recent phenomenon, for, as was suggested almost 20 years ago by G. H. Borts, the trend is for more articles on mathematical economics and fewer of a more empirical, policy-oriented, or problem-solving character.[24] (It must be pleasant to have a well-paying position that permits one to sit in some fancy office surrounded by the latest technological gadgets, far removed from most of the world's grubby, down-to-earth enigmas, and pontificate on matters that may affect the lives of millions of people.) In this, we should remember that, as George Bernard Shaw once said, you can place all of the world's economists (or the abundant papers they write) end to end and never reach a conclusion.

It is not my intent to belittle Ausubel's entire essay, for some of its content is of interest; however, I must point out that in one of his principal hypotheses he chose to ignore the dangers of utilizing either unsubstantiated or unrealistic data (which he himself had cautioned against) to justify his arguments. It is my contention that by including no sound experimental facts and instead referring to dubious projections of what might occur in the future, Ausubel not only engages in fallacious reasoning, but seriously damages the entire environmental position as well. To simply accept optimistic estimates for the future as fact without questioning them or offering any justification for this rosy view undermines his entire position. The possibility of such an unbelievably glorious future (of which only an extremely small percentage of those alive today may even hope to get a glimpse) is now and will for some time be held in check by the enormous U.S. national debt, forced ever upward by entitlement programs, as well as by as its gigantic trade imbalance. One may also wonder whether the figures for the per capita income of $150,000 for Americans were in 1991 dollars or in some devalued future dollar hardly worth the name. To counsel that, based on the information given, "waiting is our best policy" is like building a house on sand in a flood plain and hoping no storm will come. This approach, of course, closely parallels that adopted by ever so many people who when first conscious of a lump in the breast or difficulty in urinating opt against having a mammogram or a prostate biopsy and hope and wish all the while that ignoring these serious symptoms will make them go away.

There are on the market today literally hundreds of books and articles from which we may choose in an effort to determine how best to deal with any particular aspect of the multitude of environmental problems that face us. I do not mean to include in this group offerings from the 50 Simple Things You Can Do to Save the Earth genre.[25] The rise of this book on various best-seller lists was meteoric, clearly demonstrating the desire of many to avail themselves of a simple guide to rectifying such difficulties. That its popularity did not last long was basically due to its almost frivolous approach, being full of glib and childish solutions. Far too many similar efforts are now being paraded before us — each advocating some facile means of how to do our bit to "save our planet."

Of course, by far the easiest road ahead would be simply to do nothing but listen to the seductive siren songs of the more optimistic among us that we will all live wonderful lives in the bountiful world of the future. But recall that the chief intent of the songs of the beautiful mythological figures, perched high up on the fogbound rocks by the sea, was to induce mariners, by means of illusory promises, to come close enough that they would be dashed by high waves and treacherous currents to their deaths.

NOTES

Preface

1. Constance Holden, "Scientists' Campaign to Save Earth," *Science* 258 (1992): 1433.

2. As but a small sample of such threatening warnings, I submit the following: Barry Lopez, *Arctic Dreams* (New York: Scribners, 1986); Paul Kennedy, *Preparing for the Twenty-first Century* (New York: Vintage, 1993); Laurie Garrett, *The Coming Plague: Newly Emerging Diseases in a World Out of Balance* (New York: Farrar, Straus and Giroux, 1994); R. D. Kaplan, "The Coming Anarchy," *Atlantic Monthly*, February 1994, pp. 44–76.

3. For more on fraud in labeling, see Julie Hauserman, "Degradable Trash Bags a Gimmick, Firms Admit," *Wisconsin State Journal* (Madison), 25 September 1989. Ms. Hauserman states that this is "just a marketing tool!" Sen. Frank Lautenberg (D.-N.J.) claims that many "safe" products harm the environment; see his op-ed piece, "Pulling the 'Green' over Our Eyes," *New York Times*, 22 April 1991. In addition, see John Holusha, "Coming Clean on Products: Ecological Claims Faulted," *New York Times*, 12 March 1991; and Herbert Burkholz, "A Shot in the Arm for the F.D.A.," *New York Times Magazine*, 30 June 1991.

4. Genesis 1:28.

5. It was Winston Churchill who said something to the effect that democracy was not a very satisfactory political system — only the best we have been able to come up with to date. The sticking point seems to be that we can't have a democratic society without serious participation by a well-informed public. Alexis de Tocqueville was concerned about the tyranny of the masses; Spinoza was troubled that if men become enslaved by their ignorance, uninformed freedom of choice would lead to disaster; and H. L. Mencken so feared mass ignorance or the stupidity of the herd that he referred to democracy as the dictatorship of the "booboisie."

6. A good example of competitiveness in academia is that by Edward Hoagland who wrote, following the treatment he received at what many consider a rather liberal institution of higher learning, Bennington College, that "academic politics, so often a mess of razor cuts and rabbit punches, has become a tank trap lately." This essay on political correctness appeared on the op-ed page of the *New York Times* of 15 June 1991.

Outside of academia, however, the best example of this sort of arrogant, disingenuous, and basically self-serving presentation of a seriously flawed argument is that to be found in *The Bell Curve*, by Richard J. Herrenstein and Charles Murray (New York: Free Press, 1994). One might hope that such a review as that by Stephen Jay Gould in the 28 November 1994 issue of the *New Yorker* would be more than sufficient to put this dangerous proposition to rest. Unfortunately, however, it may linger with us as part of the problem.

1. A Symbol of Our Environmental Dilemma

1. *Rubber Developments*, a quarterly journal of the Malaysian Rubber Research and Development Board, has concentrated for many years on providing accurate, technical and up-to-date information on a variety of new uses and innovations in the field of natural rubber. Those interested in almost any aspect of natural rubber would do well to begin by reviewing the last few years of this journal.

2. For further reading on the Chico Mendes story, the following are suggested: Alex Schoumatoff, *The World Is Burning* (Boston: Little, Brown & Company, 1990; 377 pp., illustrated); also, Andrew Revkin, *The Burning Season: The Murder of Chico Mendes and the Fight for the Amazon Rain Forest* (Boston: Houghton Mifflin Company, 1990; 317 pp.) In his review of the latter, in *Nature* 346 (30 August 1990), Alun Anderson states, "Attention paid to his death was not fully comprehensible:—after all, Mendes was the forty-ninth rural activist to be killed in the Amazon that year." In addition to these it should be noted that the television movie *The Burning Season*, directed by John Frankenheimer and starring Raul Julia, which opened on HBO during the early fall of 1994, has attracted considerable attention to this incident.

3. Britt Robson, "The Day the Earth Stood Still," *Mpls, St. Paul*, April 1991, p. 41. In a commemoration of Earth Day, the author argues for collective commitment and willpower to overcome an economy that continues to reward waste and fails to discourage large-scale pollution.

4. William Safire, "Earth Day's 'Planetism,'" *New York Times*, 16 April 1990. In attempting to belittle the ideas of Earth Day, this columnist and former political speech writer for Richard Nixon clearly demonstrates that he is far beyond his depth when attempting to discuss environmental matters. His final point is that we should put a higher value on growth than on limitation and to emphasize this statement he claims that "Malthus was mistaken; the world can produce and then feed and shelter billions of human beings." It is somewhat pathetic to read that this self-confessed atrocious prognosticator of future events seriously suggested that "in a century or two our descendants will be coordinating with the colonists whooping it up for Mars Day and Venus Day." Mr. Safire should, as Pliny the Elder suggested, *ne supra crepidam sutor judicaret* or stick to his last of wordsmanship, at which, I believe, he is rather good.

5. Roper Poll, 1990.

6. Linda DeStefano, "Looking Ahead to the Year 2000: No Utopia but Most Expect a Better Life," *Gallop Poll Monthly* 292 (January 1990); Graham Hueber, "Americans Report High Levels of Environmental Concern and Activity," *Gallup Poll* 20 (April 1991).

7. Enzo R. Grilli, Barbara Bennett Agostini, and Maria J. 't Hooft-Welvaars, *The World Rubber Economy*, World Bank Staff Occasional Papers No. 30 (Baltimore: Johns Hopkins University Press, 1980).

8. Bruce F. Greek, "Rubber Demand Is Expected to Grow after 1991," *Chemical & Engineering News*, 13 May 1991. According to this special edition devoted to rubber, it is claimed that producers expected no growth that year but foresaw an upturn in 1992, which was certainly the case.

2. The Para Rubber Tree

1. For more on the expedition to South America by Charles-Marie de La Condamine, see J. Donald Fernie, "The Shape of the Earth," *American Scientist* 79, 2 (1991): 108–110, 79; 5 (1991): 393–395.

2. Vicki Baum, *The Weeping Wood* (Garden City, N.Y.: Doubleday, Doran & Co., 1943).

3. Ciba Review, *Rubber* (Basel, Switzerland.: Ciba Limited, 1951).

4. Russell J. Seibert, "A Study of *Hevea* (with Its Economic Prospects) in the Republic of Peru," *Annals of the Missouri Botanical Garden* 34 (1947): 261.

5. Richard E. Schultes, "The Amazon Indian and Evolution in *Hevea* and Related Genera" (with 4 plates), *Journal of the Arnold Arboretum* 37, 2 (1956): 123–147; Richard E. Schultes, "The Taming of Wild Rubber," *Horticulture*, 7 November 1976.

6. A. A. Milne, *The World of Christopher Robin* (New York: E. P. Dutton & Co., 1958), p. 128.

7. Robert Friedel, "Crazy about Rubber," *Invention & Technology*, Winter 1990, pp. 44–49.

8. P. W. Allen, *Natural Rubber and the Synthetics* (New York: John Wiley and Sons, Inc., 1972).

9. The incredibly inhumane treatment of laborers in the Belgian Congo during the nineteenth century is well described by Jeremy Bernstein in his review of three books by Henry Morgan Stanley (of "Dr. Livingston, I presume" fame). This was written under the heading "The Dark Continent of Henry Stanley" in the 31 December 1990 issue of the *New Yorker*.

10. Warren Dean, *Brazil and the Struggle for Rubber* (London: Cambridge University Press, 1987).

11. Henry A. Wickham, *Rough Notes of a Journey through the Wilderness from Trinidad to Para, Brazil by Way of the Great Cataracts of the Orinoco, Atabapo and Rio Negro* (London, 1872); Henry A. Wickham, *On the Plantation, Cultivation and Curing of Para Indian Rubber* (London, 1908).

12. P. W. Barker and E. G. Holt, *Rubber: History, Production and Manufacture*, U.S. Department of Commerce, Trade Promotion Series No. 209 (Washington, D.C.: Government Printing Office, 1940).

13. W. E. Klippert, *Reflections of a Rubber Planter* (Akron: W. E. Klippert, Peninsula Press, 1971). In this connection, it could also be pointed out that in the book *Kew Gardens for Science and Pleasure*, ed. F. Nigel Hepper (Owings Mills, Md.: Stemmer House, 1982), p. 131, the statement is made that "the true story of this enterprise [transfer of rubber seeds from Brazil] has been wildly distorted."

14. P. J. S. Cramer, *Review of Literature of Coffee Research in Indonesia*, Inter-American Institute of Agricultural Research, Miscellaneous Bulletin 15 (Turrialba, Costa Rica, 1957).

15. F. L. Wellman, *Coffee* (London: Leonard Hill, 1961).

16. J. W. Purseglove, *Tropical Crops: Dicotyledons* (New York: John Wiley and Sons, 1968), vol. 1.

17. Ernest P. Imle, "*Hevea* Rubber—Past and Future," *Economic Botany* 32 (1978): 264–277.

18. Allen M. Young, personal communication, 1993.

19. Robert Dressler, personal communication, 1992.

20. O. F. Cook, "Naming the Cultivated Rubber Tree *Siphonia ridleyana*," *Journal of the Washington Academy of Science* 31, 2 (1941): 46–65.

21. Carl D. La Rue, *The Hevea Rubber Tree in the Amazon Valley*, USDA Department Bulletin No. 1422 (Washington, D.C.: Government Printing Office, 1926).

22. Purseglove, *Tropical Crops: Dicotyledons* 1: 152.

23. Joseph Conrad, *Lord Jim* (New York: Doubleday & Co., 1899); W. Somerset Maugham, *Collected Short Stories*, vol. 4 (Harmondsworth, Middlesex, England: Penguin Books, 1963).

3. Natural to Synthetic

1. Harvey S. Firestone, Jr., *The Romance and Drama of the Rubber Industry* (Akron: Firestone Tire and Rubber Company, 1932).

2. Loren McIntyre, "Jari: A Billion-Dollar Gamble," *National Geographic*, May 1980.

3. L. G. Polhamus, *Rubber: Botany, Production and Utilization* (London: Hill, 1962).

4. Imle, "*Hevea* Rubber—Past and Future."

5. National Academy of Sciences, *Guayule* (Washington, D.C.: National Academy of Sciences, 1977).

6. Harry J. Fuller, "War-time Rubber Exploitation in Tropical America," *Economic Botany* 5, 4 (1951): 311–337. In this, Fuller states that so far as production is concerned, *H. brasiliensis* is by far the best, that *H. benthamiana* is a poor second, and that all other species fall far below this level.

7. Harry L. Fisher, "Rubber," *Scientific American*, November 1956.

8. Peter J. T. Morris, *The American Synthetic Rubber Research Program* (Philadelphia: University of Pennsylvania Press, 1989).

9. James Brooke, "For the Rubber Soldiers of Brazil, Rubber Checks," *New York Times*, 15 May 1991.

10. Dean, *Brazil and the Struggle for Rubber*.

11. W. E. Klippert, *The Cultivation of* Hevea *Rubber on Small Plantations* (Washington, D.C.: USDA, 1946).

12. P. E. Hurley, personal communication, 1991.

13. From a memorandum of U.S. Tire and Exhaust Co. of Combined Locks, Wisconsin, to its distributors, dated 30 January 1995.

4. Dream the Impossible Dream?

1. Holden, "Scientists' Campaign to Save Earth."

2. Colin Tudge, "The State of Rubber," *New Scientist*, 9 July 1981. Tudge poses the following question: "In rubber, Malaysia has an endlessly renewable resource with a guaranteed world market. All it needs to do is to produce more and more. Can it?"

3. E. P. Imle, W. E. Manis, Edilberto Camacho, and C. N. Hittle, *Permanent Mixed Crops for the Atlantic Zone in Costa Rica* (Turrialba, Costa Rica: USDA Regional Rubber Research Program, November 1953).

4. W. A. Rahaman, "Natural Rubber as a Natural Commodity," *Rubber Developments* 47, 1–2 (1994): 13–16.

5. Regis Miller of the U.S. Forest Products Laboratory in Madison, Wisconsin, informed me that the wood of the Para rubber tree has been well developed and promoted in Southeast Asia. As in the case of other species, this wood is of mixed quality. According to Dr. Miller, this is due in part to treatment applied after felling the trees which could favor the growth of a fungus that can cause "blue streak" in this species, resulting in an unwanted discoloration. This species also is equal to birch and maple so far as producing good-quality pulp. This is especially true when trees of the same clone are used, as is the case with most of the pulp from the eucalyptus grown in Brazil. Although rubber has short fibers, these are uniform in length and there are few fines, since all trees in a plantation are clones or sisters of each other.

6. Hurley, personal communication, 1991.

7. Noel Perrin, *A Reader's Delight* (Hanover, N.H.: Printed for Dartmouth College by the University Press of New England, 1988).

8. International Paper Company, "Everything You Need to Know about Recycling," advertisement, *New Yorker*, 13 November 1995, pp. 2–3; and Georgia-Pacific, "Forests," advertisement, *New Yorker*, 20 November 1995, p. 35.

9. M. A. Weaver, "Letter to Bangladesh," *New Yorker*, 12 September 1994, pp. 48–61.

10. Philip Shabecoff, "Bush Wants Billions of Trees for War against Polluted Air," *New York Times* (National Edition), 28 January 1989, p. 1.

11. Barbara Bush, *Barbara Bush: A Memoir* (New York: Charles Scribner's Sons, 1994).

12. P. E. Hurley, personal communication, 1992.

13. Ibid.

5. Disappearing Jungles—and Forests

1. René Dubos, *Man Adapting* (New Haven: Yale University Press, 1980), p. 267.

2. Joseph W. Meeker, whose 1973 book *The Spheres of Life: An Introduction to World Ecology* (New York: Charles Scribner's Sons) addresses many of the points raised in this discussion, originally pointed out this dilemma when he wrote of the person who did so much harm to humankind by helping populations to soar by ostensibly doing all of us so much good: Louis Pasteur.

3. Editorial, "The Burning of Rondonia," *New York Times*, 29 August 1988. This condemnation of what has been taking place in Brazil is based on a number of sources including Robert Repetto of the World Resources Institute. Repetto indicated that cattle ranchers, who are responsible for 80 percent of the destruction, receive sizable tax breaks without which their enterprises are inherently uneconomic. The editorial goes on to say that besides the ranchers, half a million settlers have invaded the Rondonian forest along the new Cuiaba – Porto Velho road, newly paved with a $250 million World Bank loan.

4. More recently, according to the article by Diana Jean Schemo, "Brazil Chief Moves to Take Land for Poor," *New York Times*, 13 November 1995, p. A-4, this country has been attempting, without much success, to calm tensions between homesteaders and landholders by providing land for the growing numbers of those without. *See also* Marlise Simons, "In Brazil, a Gold Rush like None Before," *New York Times*, 25 April 1988.

5. James Brooke, "Gold's Lure vs. Indian Rights: A Brazilian Conflict Sets the Amazon Aflame," *New York Times*, 21 January 1990.

6. Thomas L. Friedman, "The World Bank, 50 Years Old, Plots a New Course and Vows to Do Better," *New York Times*, 24 July 1994, p. Y-8.

7. Marlise Simons, "The Smelter's Price: Jungle in Ashes," *New York Times*, 28 May 1987.

8. Marlise Simons, "Brazil Wants Its Dams, but at What Cost?" *New York Times*, 12 March 1989.

9. Nathaniel C. Nash, "Bolivia's Rain Forest Falls to Relentless Exploiters," *New York Times*, 21 June 1993, pp. A-1, A-6.

10. An enjoyable yet informative novel that deals with the problem of the impact of missionaries on Amazonian Indians is Peter Matthiessen's *At Play in the Fields of the Lord* (New York: Random House, 1965).

11. James Brooke, "For an Amazon Indian Tribe, Civilization Brings Mostly Disease and Death," *New York Times*, 24 December 1989.

12. "Playing with Fire — Torching the Amazon," *Time*, cover story, 18 September 1989.

13. H. Jeffrey Leonard, "Environmental Hysteria Could Well Further Amazonian Destruction," *Wall Street Journal*, 16 October 1987.

14. Roger Lewin, "A Mass Extinction without Asteroids," *Science* 234 (1986): 14–15. Another article on this same subject is that by Jared Diamond in the April 1990 issue of *Discover* titled "Playing with Megadeath," in which he suggests that "the odds are good that we will exterminate half the world's species within the next century."

15. In this connection see Herman Daly, "Sustainable Development: From Concept and Theory towards Operational Principles," *Population and Development* (Hoover Institution Conference, 1989); Donald Ludwig, Ray Hilborn, and Carl Walters, "Uncertainty, Resource Exploitation, and Conservation: Lessons from History," *Science* 260 (1993): 17–18, in which the authors state, "Because past resource exploitation has seldom been sustainable, any new plan should be suspect"; and Bill Willers, "Sustainable Development: A New World Deception," *Conservation Biology* 8, 4 (1994): 1146–1148.

16. Fox Butterfield, "Maine Timber Shortage Is Seen by the Year 2000," *New York Times*, 24 October 1984.

17. Page Stegner, "Let It Be Woods," *Sierra* 76, 5 (1984): 54–61, 98.

18. S. L. Solheim, W. S. Alverson, and D. M. Waller, "Maintaining Biotic Diversity in National Forests: The Necessity for Large Blocks of Mature Forest," *Endangered Species* 4, 6 (June 1987); W. S. Alverson, D. M. Waller, and S. L. Solheim, "Forests Too Dear: Edge Effects in Northern Wisconsin," *Conservation Biology* 2, 4 (1988): 348–358; W. S. Alverson, D. M. Waller, and W. Kuhlmann, *Wild Forests: Conservation Biology and Public Policy* (Washington, D.C.: Island Press, 1994).

19. Raymond P. Guries and Jeffrey C. Stier, "Columnist Missed Point of Rainforest Ruling," *Capital Times* (Madison, Wis.), 15 March 1994.

20. Walter Kuhlmann, "A Biological Attack on Timber Primacy: Suing for Biological Diversity in the Wisconsin National Forests," *Forest Watch* 11, 1 (July 1990): 15–21.

21. Timothy Egan, "With Fate of the Forests at Stake, Power Saws and Arguments Echo," *New York Times*, 20 March 1989; John G. Mitchell, "War in the Woods: West Side Story," *Audubon*, January 1990, pp. 82–121.

22. Catherine Caufield, "The Ancient Forests," *New Yorker*, 14 May 1990.

23. Tom Wicker, "Stripping America's Forests," *New York Times*, 21 March 1989. Later that same year, an editorial in the *New York Times* of 20 September 1989, with the headline "Forest Murder: Ours or Theirs?" stated in part, "In 1947, Congress authorized the Forest Service to sign 50-year contracts with timber companies that promised to build pulp mills and create jobs. In exchange the Forest Service would guarantee the mills a steady supply of Tongass lumber at low prices. In 1980 Senator Ted Stevens fought successfully to lock in the deal. The pulp mills, one Japanese-owned, have been able to buy Tongass timber at prices averaging about $2 per 1,000 feet. The same timber, depending on quality, would fetch from $200 to $600 on the open market. In effect, the Forest Service has been selling 500-year-old trees for about the price of a cheeseburger. The Forest Service recovers only a fraction of the subsidy, which costs the taxpayers about $40 million a year.

"The companies note they'll pay higher prices under new contracts. But the prices will still be way below market. Alaska's Congressmen say the subsidy secures 1,500 jobs. But it would be cheaper just to pay each logger $35,000 a year — and it would protect the environment besides."

In this same connection, on 18 March 1991 the *Idaho Post Register* published a seven-part Special Edition on the problem of resource utilization with the title "Endangered Species."

24. Nancy Langston, *Forest Dreams, Forest Nightmares: The Paradox of Old Growth in the Inland West* (Seattle: University of Washington Press, 1995; 368 pp., illustrated).

25. Timothy Egan, "Oregon, Foiling Forecasters, Thrives as It Protects Owls," *New York Times*, 11 October 1994, pp. A-1, C-20.

26. Uli Schmetzer, "China's Bureaucratic Ax Chops Forest, Way of Life," *Chicago Tribune*, 30 April 1991.

27. Vaclav Smil, *China's Environmental Crisis: An Inquiry into the Limits of National Development* (Armonk, N.Y.: Sharpe, 1993).

28. John C. Ryan, "War and Teaks in Burma," *World Watch* 3, 5 (September–October 1990): 8–9; Steven Erlanger, "Burmese Teak Forest Falls to Pay for Border War," *New York Times*, 9 December 1990; Denis D. Gray, "Loggers Threaten Last Thai Forest," *Capital Times* (Madison, Wis.), 6 April 1988.

29. Catherine Caufield, "Pioneers of the Outer Islands," *Natural History* 3 (1984): 22–36; W. David Kubiak, "In Sarawak the Sky Is Falling," *Japan Environment Monitor* 3, 4 (July 1990).

30. Stan Sesser, "Logging the Rain Forest," *New Yorker*, 27 May 1991, pp. 42–67.

31. Marcus Colchester, "Guatemala: The Clamour for Land and the Fate of the Forests," *The Ecologist* 21, 4 (July–August 1991): 177–185.

32. Jon R. Luoma, "In Wisconsin, a Debate over Ways to Manage National Forest Growth," *New York Times*, 18 October 1988.

33. Donald M. Waller, "Testimony before the Subcommittee on Agricultural Research, Conservation, Forestry and General Legislation," *Wisconsin Academic Review*, Spring 1994, pp. 14–18.

34. John H. Cushman, Jr., "Panel Recommends Virtual End to Fishing Fleet in Georges Bank," *New York Times*, 27 October 1994, pp. A-1, A-14.

35. Garrett Hardin, "Limits to Growth Are Nature's Own," *Insight* 9, 51 (1993): 23–25.

36. Sallie Tisdale, "In the Northwest," *New Yorker*, 26 August 1991, pp. 51–52+.

37. Jerry Franklin, "Regional Management of Pacific Northwest Streams and Rivers," public lecture, University of Wisconsin, Madison, 23 September 1994.

38. Clive Ponting, *A Green History of the World* (London: Sinclair-Stevenson, 1991; 432 pp.). This was reviewed by Simon Fairlie in *The Ecologist* 21, 4 (July–August 1991).

39. John Perlin, *A Forest Journey: The Role of Wood in the Development of Civilization* (Cambridge: Harvard University Press, 1991).

40. Paul Johnson, *The Rise and Fall of the Great Powers: Economic Change and Military Conflict from 1500 to 2000* (New York: Random House, 1987), p. 675.

41. A final note in this continuing bitter debate was brought on by Mark Rey, executive director of the American Forest Resource Alliance, in a letter to the *New York Times* of 23 October 1991. In this letter he claimed, basing his argument on extremely questionable statements, that "our forests are not being overcut." He was quickly taken to task by a Mr. Eric D. Lemelson of Sherwood, Oregon, in his letter to the *Times* of 2 November 1991, in which he states, "If timber harvest levels aren't being met, it's because they were set at levels that the Forest Service, no champion of the environment, now admits are not sustainable." He adds, "Champions of the large timber companies also conveniently fail to mention that much of the Federal timber they cut in the last decade was shipped raw to Japan, thereby taking precious processing jobs away from Americans."

6. Jungle Myths and Tall Timber Tales

1. Oscar Wilde, "The Ballad of Reading Gaol," *Poems* (Oxford: Woodstock, 1994).

2. "Taxol Updated," *Nature Conservancy*, January–February 1991, p. 13.

3. Keith W. Witherup et al., "*Taxus* spp. Needles Contain Amounts of Taxol Comparable to the Bark of *Taxus brevifolia*: Analysis and Isolation," *Journal of Natural Products* 53, 5 (1991).

4. Jane E. Brody, "Gardens of Plant Tissue in Labs Seen as Factories for Vital Drugs," *New York Times*, 20 November 1990, p. B-6.

5. "Patent Granted for Drug from Yew," *New York Times*, 21 May 1991.

6. "Duplicating Yew Bark in a Lab," *New York Times*, 30 June 1991.

7. Mike Flaherty, "Forest Products Lab Logs in on Cancer Research," *Wisconsin State Journal* (Madison), 27 July 1991.

8. Milt Freudenheim, "Bristol Drops Its Yew Pact with Hauser," *New York Times*, 4 August 1993, p. Y-15.

9. Gina Kolata, "Aura of a Miracle Fades from Cancer Drug," *New York Times*, 7 November 1993, p. A-1.

10. Stephen Corry, "The Rainforest Harvest: Who Reaps the Benefit?" *The Ecologist* 23, 4 (1993): 147–153.

11. T. Gordon Roddick, letter to *The Ecologist* 23, 5 (1993): 198–199, and Stephen Corry, letter to *The Ecologist* 23, 6 (1993): 93.

12. Norman Myers, *The Primary Source: Tropical Forests and Our Future* (New York: W. W. Norton & Co., 1984).

13. Laura Tangley, "Cataloging Costa Rica's Diversity," *Bioscience* 4 (1990): 633–636.

14. Myers, *The Primary Source*.

15. Descriptions of hunter-gatherers by such researchers as Irven DeVore of

Harvard, Melvin Konner of Emory, Richard Lee of Toronto, and Mark Nathan Cohen, whose *Food Crisis in Prehistory* (New Haven: Yale University Press) was published in 1977, point out the manner by which our ancestors, during their foraging, constantly sampled everything in their environment.

16. Joseph Wallace, "Rainforest Rx," *Sierra*, July–August 1991, pp. 37–41.

17. *ABC Nightly News with Peter Jennings*, Thursday, 13 October 1994.

18. Gary Lee, "Trading Its Birthright for a Mess of Pottage: Suriname, Facing Environmental Disaster, Is Poised to Sell Off Logging Rights to Its Rain Forest," *Washington Post Weekly Edition*, 22–28 May 1995, p. 15.

19. Nigel Sizer, "Suriname's Fire Sale," *New York Times*, 14 May 1995, p. A-134.

20. Kent H. Redford, "The Empty Forest," *Bioscience* 42, 6 (1992): 412–422.

21. D. H. Janzen, "Management of Habitat Fragments in a Tropical Dry Forest: Growth," *Annals of the Missouri Botanical Garden* 75 (1988): 105–116.

22. "Unexploited Tropical Plants with Promising Economic Value" (Washington: National Academy of Sciences, 1975).

23. Purseglove, *Tropical Crops: Dicotyledons*.

24. Norman Myers, *Ultimate Security* (New York: W. W. Norton & Co., 1993), p. 182.

25. William K. Stevens, "Research in 'Virgin' Amazon Uncovers Complex Farming," *Science Times* (*New York Times*), 3 April 1990.

26. James Brooke, "Blue Jeans and Denim from Northeastern Brazil," *New York Times*, 7 April 1994, p. C-6.

27. Elizabeth Royte, "The Ant Man," *New York Times Magazine*, 22 July 1990.

28. Philip Shenon, "A Vietnamese Goat Is Imperiled by Fame," *New York Times*, 29 November 1994.

29. Malcolm Gladwell, "Rights to Life: Are Scientists Wrong to Patent Genes?" *New Yorker*, 13 November 1995, pp. 122–124.

30. Charles M. Peters, Alwyn H. Gentry, and Robert O. Mendelsohn, "Valuation of an Amazonian Rainforest," *Nature* 339 (29 June 1989): 339. After reading this article and discussing it with several colleagues, I wrote a letter to *Nature* on my observations, which were more or less those given here. Copies of this same letter were sent, at the same time, to each of the authors, but neither *Nature* nor the authors responded.

31. Polhamus, *Rubber*. This book, already cited, is the source referred to by the authors as their basis for latex yields from wild *Hevea* trees. The only yield figures given for smallholders are for 164 pounds per acre (p. 383). Additional figures for yields before and after stimulation trials give averages of 4.6 kg per tree for control trees (p. 187)—*but* these are all clonal trees under plantation conditions—not scattered, wild jungle trees.

32. N. W. Uhl and J. Dansfield, *Generum Palmarum* (Lawrence, Kans.: Allen Press, Lawrence Press, 1987).

33. "Have Your Rain Forest and Eat It, Too," *New Scientist*, 15 July 1989.

34. "Rain Forest Worth More if Uncut, Study Says," *New York Times*, 4 July 1989. This article was in press almost at the same time the original in *Nature* was published.

35. Nigel J. H. Smith, T. J. Williams, and Donald L. Plucknett, "Conserving the Tropical Cornucopia," *Environment* 33, 6 (July–August 1991): 7–9, 30–32. One might think from reading this article that none of the authors had ever been in the tropics—but apparently they have. A single example will suffice. On page 9 is a picture of a street vendor. The caption reads, "Peach palm fruits gathered in the forests of Costa Rica are sold on a street corner in San José." This statement is false, since these palms have been grown as a crop from Pre-Columbian times, and the authors would starve before finding any "in the forests of Costa Rica" as I well know (see J. R. Hunter, "The Lack of Acceptance of the Pejibaye (Peach) Palm and a Relative Comparison of Its Productivity to That of Maize," *Economic Botany* 23 (1969): 237–242. Conservation is laudatory, but to associate it, in a case such as this, with a word like *cornucopia* helps kill the very cause espoused, especially when false data or information is used.

36. K. S. Bawa, "The Riches of Tropical Forests: Non-timber Products," *Trends in Ecology and Evolution* 7 (1992): 361–363.

37. F. E. Putz, "Unnecessary Rifts," *Conservation Biology* 6 (1992): 301–302.

38. Oliver Phillips, "Using and Conserving the Rainforest," letter to *Conservation Biology* 7, 1 (1993): 6–7.

39. Richard Tremaine, "Valuing Tropical Rainforests," *Conservation Biology* 7, 1 (1993): 7–8; M. J. Balick and R. Mendelsohn, "Assessing the Economic Value of Traditional Medicines from Tropical Rainforests," *Conservation Biology* 6 (1992): 128–130.

40. Michael Parfit, "Whose Hands Will Shape the Future of the Amazon's Green Mansions?" *Smithsonian* 20, 58 (1989): 58–68.

41. Myers, *Primary Source*.

42. Karl Sax, *Standing Room Only: The Challenge of Overpopulation* (Boston: Beacon Press, 1955); Paul Ehrlich and Anne Ehrlich, *The Population Explosion* (New York: Simon & Schuster, 1990); Garrett Hardin, *Living within the Limits: Ecology, Economics and Population Taboos* (New York: Oxford University Press, 1993).

43. Warren M. Hern, "Why Are There So Many of Us? Description and Diagnosis of a Planetary Ecopathological Process," *Population and Environment* 12, 1 (1990): 9–39.

7. Everybody Plant a Tree

1. Nigel Smith, "Enchanted Forest," *Natural History*, 92 (1983): 14–20.

2. Peter Matthiessen, *The Tree Where Man Was Born* (New York: Dutton).

3. Shabecoff, "Bush Wants Billions."

4. Editorial, "Plant Trees. Then Protect Them," *New York Times*, 2 July 1990.

This includes a brief résumé of Andy Lipkis and his efforts on tree planting and indicates as well that President George Bush had promoted the idea of planting a billion trees a year for 10 years.

5. Barbara J. Eber-Schmidt, "Meanwhile in New York," letter to the *New York Times*, 21 July 1990.

6. James W. Kinnear, "A Corporate Effort," letter to the *New York Times*, 21 July 1990.

7. Ted Williams, "Don't Worry, Plant a Tree," *Audubon*, May 1991, pp. 24–33.

8. William K. Stevens, "Money Grow on Trees? No, but Study Finds Next Best Thing," *New York Times*, 12 April 1994, p. B-12.

9. John Grace et al., "Carbon Dioxide Uptake by an Undisturbed Tropical Rain Forest in Southwestern Amazonia, 1992 to 1993," *Science* 270 (3 November 1995): 778–780.

10. A typical and, from my point of view, quite misleading article on reforestation in the tropics is "Trees on Trial in Central America" (*American Forests*, September–October 1990) by Chris Wille. The suggestion that "on this isthmus of fast-vanishing forests, a plantation project may win sorely needed converts to the science of silviculture" is probably quite spurious and, with its strong implication that trials of this nature will soon have everything under control, does little to allay concerns about the current situation. The article might have been improved by using pictures of better-looking saplings, but then, perhaps there were not any available.

A far sounder and more honest analysis of this matter is contained in a letter to *Global Ecology and Biogeography* (1 [1991]: 33–35) by Justine Dunn. Rather than go through trials, which are more directed toward satisfying granting agencies than the local farmers whom they are theoretically designed to assist, Dunn suggests, "scientists must appreciate the worth of information that farmers have accumulated over centuries, rather than knowledge gained over a few years using complex research methods."

11. For further information on the minimal and often dismal success of the Green Revolution and the Food and Agriculture Organization of the United Nations, see the May–June 1991 issue of *The Ecologist*, which is almost completely devoted to this matter.

12. Eldon Kenworthy, "The Tropical Forestry Initiative and New Thinking about Economic Development in Costa Rica," *Environmental Review* 2, 10 (October 1995).

13. James Brooke, "High Profile on Environment for Brazilian Pulp Company," *New York Times*, 1 June 1992, pp. C1, C3.

14. Mark E. Harmon, William K. Ferrell, and Jerry F. Franklin, "Effects on Carbon Storage of Conversion of Old-growth Forests to Young Forests," *Science* 247 (9 February 1990): 699–702. This paper indicates that conversions of old-growth forests to young fast-growing forests will not automatically decrease atmospheric carbon dioxide as has been suggested by many who wish it might be so.

15. Michael de C. Hinds, "Do Disposable Diapers Ever Go Away?" *New York Times*, 10 December 1988; Lawrence E. Joseph, "On Disposables," *New York Times Magazine*, 23 September 1990.

16. The Georgia-Pacific advertisements referred to appear on pages 50 and 51 in the 13 May 1991 and on page 15 of the 19 August 1991 issues of *Forbes*.

17. Robert L. Heilbroner, "Reflections (Predicting the Economy)," *New Yorker*, 8 July 1991.

18. *New York Times Magazine*, 26 November 1995, p. 24.

19. Bill McKibben, "An Explosion of Green," *Atlantic Monthly*, April 1995, pp. 61–83.

8. The Role of Diversity

1. Daniel Janzen, "The Unexploited Tropics," *Bulletin of the Ecological Society of America* 51 (1972): 4–7.

2. Alan Burdick, "Invasion of the Nature Snatchers: Will the Brown Tree Snake, Having Invaded Guam, Ravage Hawaii? How Alien Species Are Flattening the World," *New York Times Magazine*, 12 November 1994, pp. 49–86.

3. John D. Castello, Donald J. Leopold, and Peter J. Smallidge, "Pathogens, Patterns, and Processes in Forest Ecosystems," *Bioscience* 45, 1 (1995): 16–24.

4. Alfred Russel Wallace, *The Malay Archipelago* (New York: Oxford University Press, 1990; 648 pp. [originally published in 1869]).

5. Paul W. Richards, *The Tropical Rain Forest* (1952; reprint, Cambridge: Cambridge University Press, 1964).

6. Lawrence Slobodkin, *Growth and Regulation of Animal Populations* (New York: Holt, Rinehart and Winston, 1961).

7. E. O. Wilson, "Is Humanity Suicidal?" *New York Times Magazine*, 30 May 1993, pp. 24–28.

8. Anne Raver, "Silent Cutback Victim: New York's Dying Trees," *New York Times*, 27 August 1991. See also William K. Stevens, "Time Is Running Out for Eastern Hemlock," *New York Times*, 20 November 1991. A newly imported sucking insect is reported to be decimating the eastern hemlock, and according to this article, which corroborates the problems of predation, this species may soon go the way of the chestnut and elm.

9. Douglas Martin, "Street Trees Are Dying for Lack of Care," *New York Times*, 30 May 1994, p. Y-16.

10. Donovan Webster, "Heart of the Delta," *New Yorker*, 8 July 1991 (an excellent description of spraying crops with agricultural chemicals); J. Robert Hunter, "Is Costa Rica Truly Conservation Minded?" *Conservation Biology* 8, 2 (1994): 592–595.

11. R. H. MacArthur and E. O. Wilson, *The Theory of Island Biogeography* (Princeton: Princeton University Press, 1967; 203 pp.).

12. William Morris, *News from Nowhere* (1890; reprint, New York: Routledge Chapman & Hall, 1972). This is a classic description of a utopia in which peace

and tranquillity prevail and the principal social and economic evils of the late nineteenth century are overcome.

13. Adam Smith, *Inquiry into the Nature and Causes of the Wealth of Nations*, edited, with an introduction, notes, marginal summary, and enlarged index by Edwin Cannan; with an introduction by Max Lerner (1888; reprint, New York: Modern Library, 1937); Sue Hubbell, *A Book of Bees* (New York: Random House, 1988).

14. Richard B. Norgaard, "The Process of Loss: Exploring the Interactions between Economic and Ecological Systems," *American Zoologist* 34 (1994): 145–158.

15. Redford, "Empty Forests."

16. James Brooke, "Saving Scraps of the Rain Forest May Be Pointless, Naturalists Say," *New York Times*, 14 November 1989.

17. Craig L. Shafer, "Values and Shortcomings of Small Reserves," *Bioscience* 45 (1995): 80–88.

9. Impossible Dream into Inevitable Nightmare

1. "We have a long, rough voyage ahead of us, and I cannot say where it will end, because it is not over yet. We are still the offspring of the Romantic movement, and still victims of the Fallacies of Hope" (Kenneth Clark, *Civilisation: A Personal View* [New York: Harper and Row, 1969]).

2. Hugh H. Iltis, "Tropical Deforestation and the Fallacy of Agricultural Hope," in *Conference on the Global Environment and Human Response towards Sustainable Development, Tokyo, 11–13 September 1989* (United Nations Environmental Programme and the Government of Japan).

3. William K. Stevens, "Latest Endangered Species: Natural Habitats of America," *New York Times*, 14 February 1995, pp. A-1, B-10.

4. Reed F. Noss, Edward T. LaRoe III, and J. Michael Scott, "Endangered Ecosystems of the United States: A Preliminary Assessment of Loss and Degradation," Biological Report 28 (Washington, D.C.: U.S. Department of the Interior, National Biological Service, 1995).

5. "Forecast for 2050: Scarcities Will Force a Leaner American Diet," *New York Times*, 18 February 1995, p. Y-5.

6. Al Gore, *Earth in the Balance: Ecology and the Human Spirit* (Boston: Houghton Mifflin, 1992).

7. James Brooke, "Rubber Trees Grow Again in Brazil," *New York Times*, 2 July 1995, p. Y-7.

8. Garrett Hardin, ed., *Population, Evolution, and Birth Control* (Santa Barbara: University of California, 1969).

9. James Brooke, "Brazilian Removes Environmental Chief," *New York Times*, 22 March 1992, and "Cleaning the Environment for Environmentalists," *New York Times*, 14 May 1992.

10. James Brooke, "Science Desk: The Environmental Page," *New York Times*, 4 April 1991, section C, p. 4, col. 1.

11. Allen L. Hammond, ed., *World Resources 1990 – 1991 Report*, International Institute for Environmental Development with the UN Environmental Programme (New York: Basic Books, 1992).

12. Karl Butler, "Amazon Yields Little Rubber," *Syracuse Post-Standard*, 15 December 1990.

13. Ray F. Dawson and F. W. Owen Smith, "History and Technological Significance of *Hevea* Rubber Production in Guatemala," *HortTechnology* 2, 3 (July – September 1992): 321– 323.

14. E. P. Imle, personal communication.

15. Tudge, "The State of Rubber."

16. Smith, *Wealth of Nations*.

17. Parfit, "Whose Hands Will Shape the Future of the Amazon's Green Mansions?"

10. What to Do with a Used Tire

1. Joyce Purnick, "The Foul Mystery of North River," The Editorial Notebook, *New York Times*, 6 December 1989, p. A-30.

2. William J. Broad, "Russians Describe Extensive Dumping of Nuclear Waste," *New York Times*, 27 April 1993, pp. A-1, B-8.

3. Timothy Egan, "Eskimos Learn They've Been Living amid Secret Pits of Radioactive Soil," *New York Times*, 6 December 1992, p. 16.

4. Michael Satchell, "Fight on Pigeon River," *U.S. News & World Report*, 4 December 1989.

5. Stephen Labaton, "Asbestos Cases Pose Test for a Court Ringmaster," *New York Times*, 16 August 1991; Barnaby J. Feder, "Asbestos Cleanup Has Few Winners," *New York Times*, 26 September 1991, p. D-8.

6. Smith, *Wealth of Nations*.

7. "Solution Sought for Tire Dumps," *Wisconsin State Journal* (Madison), 14 November 1988, p. 4-B.

8. Sam Howe Verehovek, "Fiery 'Mountains of Tires' Defy Fire-fighters at New York Dump," *New York Times*, 1 March 1990.

9. John McPhee, "Duty of Care," *New Yorker*, 28 June 1993.

10. David Pandarad, "Bill on Illegal Dumping, Burning of Tires Passes Senate," *Atlanta Constitution*, 24 February 1993, p. D-3.

11. Sabra Chartrand, "Flood Levees from Old Tires," *New York Times*, 19 July 1993.

12. "Earth Almanac: Old Tires Burn for Power, Add Rubber to the Road," *National Geographic*, July 1992; Thomas P. Lippman, "At Connecticut Plant, Tires to Burn New Tracks in Energy Production," *Washington Post*, 21 July 1991, p. A 3.

13. Barnaby J. Feder, "Shrinking the Old-Tire Mountain: Progress Slow," *New York Times*, 9 May 1990.

14. Jonathan P. Hicks, "A Whole New Dimension to Retreads," *New York Times*, 17 November 1991.

15. Matthew L. Wald, "Turning a Stew of Old Tires into Energy," *New York Times*, 27 December 1992.

16. "Too Many Tires," *New York Times Magazine*, 2 October 1994, p. 20.

17. John H. Chafee, letter to the *Wall Street Journal*, 7 October 1993. In his letter, Senator Chafee notes that scrap tires present significant environmental problems and recycling these into asphalt is a viable solution.

18. Feder, "Shrinking the Old-Tire Mountain."

11. Are We Capable of Doing the Right Thing?

1. K. G. McIndoe, *The Rubber Tree in Liberia: A Story of the Introduction of Hevea brasiliensis to Liberia*. (Dunedin, New Zealand: John McIndoe, 1968). In this connection, a very impressive, full-color publication titled *Firestone Plantations Company in Liberia* demonstrates the amazing development of this plantation and its impact on the entire country.

2. Heilbroner, "Reflections."

3. Ted Williams, "He's Going to Have an Accident," *Audubon*, March 1991, pp. 30–39.

4. Timothy Egan, "In West, a Showdown over Rules on Grazing," *New York Times*, 19 August 1990.

5. Richard Conniff, "Federal Lands," *National Geographic*, 185, 2 (1994): 2–39.

6. Peter Passell, "Water, water everywhere . . ." *New York Times*, 29 October 1992, p. C-2; John McPhee, "Water War," *New Yorker*, 26 April 1993, p. 120; Special Edition: "Water: The Power, Promise and Turmoil of North America's Fresh Water," *National Geographic*, November 1993.

7. Marc Renner, *Cadillac Desert: The American West and Its Disappearing Water*. (New York: Viking Penguin, 1993).

8. Timothy Egan, "Wingtip 'Cowboys' in Last Stand to Hold on to Low Grazing Fees," *New York Times*, 29 October 1993.

9. Editorial, "Bruce Babbitt's Landscape, at Risk," *New York Times*, 31 October 1993, p. 15-E.

10. Hardin, *Living within the Limits*.

11. Editorial, "Preaching to Brazil from Hawaii," *New York Times*, 24 July 1990.

12. Katherine P. Ransel, "The Last Salmon Run," *New York Times*, 18 February 1995, p. 15.

13. Katherine Bishop, "Militant Environmentalists Planning Summer Protests to Save Redwoods," *New York Times*, 19 June 1990.

14. Christopher Manes, *Green Rage: Radical Environmentalism and the Unmaking of Civilization* (New York: Little, Brown, 1990).

15. Wallace Stegner, *Where the Bluebird Sings to the Lemonade Springs: Living and Writing in the West* (New York: Random House, 1992).

16. Baum, *Weeping Wood*.

17. Jonathan P. Hicks, "Firestone to Sell 75% of Tire Unit in $1 Billion Deal with Japanese," *New York Times*, 17 February 1988.

18. Fred H. Hayward, personal communication, 1992. In this connection, see also Jeffrey Goldberg, "A War without a Purpose in a Country without Identity," *New York Times Magazine*, 22 January 1995, pp. 36 – 39.

19. Howard W. French, "Rebels without a Cause Plunder Sierra Leone," *New York Times*, 17 February 1995.

12. High-Tech to the Rescue?

1. John Perlin, *A Forest Journey: The Role of Wood in the Development of Civilization* (Cambridge: Harvard University Press, 1991).

2. John H. White, Jr., "Changing Trains," *Invention & Technology*, Spring – Summer 1991, pp. 35 – 40 (on the impact and later demise of railways, particularly in the United States); Curt Wohleber, "The Annihilation of Time and Space," *Invention & Technology*, Spring – Summer 1991 (review of the conversion of sailing ships to steam).

3. Lester C. Thurow, *The Zero-Sum Society: Distribution and the Possibilities for Economic Change* (New York: Basic Books, 1980).

4. Michael Adas, *Machines as the Measure of Men: Science, Technology, and Ideologies of Western Dominance* (Ithaca, N.Y.: Cornell University Press, 1990). This is an excellent presentation not only of how Europe, particularly England and France, came to dominate much of the world (especially Africa and Asia) by means of technological innovations but also of how a general attitude developed that by these same means human beings could develop complete dominance over nature as well.

5. T. A. Heppenheimer, "The Man Who Made Los Angeles Possible," *Invention & Technology*, Spring – Summer 1991, pp. 11–18. This is the story of how, through the incredible and persistent efforts of William Mulholland, water was brought from hundreds of miles away to southern California.

6. Sheryl WuDunn, "Chinese Suffer from Rising Pollution as Byproduct of Industrial Boom," *New York Times*, 28 February 1993, p. Y-11.

7. P. Brodeur, "The Cancer of the Slater School," *New Yorker*, 7 December 1992, pp. 86 – 94+. This article discusses the possible role of electric power lines' magnetic fields in Fresno, California; "Electromagnetic Fields," *Consumer Reports*, May 1994, pp. 354 – 359.

8. Keith Schneider, "Bush Aide Assails U.S. Preparations for Earth Summit," *New York Times*, 1 August 1992, pp. A-1, A-9.

9. Newt Gingrich et al., *Contract with America* (Atlanta: Turner Publishing Company, 1994).

10. Alvin and Heidi Toffler, *Creating a New Civilization* (Atlanta: Turner Publishing Company, 1995).

11. Barbara Ehrenreich, "The Politics of the Third Wave," a review of *Creating a New Civilization*, in *New York Times Book Review*, 7 May 1995, p. 9.

12. Hendrick Hertzberg, "Marxism: The Sequel — There's Something Oddly Familiar about Mr. Gingrich's Ideology," *New Yorker*, 13 February 1995, pp. 6 – 7.

13. Jean Pierre Lasota, "Darkness at Noon: Time Is Running Out for Poland's Environment," *The Sciences*, July–August 1987, pp. 23–29.

14. William J. Broad, "Scientists Fear Atomic Explosion of Buried Waste," *New York Times*, 5 March 1995, pp. A-1, A-9.

15. "Forecast for 2050: Scarcities Will Force a Leaner American Diet," *New York Times*, 18 February 1995, p. 5.

16. David Pimentel, "Agriculture's Relation to Civilization," *Bioscience* 45, 6 (1995): 44–45. A review of Otto T. Solbrig and Dorothy J. Solbrig, *So Shall Ye Reap: Farming and Crops in Human Affairs*.

17. Ann Misch, "Purdah and Overpopulation in the Middle East," *World Watch*, November–December 1990, pp. 10, 11, 34.

18. Hugh H. Iltis, "Conservation, Contraception and Catholicism, a 20th Century Trinity," *The Biologist* 54, 1 (February 1972): 35–47.

19. Ansley J. Coale et al., "Recent Trends in Fertility and Nuptiality in China," *Science* 251 (25 January 1991): 389–393.

20. At the American Association for the Advancement of Science (AAAS) annual meeting for 1994, held in San Francisco in February, Dr. David Pimentel of Cornell University made the statement that unless we could manage to control our populations so that the world's total, 100 years from now, would be only 2 billion (it is now rapidly approaching 6 billion), the earth would not be a fit place for *Homo sapiens.*

21. Peter M. Vitousek et al., "Human Appropriation of the Products of Photosynthesis," *Bioscience* 36, 6 (June 1986): 368–380.

22. Aldo Leopold, *A Sand County Almanac, and Sketches Here and There* (New York: Oxford University Press, 1949).

23. Peter Miller, "A Comeback for Nuclear Power?" *National Geographic*, August 1991, pp. 60–89; William J. Broad, "Breakthrough in Nuclear Fusion Offers Hope for Power of Future," *New York Times*, 11 November 1991.

24. Malcolm W. Browne, "Reactor Passes the Point of No Return in Uphill Path to Fusion Energy," *Science Times–New York Times*, 7 December 1993, p. B-7.

25. Lyman Spitzer, Jr., "Harnessing the Sun," *New York Times*, 7 December 1993, p. Y-15.

26. Warren E. Leary, "The Use of Clean, Plentiful Hydrogen as Fuel Is Moving Closer to Reality," *New York Times*, 16 April 1993, p. Y-10.

27. Peter G. Wolynes, "Don't Look to Hydrogen for Future Fuel," letter to the *New York Times*, 21 April 1995.

28. Barry Commoner, "Free Markets Can't Control Pollution," *New York Times*, 15 April 1990, p. 13.

29. P. E. Hurley, personal communication, 1995.

30. The editorial in *Science* (19 June 1992) by Philip H. Abelson on "Exaggerated Carcinogenicity of Chemicals" brought forth three separate letters — first from David P. Rall, then from David A. Dankovic, Lester T. Stayner, Randall Smith, and A. John Bailer, and finally from Philip J. Landrigan — together with

Abelson's reply in the 4 September 1992 issue of this journal. Each letter took issue with Abelson's statements relative to the carcinogenicity of butadiene. Indeed, sufficient evidence was presented to suggest strongly that this substance, the basis for synthetic rubber production, may well present a serious health problem.

31. Chip Brown (Associated Press), "1,300 Texans Sue Factory over Stench," *Wisconsin State Journal*, 18 November 1991.

13. Roll Out the Barrel

1. Richard A. Kerr, "Oil and Gas Estimates Plummet," *Science*, 22 September 1989, p. 1330.

2. M. K. Hubbert, National Academy of Sciences – National Research Council Committee, *Resources and Man* (San Francisco: Freeman, 1969), p. 163.

3. Daniel B. Hawkins, "U.S. Oil and Gas Consumption: Is Another Crisis Ahead?" Letter to *Science* 247 (16 March 1990).

4. Robert L. Hirsch, "U.S. Oil and Gas Consumption: Is Another Crisis Ahead?" Letter to *Science* 247 (16 March 1990).

5. Cutler J. Cleveland, "Yield per Effort for Additions to Crude Oil Reserves in the Lower 48 United States, 1946 – 1989," *American Association for Petroleum Geologists Bulletin* 76, 6 (1992): 948 – 958.

6. Agis Salpukas, "Long-term Oil Strain Seen," *New York Times*, 31 October 1994, p. C-5.

7. Robert L. Hirsch, "Impending United States Energy Crisis," *Science* 235 (1990): 1467 – 1473.

8. *The Economist*, 28 July 1990. This unsigned editorial was reprinted under the title "Hey, America, Lighten Up a Little" on the op-ed page of the *New York Times* of 5 September 1990.

9. Alan Tonelson and Andrew K. Hurd, "The Real Cost of Mideast Oil," *New York Times* op-ed section, 4 September 1990.

10. Edward A. Gargan, "Oil Prices Plunge after OPEC Fails to Cut Output," *New York Times*, 29 March 1992, p. C-1.

11. Richard Stevenson, "Risks Rise in North Sea as Oil's Price Declines," *New York Times*, 5 April 1993, pp. C1, C8; James Brooke, "Pollution of Rain Forest Is Tied to Oil in Ecuador," *New York Times*, 22 March 1994, p. B-7; James Brooke, "With Oilfields as Battleground Colombia Adopts New Tactics in Rebel War," *New York Times*, 16 April 1993, p. Y-6; Agis Salpukas, "For Oil Industry, That Next 'Elephant' Proves Elusive," *New York Times*, 20 March 1994, p. F-5.

12. Agis Salpukas, "New Ideas for U.S. Oil," *New York Times*, 16 November 1995, pp. C-1, C-18.

13. Agis Salpukas, "Siberian Oil Venture by 4 Companies," *New York Times*, 12 April 1994.

14. Agis Salpukas, "2,860 Feet under the Sea, a Record-breaking Well," *New York Times*, 24 April 1994, p. F-9.

15. Joe Kane, *Savages* (New York: Knopf, 1995; 273 pp., illustrated).

16. William Boyd, "In Memoriam: Death of a Writer," *New Yorker,* 29 November 1995, pp. 51–55. This is as thorough a presentation of what has been taking place in Nigeria as I have read. In addition it is a tender tribute to a friend.

17. Kevin Phillips, *The Politics of Rich and Poor: Wealth and the American Electorate in the Reagan Aftermath* (New York: Random House, 1990).

18. Sylvia Nasar, "Those Born Wealthy or Poor Usually Stay So, Study Says," *New York Times,* 18 May 1992, pp. A-1, C-7.

19. Hardin, *Living within the Limits.*

20. Richard Stone, "A Big Chill Drops Geothermal Energy," *Science* (Briefings), 22 November 1991.

21. David Pimentel, "Energy Security, Economics, and the Environment," *Journal of Agriculture and Environmental Ethics* 4, 1 (1991): 1–13. In this article, which was republished the following year in *Focus of the Carrying Capacity Network* 2, 3 (1992): 36, 38–43, Pimentel states, "Ethanol production is energy inefficient, requiring considerably more energy than is contained in the ethanol produced."

22. Farrington Daniels, *Direct Use of the Sun's Energy* (New York: Ballantine Books, 1974 [originally published in 1964]).

23. Barbara and David Porter, *Alternative Sources of Energy: A Bibliography of Solar, Geothermal, Wind, and Tidal Energy, and Environmental Architecture* (New York: Scarecrow Press, 1975).

24. Amory B. Lovins et al., *The Energy Controversy: Soft Path Questions and Answers* (San Francisco: Friends of the Earth, 1979), ed. Hugh Nash; Amory B. Lovins and L. Hunter Lovins, *New York Times* op-ed section, 3 December 1990; David J. Houghton and L. Hunter Lovins, "There's More than One Way to Save Gas," letter to the *New York Times,* 31 March 1991.

25. Harold M. Hubbard, "The Real Cost of Energy," *Scientific American* 264, 4 (April 1991): 36–42.

26. Richard Heede and Robert Bishop, "Corporate Wealth through Waste," *Sierra,* July–August 1991, pp. 16–18.

27. Peter Passell, "Cheap Oil, Expensive Cartel," *New York Times,* 20 March 1991.

28. Daniel Yergin, *The Prize: The Epic Quest for Oil, Money and Power* (New York: Simon & Schuster, 1990; illustrated).

29. Mary Anne Weaver, "Hunting with the Sheikhs," *New Yorker,* 15 December 1992, pp. 51–52+.

30. Leslie H. Gelb, "Oil Facts and Follies," *New York Times,* op-ed section, 19 March 1991.

31. "Russians Struggle to Clean Up Spill," *New York Times,* 1 November 1994, p. A-6.

32. Agis Salpukas, "Squeezing U.S. Oilfields' Last Drop," *New York Times,* 13 January 1995, pp. C-1–2.

33. Tim Appenseller, "Fire and Ice under the Deep-Sea Floor," *Science* 252 (1991): 1790–1792.

34. Melvin Calvin, "Fuel Oils from Euphorbs and Other Plants," *Botanical Journal of the Linnean Society* 94, 1–2 (1987): 97–110.

35. Marc S. Reisch, "Rubber: Slow Growth Ahead," *Chemical and Engineering News*, 10 May 1993, pp. 24–33.

36. Daniel Yergin, "Oil Business, Not Oil Politics," *New York Times*, 2 August 1991, p. A-15.

37. "Michelin Plans to Cut at Least 16,000 Jobs," *New York Times*, 18 May 1991, p. C-4.

38. Jonathan P. Hicks, "Chasing Few Buyers with Too Many Tires," *New York Times*, 3 February 1991, p. F-5.

39. Agis Salpukas, "Petrochemical Profits Are Helping Oil Companies," *New York Times*, 20 October 1994.

40. Thomas Friedman, "OPEC's Lonely at the Tap, but China's Getting Thirsty," *New York Times*, 3 April 1994, p. E-3.

41. Barry Commoner, "Free Markets Can't Control Pollution," *New York Times*, 15 April 1990, p. 13.

14. The Para Rubber Tree and Global Ecology

1. T. M. Lewinsohn, "The Geographical Distribution of Plant Latex," *Chemoecology* 2 (1991): 64–68. In this article are listed forty different plant families members of which contain latex.

2. David E. Dussourd, "The Vein Drain; or, How Insects Outsmart Plants," *Natural History*, February 1990, pp. 44–49.

3. Myron P. Zalucki and Lincoln Brower, "Survival of First Instar Larvae to Cardiac Glycoside and Latex Content of *Asclepias humistrata* (Asclepiadaceae)," *Chemoecology* 3 (1992): 81–93.

4. The majority of plants that produce latex in some form, according to James Bonner and Arthur W. Galston ("The Physiology and Biochemistry of Rubber Formation in Plants," *Botanical Review* 13, 10 [December 1947]: 543–591), are to be found in the moist and humid tropics. Actually, the list of plant families exhibiting this characteristic is quite large.

5. Polhamus, *Rubber*.

6. H. W. Bates, *The Naturalist on the River Amazons* (reprint, Berkeley: University of California Press, 1962), p. 38.

7. Paul H. Allen, *The Rainforests of Golfo Dulce* (Gainesville: University of Florida Press, 1956; 417 pp.).

8. Eldon Newcomb, personal communication, 1991.

9. Lynn Margulis, personal communication, 1991.

10. A. A. Cook, *Diseases of Tropical and Subtropical Field, Fiber, and Oil Plants* (New York: Macmillan, 1981).

11. See J. Robert Hunter, "Reconsidering the Functions of Latex," *Trees: Structure and Function* 9 (1994): 1–5.

12. R. C. Kline, E. Parry, and E. L. Gershey, "Safety in the Laboratory," *Nature* 341 (1989): 288.

13. Beverly Merz, "The Case of the Mysterious Epidemic," *Good Housekeeping*, March 1992, pp. 112–114+.

14. The debate over changes in the earth's climate and atmosphere has been a long and intensive one ranging from the importance of El Niño to depletion of stratospheric ozone. Without meaning to slight anyone, a very partial list of players in this drama includes Paul J. Crutzen, James E. Hansen, Richard S. Lindzen, Francesco Loreto, James Lovelock, Russell K. Monson, Harold A. Mooney, Reinhold A. Rasmussen, F. Sherwood Rowland, Stephen H. Schneider, Thomas D. Sharkey, Peter Vitousek, Fritz Went, and George Woodwell. In this connection there are literally hundreds of books and articles devoted to this subject. Two general articles on this wide topic give an overall view: Robert M. White, "The Great Climate Debate," *Scientific American*, July 1990; and Patrick McCully, "Discord in the Greenhouse: How WRI [Washington-based World Resources Institute] Is Attempting to Shift the Blame for Global Warming," *The Ecologist* 21, 4 (June–July 1991).

15. James Lovelock, *Gaia* (New York: Oxford University Press, 1979); James Lovelock, personal communication, 1991.

16. A. Cailleux, M. Cogny, and P. Allain, "Blood Isoprene Concentrations in Humans and in Some Animal Species," *Biochemical Medicine* 47 (1992): 157–160.

17. Edward S. Rubin et al., "Realistic Mitigation Options for Global Warming," *Science* 257 (1992): 148–149, 251–266.

18. Lewis Thomas, *The Lives of a Cell: Notes of a Biology Watcher* (New York: Bantam Books, 1975).

19. Connie Barlow and Tyler Volk, "Gaia and Evolutionary Biology," *Bioscience* 42, 9 (1992): 686–692.

20. Kevin Jardine, "Finger on the Carbon Pulse: Climatic Change and Boreal Forests," *The Ecologist* 24, 6 (1994): 220–224.

21. William K. Stevens, "Skeptics Are Challenging Dire 'Greenhouse' Views," *New York Times*, 13 December 1989, pp. 1, A-7.

22. Kathleen B. Hogan, John S. Hoffman, and Anne M. Thompson, "Methane on the Greenhouse Agenda," *Nature* 354 (21 November 1991): 181–182.

23. Polhamus, *Rubber*.

24. C. C. Webster and W. J. Baulkwill, *Rubber* (London: Longman, 1989).

25. Fritz Went, "Blue Haze in the Atmosphere," *Nature* 187 (1960): 641.

26. Reinhold A. Rasmussen and M. A. K. Khalil, "Isoprene over the Amazon Basin," *Journal of Geophysical Research* 93 (1988): 1417–1421; Francesco Loreto and Thomas D. Sharkey, "A Gas-Exchange Study of Photosynthesis and Isoprene Emission in *Quercus rubra* L.," *Planta* 182 (1990): 523–531; Russell K. Monson and Ray

Fall, "Isoprene Emission from Aspen Leaves," *Plant Physiology* 90 (1989): 267–274.

27. Thomas D. Sharkey and Eric Singsaas, "Why Plants Emit Isoprene," *Nature* 374 (27 April 1995): 769.

28. Francesco Loreto, personal communication, 1991.

29. Leo Salter and C. Nicholas Newitt, "Ozone-Hydrocarbon Interaction in Plants," 1992.

30. Colin Tudge, *Global Ecology* (New York: Oxford University Press, 1991), p. 88.

31. V. C. Runeckles and B. I. Chevone, "Crop Response to Ozone," in *Surface Level Ozone Exposures and Their Effects on Vegetation*, ed. A. S. Lefohn (Chelsea, Minn.: Lewis, 1992), pp. 189–270; S. E. Paulson, R. C. Flagan, and J. H. Seinfeld, "Atmospheric Photo-oxidation of Isoprene, II: The Ozone-Isoprene Reaction," *International Journal of Chemical Kinetics* 24 (1992): 103–125.

32. Tudge, *Global Ecology*.

33. Frank H. Murkowski, "U.S. Forest Harvest Is Nothing like the Tropics," letter to the *New York Times*, 30 September 1990.

34. G. M. Woodwell, "CO_2 Reduction and Reforestation," letter to *Science* 242 (16 December 1988): 1493.

35. Thomas D. Sharkey, personal communication, 1993.

36. Eugene P. Odum, *Fundamentals of Ecology* (Philadelphia: W. B. Saunders Company, 1971).

37. Ludwig Boltzmann, "The Second Law of Thermodynamics" (1886), in *Theoretical Physics and Philosophical Problems*, ed. Brian McGuinness (Boston: Reidel Pub. Co., 1974).

15. "Man's Inhumanity to Man"

1. Robert Burns, "Man Was Made to Mourn," Stanza 7.

2. René Dubos, *Man Adapting* (New Haven: Yale University Press, 1965), pp. 101–102.

3. C. J. Krebs and J. H. Myers, "Population Cycles in Small Mammals," *Advances in Ecological Research* 8 (1982): 267–399; C. J. Krebs, *The Message of Ecology* (New York: Harper & Row, 1988), pp. 24–27.

4. R. C. Peterson, *Wolf Ecology and Prey Relationships on Isle Royal* (Washington, D.C.: U.S. Government Printing Office, 1978).

5. Editorial, "The Cemetery Called East Timor," *New York Times*, 25 September 1992, p. A-12.

6. Calvin Sims, "'Dirty War' Admission Ungags Argentina," *New York Times*, 27 April 1995, p. A-5.

7. Herbert Spencer, *The Principles of Biology: Indirect Equilibrium*: "This survival of the fittest which I have sought to express in mechanical terms, is that which Mr. Darwin has called 'natural selection' or the preservation of favored races in the struggle for life."

8. Editorial, "The Rich Get Richer Faster," *New York Times*, 18 April 1995, p. A-14.

9. Lester C. Thurow, "A Surge in Inequality," *Scientific American* 256, 5 (1987): 30–38.

10. Robert Wright, "The Biology of Violence," *New Yorker*, 13 March 1995, pp. 68–77.

11. Hugh H. Iltis, Orie L. Loucks, and Peter Andrews, "Criteria for an Optimum Human Environment," *Bulletin of the Atomic Scientists* 26, 1 (1970): 2–6.

12. Paul R. Ehrlich, "Shared Sensibilities," *Natural History*, November 1984; E. O. Wilson, *Biophilia: The Human Bond to Other Species* (Cambridge, Mass.: Harvard University Press, 1984; 159 pp.).

13. Richard Harwood, "Death in the 20th Century," *Washington Post National Weekly Edition*, 1–7 May 1995, p. 27.

14. Plato, *Dialogues: Apology, Crito, Phaedo, Symposium and Republic*, ed. J. D. Kaplin (New York: Pocket Books, 1950).

15. Paul R. Ehrlich et al., "Global Change and Carrying Capacity: Implications for Life on Earth," *Stanford Institute for Population and Resource Studies* (Stanford Institute, 1989); Joel E. Cohen, "Population Growth and Earth's Human Carrying Capacity," *Science* 269 (1995): 341–346.

Epilogue

1. Michael Oppenheimer and Robert Boyle, *Dead Heat: The Race against the Greenhouse Effect* (New York: Basic Books, 1994). In the beginning, these authors quote H. G. Wells's statement that "human history becomes more and more a race between education and catastrophe" — something all should contemplate now that educational systems worldwide have become increasingly dismal and lacking.

2. Stephen W. Hawking, *A Brief History of Time: From the Big Bang to Black Holes* (New York: Bantam Books, 1988).

3. Alan Riding, "Paris Meeting Backs U.N. Proposal to Combat AIDS," *New York Times*, 2 December 1994, p. 12-A.

4. Calvin Sims, "A Hole in the Heavens (Chicken Little Below?)," *New York Times*, 3 March 1995, p. A-4.

5. Heilbroner, "Reflections."

6. Voltaire (François Marie Arouet), *Candide, or Optimism*, trans. and ed. Robert M. Adams, 2d ed. (New York: W. W. Norton & Co., 1991).

7. John Maddox, *The Doomsday Syndrome* (New York: McGraw-Hill, 1972).

8. Julian Simon, "Resources, Population, Environment: An Oversupply of False Bad News," *Science* 208 (1980): 1431–1437.

9. Gregg Easterbrook, *A Moment on the Earth: The Coming Age of Environmental Optimism* (New York: Viking, 1995).

10. Thomas Robert Malthus, *An Essay on the Principle of Population* (London, 1798).

11. Garrett, *The Coming Plague*.

12. Peter Raven, "Review of *A Moment on the Earth*," *Amicus Journal*, Spring 1995, pp. 42 – 45.

13. Among the many that could be cited I include Ehrlich and Ehrlich, *The Population Explosion*; Katherine S. Newman, *Declining Fortunes: The Withering of the American Dream* (New York: Basic Books, 1993); Paul Kennedy, *Preparing for the Twenty-first Century* (New York: Random House, 1994); Zbigniew Brzezinski, *Out of Control: Global Turmoil on the Eve of the Twenty-first Century* (New York: MacMillan, 1993); and Haynes Johnson, *Divided We Fall: Gambling with History in the Nineties* (New York: W. W. Norton & Co., 1994). In addition to these books, Robert Kaplan's article in the February 1994 issue of the *Atlantic Monthly*, titled "The Coming Anarchy: How Scarcity, Crime, Overpopulation, Tribalism and Disease Are Rapidly Destroying the Social Fabric of Our Planet," and William E. Rees, "Reducing Our Ecological Footprints," *Siemens Review* 62, 2 (1995): 30 – 35, are also excellent, the latter particularly from an ecological-economic standpoint.

14. A. M. Rosenthal, "The Fear of Refugees," *New York Times*, 16 September 1994; John Tagliabue, "Sunny Italy Turns Scowling Face to Immigrants: A Land of Emigrants Has Trouble Handling a Reverse Tide," *New York Times*, 5 January 1995. See also Peter Brimelow, *Alien Nation: Common Sense about America's Immigration Disaster* (New York: Random House, 1995).

15. Bob Herbert, "A Nation of Nitwits," *New York Times*, 1 March 1995, p. A-15.

16. *Amicus Journal* 17, 4 (Winter 1996): Donella Meadows, "This Land Was Your Land: Three Views of a Theft in Progress"; Karl Hess, Jr., and Johanna Wald, "Eating the Land Away"; Will Nixon, "The Arctic Wildlife Refuge Also Protects People."

17. Thomas E. Lovejoy, "Will Expectedly the Top Blow Off?" *Bioscience*, 1995, Supplement, pp. S3 – S6.

18. Stephen Engelberg, "Forestry Company Helps Write a Law to Derail Inquiry," *New York Times*, 26 April 1995, p. A-1.

19. Paul R. Ehrlich, "The Loss of Diversity: Causes and Consequences," in *Biodiversity*, ed. E. O. Wilson (Washington, D.C.: National Academy Press, 1988), pp. 21 – 27; editorial, "Shevardnadze Feared for Fate of World," *Wisconsin State Journal*, 21 November 1991.

20. Robert L. Heilbroner, *The Human Prospect* (New York: W. W. Norton & Co., 1975).

21. Gro Harlem Brundtland, "How to Secure Our Common Future," *Scientific American*, September 1989, p. 190.

22. In the article "Group of 100," in defense of whales the statement is made that "Norway, as an IWC member nation, has defied the global moratorium and in 1993 hunted minke whales for commercial sale" (*New York Times*, 10 May 1994, p. A-7).

23. Jesse H. Ausubel, "A Second Look at the Impacts of Climate Change," *American Scientist* 79 (May/June 1991): 210 – 221.

24. Wassily Leontief, "Academic Economics," letter to *Science* 217 (9 July 1992):

104–105. G. H. Borts was the editor of the *American Economic Review* when, according to Leontief, he suggested that "articles on mathematical economics and the finer points of economic theory occupy a more and more prominent place than ever before."

25. *50 Simple Things You Can Do to Save the Earth* (Berkeley: Earth Works, 1989).

INDEX